MW01147867

PEDDLERS, MERCHANTS, AND MANUFACTURERS

PEDDLERS, MERCHANTS, AND MANUFACTURERS

How Jewish Entrepreneurs Built Economy and Community in Upcountry South Carolina

DIANE CATHERINE VECCHIO

THE UNIVERSITY OF
SOUTH CAROLINA PRESS

© 2023 University of South Carolina

Published by the University of South Carolina Press
Columbia, South Carolina 29208

uscpress.com

Manufactured in the United States of America

32 31 30 29 28 27 26 25 24 23
10 9 8 7 6 5 4 3 2 1

Library of Congress Cataloging-in-Publication Data
can be found at https://lccn.loc.gov/2023037649.

ISBN: 978-1-64336-452-0 (hardcover)
ISBN: 978-1-64336-453-7 (ebook)

FOR JOHN

And our beautiful family:

AJ, Elizabeth, Rocco, and Nico; Cory, Paige, Koda, Julian, and Ruby;
Benjamin; Kelsea, Todd, Azra, Caroline, and Rollins

CONTENTS

Acknowledgments   ix

Introduction   1

CHAPTER 1
The Lure of South Carolina   7

CHAPTER 2
Foundations of Jewish Enterprise in the Upcountry   34

CHAPTER 3
Creating Community   52

CHAPTER 4
Jewish Business and Industry in the Interwar Years   70

CHAPTER 5
The Promise of American Life   94

CHAPTER 6
The Upcountry Goes to War   107

CHAPTER 7
Jewish Garment Manufacturing   119

CHAPTER 8
Jewish–Black Relations   153

CHAPTER 9

The Jewish Role in a New Economy *182*

Epilogue *199*

Glossary 203
Notes 205
Bibliography 243
Index 257

ACKNOWLEDGMENTS

During years of researching and writing about Upcountry Jews many people provided me support, encouragement, and important insights. I owe a debt of gratitude to Mark Bauman, who encouraged me to write this book, convinced there was an important story to share about Jews and business in Upcountry South Carolina. His meticulous reading of various chapters helped bring this book to fruition. I would like to thank friends and scholars who gave generously of their time to read and comment on specific chapters. They include Hasia Diner, Dale Rosengarten, Melissa Walker, Steve O'Neill, Betsy Wakefield Teeter, Su Su Johnson, George Dean Johnson, and my stepdaughter, Kelsea Turner. I owe the greatest debt of thanks to my husband, John Stockwell, who read, commented on, and critiqued every chapter of this book. His total support of my scholarly work, and this book sustained me throughout the entire process.

Many thanks to Rabbi Yossi Liebowitz for his insights and our many discussions of Judaism and the congregation of Temple B'nai Israel. The late Ben Stauber helped me mine through decades of temple papers stored in B'nai Israel's attic. Joe Wachter, a font of information about the Jews of Spartanburg, shared his knowledge of the Jewish community. Thank you to John Cutchin who toured me around Jewish business and industry sites in Easley.

William (Bill) Barnet, Kathy Dunleavy, Karen Mitchell, and Su Su Johnson enlightened me on past politics and race issues in Spartanburg. The Reverend Jesse Jackson shared his experiences as a young Black man growing up in Greenville over several days of interviews, meals, lectures, and classroom visits at Furman University.

The following librarians, archivists, and public historians helped me locate important documents, records, and photographs: Alyssa Neely with Special Collections at the College of Charleston; Brad Steineke, Charity Rouse, Christen Bennett, Harrison Gage, and Andy Flint with the Archives and Special Collections at the Spartanburg Public Library; Kristina Hornbeck at the Upcountry History Museum; Libby Young at the James B. Duke Library, Furman University; the Special Collections staff at Furman University; Brenda Burk at Clemson University; and Lee Grady, the reference archivist at the Wisconsin Historical Society. The library staff in the South Carolina Room at the Greenville Public Library and the Union County Historical Society procured files on Jewish residents, and the staff at the Greenville County Historical Society provided me with historic photographs of Greenville. The office staff at Spartanburg's B'nai Israel and Greenville's Temple of Israel and Beth Israel provided me with temple and Hadassah records.

My dear friend and former student Courtney Tollison Hartness along with Judith Bainbridge shared their knowledge of Greenville's history, and Russell Booker, former superintendent of Spartanburg's District Seven, provided sources for tabulating high school graduates. My granddaughter Azra Erbatu helped me record demographic information of Jews in the Upcountry from Ancestry.com. I also thank Furman University for providing me with a research grant during the formative period of this book and the overreaders for providing excellent insights and suggesting important revisions on the manuscript. Many thanks to Production Editor Kerri Tolan and the EDP staff and much gratitude toward Cathy Esposito's assistance in selecting photographs. Finally, I thank my Acquisitions Editor Ehren Foley at the University of South Carolina Press for his encouragement, support, guidance, and speedy responses to my queries.

I am especially indebted to the individuals who agreed to be interviewed for this book. Sadly, several of them have passed away, never having had the opportunity to see this book in print. Without their insights this book would not have been possible. I also apologize to members of the Upstate Jewish community that I could not interview.

Sections of this book appeared as articles in the following books and journals: "Making Their Way in the New South: Jewish Peddlers and Merchants in the South Carolina Upcountry," *South Carolina Historical Journal* 113, no. 2 (April 2012): 100–124; "Max Moses Heller: Patron Saint of Greenville's Renaissance," in *Doing Business in America. A Jewish History,* edited by Hasia R. Diner, Casden Institute for the Study of the Jewish Role in American Life, vol. 16, Purdue University Press, 2018; and "New Jewish Women: Shaping the Future of a 'New South' in the Palmetto State," *Southern Jewish History* 23 (2020): 43–75.

In this book, which examines Jewish immigrants and entrepreneurs, I am struck by the similarities to other immigrant groups who came to America,

worked hard, embarked on business opportunities, and stressed the importance of education to their children. As the daughter of an immigrant Italian father who built a business from the bottom up, I saw his achievements,
both materially and socially, as equal only to the pressure he put on me and
my three siblings to achieve success through education. It worked. My sister
Denise became a medical social worker, my brother Alex, a research chemist
and our youngest sister, Rosemarie, with a nursing degree and an MBA, vice
president of the Miami Jewish Hospital at the time of her untimely death.
As for me, I obtained a PhD in history and now dedicate my work to the
immigrants who paved the way for our success.

Introduction

In 1908, Nathan Shapiro, a Russian Jew who served in the czar's army, slipped out of Russia and immigrated to the United States as soon as he had saved enough money for the voyage. He joined a cousin in Baltimore who encouraged him to start peddling. His cousin, whom he called Levine, bought train tickets and advanced Shapiro the money he needed to purchase supplies. The cousins traveled to the South and settled in Union, a small town in the South Carolina Upcountry, where Levine had previously peddled.[1] After years of peddling goods in Union County, Shapiro had enough money to open his own business. He bought a round-trip train ticket to Baltimore and purchased stock from the Baltimore Bargain House where Jacob Epstein, a well-known Jewish wholesaler, extended him credit for goods. After peddling for several years, Shapiro became a successful merchant after opening a dry goods store in downtown Union in the 1920s.[2]

Decades earlier, Polish-born Wolf Rosenberg established Rosenberg & Company, a dry goods store in in the Upcountry town of Abbeville, in 1872, having moved there from Chester, South Carolina. Within three years, Rosenberg relocated the business to a larger store and brought his brothers and nephew into the business. They opened another store in 1882 and continued to prosper. By 1895, the local newspaper boasted: "Rosenberg & Co. has attained greater financial success than any other firm in town. They own more bank stock and more town property than any other firm in Abbeville County."[3]

Across the Atlantic as a youth, Andrew Teszler escaped Nazi-occupied Hungary and lived in England until he could emigrate to the United States with his brother, Otto. Raised in a prominent Hungarian textile-manufacturing family, the Teszler brothers attended North Carolina State University, a leading institution in textile education and research. In 1959, Andrew Teszler approached David Schwartz, the president and chairman of the board of Jonathan Logan Inc., a leading manufacturer of women's apparel. Teszler convinced Schwartz of a lucrative market in double-knit garments, a trend

that started years earlier in Europe, and Schwartz established a vertically integrated manufacturing facility in Spartanburg with Teszler leading the company. Teszler successfully operated Butte Knit, the largest manufacturing firm
in Spartanburg during the 1960s and 1970s with 4,000 employees.

Jewish peddlers, merchants, and manufacturers are the subject of this
book. These entrepreneurs represent the diverse economic experiences of
Jews who settled in Upcountry South Carolina in the late nineteenth and early
twentieth centuries. In many respects these peddlers and merchants resemble
the experiences of Jews who migrated to numerous southern destinations.
From Virginia to Alabama, and North Carolina to Louisiana, German and
East European Jews started their lives in the United States as peddlers, as did
Nathan Shapiro, and merchants such as Wolf Rosenberg. A smaller number
of Jewish manufacturers migrated to the South and established textile companies as did the Teszlers.

Jews came to the South in smaller numbers than those who settled in the
Northeast or the upper Midwest and were motivated by factors different from
those attracted to major urban centers such as New York and Chicago. The
large numbers of Jews who settled in urban centers found work in the needle
trades while Jewish migrants came to the South for business and commercial
opportunities.

Peddlers, Merchants, and Manufacturers focuses on Jews and business
enterprises in a region comprised of ten counties in the northwestern part
of the state known as the "Upcountry," as distinct from the "Lowcountry"
(Charleston and the coastal regions), and the "Midlands" (Columbia and
surrounding cities). The story of Jews and their rise in business and manufacturing cannot be accounted for without examining the rise of textile
manufacturing in the Upcountry. This region experienced dynamic growth
in the mid- to late nineteenth century as the cotton textile industry developed and the concept of a New South advanced. With access to cotton fields
and developed transportation networks, coupled with South Carolina's
generous tax incentives, cheap labor, abundance of workers, and a history
of anti-unionism, Greenville and Spartanburg became a center for textile
manufacturing.

Forward-looking South Carolinian investors, along with northern textile entrepreneurs, paved the way for the domination of manufacturing that
defined a century of upcountry economic history. By 1899, Spartanburg was
promoting itself as "the Lowell of the South," as it successfully competed with

the Massachusetts center of textile manufacturing in the North. Continued economic difficulties and labor strikes in New England's textile industries led to bankruptcies and mill closings, forcing more northern textile manufacturers to look south for relocation.

Why study the history of Jews in the Upcountry of South Carolina? Because Jewish migration to this region illustrates how entrepreneurial Jews, whether peddlers, merchants, or manufacturers, carefully chose areas ripe for business opportunity. Jews settled in the upcountry of South Carolina beginning in the late nineteenth century, even though there were few Jewish compatriots and no established Jewish life. The earliest Jews to inhabit the Upcountry were peddlers drawn to the region by kinship networks and the prospect of selling goods to rural folk who had little or no access to local markets. Many peddlers saved enough money to eventually open their own shops. By the first quarter of the twentieth century, Jewish merchants dotted the towns and cities of Upcountry South Carolina, many of whom migrated there from regions in the North and South because of the economic potential for business.

Beginning in the early twentieth century, northern Jewish clothing manufacturers relocated to the Upcountry as New England cotton textile manufacturers had done earlier. Most of these Jewish manufacturers had operated garment factories in the northeast and sought less expensive means of producing goods.

Jewish-owned manufacturing companies ranged from small factories employing fewer than one hundred employees to major companies with a workforce of several thousand. They manufactured shirts, men's suits, women's apparel, workers' clothing, undergarments, and children's wear. During World War II, they received government contracts and produced uniforms and parachutes for American soldiers.

Emigrant Jews from Russia had established several Jewish-owned upcountry garment companies. New York transplants, the sons of Jewish immigrants who initially settled in the northeast founded most companies. Some of these entrepreneurs became deeply involved in their communities and synagogues, while others simply operated their business and remained aloof from local religious and community life.

The history of capital relocation from the North to the South has overlooked Jewish manufacturers in the Upcountry. Publications abound on the New England textile manufacturers who established cotton mills in South

Carolina, but Jewish garment manufacturers have gone unnoticed. Thus, this book adds an important corrective to the history of manufacturing in South Carolina as well as an important addition to Jewish economic history.

In many ways, the economic lives of Jews in the Upcountry were like those in other parts of the state. Regardless of where they settled, Jews peddled and merchants conducted business, from the Upcountry to the coast. But differences also existed. The contrast between Charleston, a major trading and commercial center, and the Upcountry, a future textile manufacturing hub, offered diverse opportunities for Jews. Both regions exemplify the significance of economic prospects that pulled Jewish migrants to a specific locality.

The Jewish presence in South Carolina is well documented by historians with studies of Charleston, where American Jewish history began in the early seventeenth century. By 1800, Charleston had the largest Jewish community in America with 500 people. Interest in the Jews of Charleston is well deserved as it was the center of a prosperous and culturally elite Jewish population. However, the Jews of the Upcountry have gone unnoticed.

And it is no wonder. While Charleston flourished as a vital port city, the Upcountry was a backcountry region settled by Scots-Irish, situated at the foothills of the Blue Ridge Mountains, and dominated by agriculture and cotton production. That began to change in the post–Civil War era, however, when significant transformations took place in cotton manufacturing. With the prospect of a growing economy from textiles, entrepreneurial Jews found their way to a promising location for business. These were pioneers, people on the move in search of locations ripe for commercial activity.

This study demonstrates how immigrant entrepreneurial success transpired, according to opportunity structures, group characteristics, and strategies. Jews took advantage of migration networks, mobilizing resources and moving into regions where market conditions were promising and profitable.

Jews who relocated to the Upcountry employed various strategies to succeed in an unfamiliar environment. These include following social and familial networks, residing with other Jews as extended-family household members (or as paying boarders), providing financial and business support in professional endeavors, and hiring other Jews (particularly family members) in business establishments. Jews relied on credit networks, often pooling their resources to start a business.

The history of small Jewish communities in America has become increasingly significant since the 1970s when local and community history became a serious tool for examining the immigrant experience. Lee Shai Weissbach's publication of *Jewish Life in Small-Town America* shifted the focus from Jewish life in large urban areas such as New York City to the myriad of small and medium-sized American towns that became the destination of tens of thousands of Jewish migrants.[4] There is no question of the significance of New York Jewry, but their experiences do not reflect those of Jews who settled in villages, small towns, and medium cities in the West, Middle West, and South.

There are, however, similarities between migrant urban Jews and small-town Jews. By examining the Jewish experience in Upcountry South Carolina, contrasts and similarities with urban Jews are apparent. For example, Jews who settled in New York City in the late nineteenth century worked in the needle trades and became urban laborers. In contrast, Jews in the Upcountry were never part of the working class. Rather, as businesspeople, they occupied the middle class and upper-middle class of merchants and manufacturers.

As Jews gained an economic foothold in the Upcountry, they established synagogues and religious organizations. They also engaged with the non-Jewish community by joining service and fraternal organizations, such as the Elks Club, Rotary, and Lions Club.

In an economic atmosphere dominated by working-class, native-born southerners, this volume reveals how daughters and sons of Jewish businesspeople pursued education, both at secondary and university levels, at rates greater than the general population. American-born daughters of Jewish immigrants worked in their family's business enterprises and entered white-collar occupations where they worked as secretaries, clerks, and stenographers. While European-born Jewish women rarely worked outside of the home, they contributed to the family economy by taking in Jewish boarders, an invisible form of earning income.

Business-class Jews acculturated by becoming homeowners, achieving citizenship, and fighting for their country during the world wars. During World War II, several Upcountry Jews became decorated war heroes, a fact that disputes false anti-Semitic charges that Jews shirked their responsibilities in wartime. Jewish war service solidified their status as loyal American citizens.

In the post–World War II era, Jewish textile and garment manufacturers relocated to the Upcountry and made significant contributions to the industry with creative innovations in clothing apparel and fabric design. Apparel manufacturers, such as Butte Knit in Spartanburg, created and produced double-knit garments, and other manufacturers perfected new methods of dying and knitting. Garment manufacturers emigrated from Europe, but most were American-born sons of immigrant Jews from the Northeast. Attracted to the South by low labor costs, transportation networks, state incentives, which included tax exemptions, and a tradition of anti-unionism, Jewish manufacturers found a welcoming environment in Upcountry South Carolina, where they provided thousands of jobs to local residents.

Jewish–Black relations, which developed initially as interactions between Jewish merchants and their Black clientele, were positive overall. During the civil rights era, racial tensions deepened in the Upcountry as local leaders, such as Jesse Jackson, sparked a movement. At the height of the civil rights unrest, Upcountry Jews, who privately supported the goals of the civil rights movement, remained on the sidelines and rarely spoke out. These were behaviors that Upcountry Jews shared with Jews in small towns throughout the South.

In the late twentieth and early twenty-first centuries, Jewish business leaders became important community builders and mayors of the largest cities in the Upcountry, continuing a long tradition of Jews elected to manage towns and cities in South Carolina. Even though Jews had overwhelming support of their communities, anti-Semitism reared its ugly head in mayoral and legislative races. Furthermore, Jews faced exclusion from private social and golf clubs, a prohibition that would not be lifted until the 1970s.

By illuminating how Jews negotiated their place in Upcountry South Carolina, this work is a case study of a specific geographical location and an economic environment that attracted Jewish migrants. It examines Jewish immigration history through the lenses of regional economic history, social history, and labor history. It follows the Upcountry's transition from a major cotton textile manufacturing region to a center of industrial diversification and international investments, where community leaders actively courted international businesses and created model communities of globalization. The Greenville-Spartanburg corridor is today the site of the largest per capita diversified foreign investment in the United States, an economic environment attracting a new class of Jewish migrants: professionals and upper-managerial executives. The Upcountry has reinvented itself many times since the nineteenth century, and Jewish migrants have played a significant role in those changes.

CHAPTER 1

The Lure of South Carolina

Moses Lindo, a Sephardic Jew who emigrated from London to Charleston in 1756, became a prominent indigo merchant and authority on dyes.[1] From field to market, Lindo promoted the planting, cultivation, processing, and merchandising of the deep blue dye made from the leaves of the indigo plant.

From its earliest days as a British colony to its maturation as an important southern state, South Carolina provided Jews with an economic incentive for immigrating to America. Jewish settlement in the British colony dates to the seventeenth century and was concentrated in the port city of Charleston, a major Atlantic trade center. Jews came as traders and merchants connecting transatlantic centers with Charleston.[2]

Most Jews who lived in the booming port city were Sephardim who had been expelled from Spain and Portugal and came to South Carolina after migrating first to the Netherlands or England.[3]

Only a handful of Jews resided in Charleston in 1697, but their numbers continued to grow slowly throughout the eighteenth century. The experiences of early settler Jews in the colony of Carolina demonstrate what historian Mark Bauman observed, that "colonial Jewry was part of a transatlantic Jewry linked by business, family, and religion."[4] The increasingly important trade center needed people with trading skills and contacts and the Jews had both.

Many mid-eighteenth-century Jewish immigrants who settled in Charleston were Sephardim from London, descended from wealthy merchant families and engaged in business, trade, finance, and agriculture. Mordecai Cohen and Isaiah Moses, along with several other Jewish immigrants, established themselves as lowcountry planters in the late eighteenth century.[5] Before becoming a planter, Polish-born Cohen started out as a peddler and a shopkeeper. By the late eighteenth century, he was one of the wealthiest men in South Carolina.[6]

The economic opportunities for entrepreneurial Jews in Carolina were endless. Furthermore, Jews were permitted to worship as they saw fit, another reason for European Jews to look across the Atlantic as a potential site of settlement free from the persecutions they suffered in the Old World.

The Jewish population of the state grew rapidly after the war for independence. When Columbia became the capital of South Carolina in 1786, Jewish men from Charleston were among the first to buy town lots in the city.[7] Jews also settled in other parts of the state, particularly Georgetown, north of Charleston, the second largest seaport in South Carolina and the second oldest Jewish settlement in the state.[8]

While the Sephardim immigrated to South Carolina during the colonial period, later Jewish arrivals tended to be Ashkenazim, most of whom came from German-speaking Central Europe with a smaller percentage from East Europe.[9]

Central and East European Jews filled a different economic niche than their Sephardim predecessors as peddlers and merchants, a pattern typical throughout the United States.[10] Many made their way into the South Carolina interior peddling clothing, needles, tobacco products, dry goods, hardware, and jewelry. From their Midlands routes of the 1840s and 1850s, their extensive territory soon expanded to the backcountry,[11] an area dominated by the Scots-Irish, who had settled there before the Revolutionary War.[12]

Many factors led to a dramatic increase in East European Jewish immigration during the late nineteenth century, among them pogroms, persecution, and the prospect of conscription into the Russian army. They also fled Europe for economic reasons. In addition to finding jobs in America's sprawling industrial cities, of the northeast, many East European Jews were also motivated to start businesses and control their lives through entrepreneurial activities.

As several historians have noted, Jewish immigration to the United States was "grounded in the material realities of emerging markets, explosive demographic growth, and fledgling pluralistic democracies."[13] Hasia Diner and Adam Mendelson, historians of the Jewish experience in America, discount the argument made by which scholars contend that Jewish immigration was solely the result of old-world push factors such as violent anti-Semitism and discriminatory religious limitations. They emphasize the risks taken by Jews to secure economic advancement in other lands.[14] As Diner maintains: "The beckoning of newly opened territory for commerce in widely scattered places more powerfully pulled them out of their old homes than did persecution push them out."[15]

With the growth of the United States as an industrial power in the late nineteenth century, thousands of jobs became available to Jews and other immigrants who arrived between 1880 and 1924. Industrializing cities such as Cleveland attracted Slovaks and Italians who found jobs in the steel and automotive industries; Philadelphia and New York City provided thousands of jobs to Jews and Italians in the needle trades, while Irish and Polish workers dominated Chicago's meatpacking plants. Smaller towns and cities such as Endicott, New York, drew Italians and Slovaks to their shoe manufacturing companies, while Jewish immigrants in Johnstown, Pennsylvania, and Italians in Milwaukee, Wisconsin, formed tightly knit entrepreneurial ethnic niches.

Jews migrated to the South in smaller numbers than those who settled on the northeast coast or even in the Midwest, and for many the region provided a secondary destination after settling in other parts of the country. Jews who migrated to the South were motivated by varied factors from those who settled in the North. Jewish migrants to southern destinations determined that their future was in business and commercial activity, not in sweatshops or garment factories. "The possibility of frequent failure and relocation," according to historian David Gerber, "enabled [these] Jews to become risk takers who might well be considered exemplary American capitalists."[16]

One of the major characteristics of Jewish migration in the South was the incessant mobility of a people who were on the move in search of locations ripe for commercial activity. During the nineteenth and early twentieth centuries Jewish "risk takers" were attracted to areas of the South characterized by improved transportation networks, industrialization, and urbanization.

One of these regions was the South Carolina Upcountry, an area that was shifting from an agricultural to an industrialized society. The changes brought about by industrialization—particularly textile mills—stimulated business and commercial activities. The movement of Jews to this region of the Piedmont reveals how the potential for economic opportunities and business ventures enticed Jewish migrants to South Carolina's Upcountry. Somewhat ironically, the mills of the South provided the textiles for many of the sweatshops and factories of the North.

THE UPCOUNTRY

In the late nineteenth century, the Upcountry, with its growing commerce, transportation system, and profits from cotton was an attractive place for business. Jewish migrants came from Charleston and other regions of the

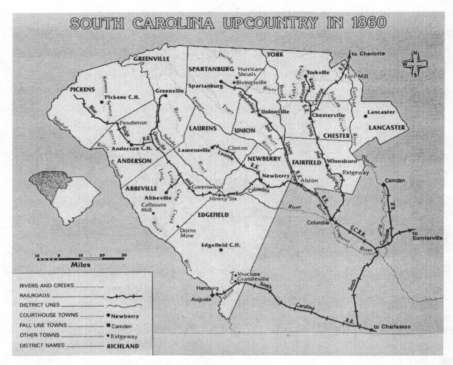

Map of the South Carolina Upcountry 1860. Courtesy of the Spartanburg Public Library, Kennedy Room.

Lowcountry, while most came from the North and still others from Central and East Europe.

In the nineteenth century, South Carolinians referred to the far western counties in the Piedmont as the "Upcountry." Bordered on the north by North Carolina and on the west and south by Georgia, the region comprises fifteen counties: Oconee, Pickens, Greenville, Spartanburg, Cherokee, York, Anderson, Laurens, Union, Chester, Abbeville, McCormick, Greenwood, Edgefield, and Newberry.[17] In the twentieth century, this region would become known as the "Upstate."

Inhabited by native Cherokee and Catawba, the backcountry of South Carolina was resettled in the late 1700s when Scots-Irish, English, and German families and a small population of Swedes migrated from Pennsylvania and Virginia through the Appalachian Mountains into the Carolinas.

The American Revolution brought notoriety to what would become Spartanburg County (named for the Spartan Rifles, a local regiment) when

Daniel Morgan of the Continental Army defeated Banastre Tarlton and his British legions at the Battle of Cowpens, considered a major turning point in the war.[18]

The two largest communities in the Upcountry, Spartanburg and Greenville, were organized after independence. Spartanburg had its beginnings as a county in the first session of the post–Revolutionary War state legislature on January 1, 1782. Greenville County came into existence in 1786 and was named after Revolutionary War hero Nathaniel Green. The growth of the newly designated courthouse village of Spartanburgh (as it was spelled then), gauged in the first official United States census of 1790, showed that the county's population was 8,800. Of that number 7,913 were white, 860 were enslaved, and twenty-seven were listed as free persons, not white.[19] The Greenville population in 1810 was more than 13,000, an increase of eighty-seven percent over the previous ten years. The enslaved population also grew while the number of enslavers increased from 314 to 443 during the same period.[20]

Most people living in the Upcountry during the eighteenth century were subsistence farmers who supported themselves by growing wheat, grain, tobacco, and corn and raising hogs and cattle. However, during the early decades of the next century, short-staple cotton production spread into the South Carolina interior where upcountry soil proved receptive to the cultivation of the new staple crop.[21] According to southern historian Lacy Ford, "In 1793, the entire state produced only 94,000 pounds of cotton . . . but by 1811 the Upcountry exported more than 30 million pounds of short-staple cotton."[22]

With the emergence of this profitable cash crop, many upcountry families increased their landholdings and became successful cotton planters, which resulted in an increased number of families who enslaved.[23] While serving as Andrew Jackson's vice president between 1825 and 1832, John C. Calhoun's upcountry home consisted of a sprawling 500-acre cotton plantation along the Seneca River in Pickens District where he enslaved forty-two people who worked his cotton fields.[24]

Industry and manufacturing were also developing during this time and contributed to diversification in the Upcountry's economy. The manufacture of muskets and other firearms was a major industry in the Greenville district. More important, the textile industry was laying a modest foundation for the post–Civil War industrial revolution.[25] Two textile plants had been built in Spartanburg County in 1816 and 1818 by two sets of brothers who were native New Englanders.

The Upcountry's population continued to grow. The 1820 census for Spartanburg revealed a population of 16,989 people of European origin compared to 8,800 in 1790, an increase of nearly seventy-five percent. The number of enslaved increased almost four-fold, from 866 to 3,308, a result of intensifying cotton cultivation.[26]

In Spartanburg County, B. B. Foster owned forty-three enslaved persons who worked his cotton plantation near Glenn Springs. Others enslaved picked cotton on Thomas Williamson's plantation in Woodruff where a Georgian-style home built in 1793 (now known as the Nicholls-Crook Plantation House) overlooked 1,000 acres. At the Price House in Woodruff, twenty-eight enslaved people worked the 2,000-acre plantation.[27]

In 1850 eighty-two persons in Greenville each owned twenty or more enslaved individuals, thereby qualifying as planters. Vardry McBee remained the largest landowner in the Greenville district at the end of the antebellum period with thirty-seven enslaved people in 1850 and fifty-six a decade later. According to Greenville historian A. V. Huff, "Only seven persons owned more in 1860, and only Colonel T. Edwin Ware owned more than one hundred . . . slaves."[28]

Although most of those enslaved worked in agriculture, South Carolina historian Steve O'Neill notes that "the hiring-out of slaves by owners was a common practice in South Carolina and throughout the South." Indeed in Greenville, enslaved people were hired from their enslavers to work on the construction of the campus of Furman University during the 1850s.[29]

Beginning in 1817 the state authorized expenditures for the building of roads and canals that improved transportation and lowered the cost of moving goods.[30] Progress in the Upcountry slowed during the 1840s, however, when soil exhaustion and erosion became serious problems for the state's farmers. Many farmers left the state for fresh opportunities and land further west.[31]

At the end of the decade, however, South Carolina began to pull out of its slump. Upcountry farmers produced more cotton than ever before even though they had been warned by reformers to wean themselves from their reliance on the crop.[32] Rising profits from the cotton boom, claims historian Lacy Ford, "sparked an important commercial quickening in upcountry towns during the 1850s."[33] Cotton prices, land values, and the value of the enslaved were all high and "upcountry planters were clearly at the height of their economic power" as cotton production expanded.[34]

Beginning in the 1850s, a flurry of railroad building, backed by northern investors, created a far-reaching transportation system in South Carolina.

By 1860 eleven railroads operated in the state. In the Upcountry alone 400 miles of track were laid between 1848 and 1860, establishing rail connections for every district in the region and the major commercial centers of Columbia and Charleston.[35] This extension of railroads into the Upcountry in the 1850s and the establishment of banking systems contributed to Spartanburg and Greenville becoming important upcountry market centers.

Minor industries dotted the Upcountry with iron-manufacturing establishments such as Berwick's Iron Works and the South Carolina Manufacturing Company in Spartanburg.[36] Greenville also became a center of iron mining and smelting industries, and during the Civil War the city was used as an armory to manufacture rifles.[37] Four foundries produced farming implements and building materials essential to an expanding agricultural society.[38] The iron industry developed into one of the leading industries in the region because of large iron ore deposits found in the foothills of the Appalachian Mountains and the upper regions of the Upcountry. Manufacturing grew slowly but steadily. Grist milling was the largest single industry in the Upcountry in the mid-nineteenth century, followed by carriage making.

A small but vital business district developed in the marketing centers of Spartanburg and Greenville and provided goods and services to the growing villages. Boasting of Spartanburg in April 1851, the editor of the *Carolina Spartan* wrote: "We observe the signs of growth and of progress all around us. We have in successful business operation thirteen dry goods establishments; two saddlery and harness establishments; three excellent hotels; three commodious churches . . . two academies, male and female; two-day schools for smaller pupils; lawyers and doctors aplenty and . . . kind and courteous people."[39]

It's not surprising that the Upcountry with its growing commerce, expanded transportation systems, and profits from cotton attracted Jewish migrants. In the mid-nineteenth century a handful of Jews arrived in Greenville and several rural communities in the Upcountry.

Historian Anton Hieke noted that "Jews generally came to the region [South Carolina Upcountry] for two reasons: having family and friends already living there, and economic considerations."[40] The Visanska, Rosenberg, and Winstock families demonstrate how Jewish family members followed each other to Abbeville through chain-migration networks. These same families became successful and prosperous when they combined their fortunes through marriage.

The legacy of the Russian-Polish Winstock family started when Moses Winstock immigrated to Charleston in the 1840s and purchased a wholesale jewelry concern that evolved into a peddler's supply company. In 1854 he moved his family to the upcountry town of Due West, located in Abbeville District, where the climate was cooler and drier, to escape the stifling heat and humidity of Charleston.[41]

Winstock's growing financial success allowed him to build several brick stores and purchase a 525-acre plantation nearby where he planted cotton and corn. His daughter, Rebecca, helped consolidate the family's prosperity when she married Abraham Rosenberg of Rosenberg & Company in Abbeville. The Rosenberg family owned more than twenty buildings and nearly 8,000 acres of land in Greenwood County where they harvested timber.[42] The Winstock and Rosenberg families reveal how Jewish kinship networks created and maintained opportunities for upward mobility.

During the mid-nineteenth century, several German Jews made their way to Greenville. The most prominent was Simon Swandale, whose original surname may have been Schwan. Swandale became a leading business figure in the growing community. Born in Hamburg in 1809, he came to the United States as a young man, trained as a tailor in New York City, and soon became a fabric peddler. Swandale visited Greenville at least once prior to establishing a business in 1841. Swandale partnered with a man named Moses McCary, and the merchant tailors boasted that the goods available at their shop, Swandale and McCary, were of "superior quality." Their "French and English broadcloths, doeskins and cassimers, rich satin cravats, silk and cotton undershirts and gentlemen's accessories, including canes and umbrellas,"[43] were goods as fine as one may purchase on the fashionable streets of New York City. Throughout the 1840s Swandale made frequent trips to New York to buy fabrics and fancy goods including striped, plaid, and plush vests; velvet and silk robes; and ready-made shirts for his Greenville store.[44] These merchants and others like them created a consumer marketplace for their small-town clientele. Swandale and McCary provided merchants, bankers, and the small but growing business class access to quality merchandise in a convenient downtown location.

Looking for an opportunity to improve his economic status, Isak Eisenmann, a farmer, left Baden (southwestern Germany) in 1850 in financial difficulty and immigrated to South Carolina where some of his "siblings already reside[d], in order to find a better livelihood." Isak's three brothers had already established themselves as merchants in Darlington.[45]

During the next several decades, Jewish merchants would dominate retail trade in Greenville, Spartanburg, and small towns throughout the Upcountry. Their expertise in merchandising and tailoring allowed them to offer New York-style clothing to their customers. Many Jewish merchants, like Swandale, were part of an ethnic network emanating from New York and Baltimore that helped immigrants gain a foothold in their new surroundings.[46]

With a burgeoning Jewish economy in ready-made clothes and peddler supplies centered in Baltimore, merchants made connections with other Jews throughout the South. In an age when immigrant Jews had few other sources of credit, Goldstein and Weiner remark that "these networks allowed immigrant Jews to connect Baltimore to markets across many states."[47] In addition, several upcountry businesspeople had migrated to the South after having lived in Baltimore. The contacts that Jewish merchants had with New York and Baltimore firms often provided them with goods on credit and the opportunity to reflect a cosmopolitan identity.

THE BUSINESS OF UPCOUNTRY RESORTS

The prominence of the Upcountry grew during the nineteenth century as it also became a tourist destination—an "important factor in the development of the economy, culture, and infrastructure of upcountry South Carolina."[48] The Upcountry was cooler than other parts of the South—especially the oppressively humid Lowcountry—and possessed beautiful views of the Blue Ridge Mountains. Newly built resort hotels were often located at the site of mineral springs, which made them even more appealing.[49] Melissa Walker, a southern historian found that "entrepreneurs developed several resorts in the upcountry districts and tourism became an important vehicle through which upcountry business leaders built the local economy."[50] Wealthy residents escaped the heat, humidity, and malaria of the Lowcountry by fleeing to the cooler, drier locations of the Upcountry.[51]

Edmund Waddell established Prospect Hill, one of the first resort hotels in Greenville in 1815 and Colonel William Toney opened the Mansion House in 1824, which had a reputation of being one of the finest "hostelries" in the South.[52] In Spartanburg, the earliest hotels were the Walker House Hotel and the Palmetto House. Pacolet Springs in the Spartan district was one of the first mineral springs hotels to open, followed by Limestone Springs, near the village of Gaffney in northern Spartanburg County. In Greenville, Chick Springs developed and attracted influential visitors from around the state.[53]

The most popular resort hotel by far was the Glenn Springs Hotel, located in a village a few miles southeast of Spartanburg. Known for its mineral springs, the lore of the healing waters soon spread and became popular with South Carolinians suffering from various afflictions. The resort sold bottled spring water and offered cold, warm, and shower baths for their guests. Glenn Springs became a popular resort for some of South Carolina's most influential leaders including a governor who moved his office to the resort for several weeks each summer.

South Carolina Congressman Preston Brooks had a home nearby and frequently dined at the Glenn Springs Hotel while other notable visitors included Mrs. John C. Calhoun and Edmund C. Ruffin, the passionate secessionist from Virginia.[54] Jewish Charlestonians were among those who frequented the Glenn Springs resort. Many of them, Jews who had left East Europe in the decades before and after World War I, were businesspeople referred to as "uptown Jews."[55] That Jews gained admittance to the resort suggests that no exclusionary laws forbade Jews from enjoying the resort along with non-Jews.

In 1852, Simon Swandale and William H. Irvine of Spartanburg purchased Toney's Mansion House in Greenville.[56] The grand hotel was a destination vacation that drew visitors from all over the South, including John C. Calhoun, who made it his headquarters when he was in Greenville.[57] For twenty-five years, Swandale welcomed guests to the resort, which had a massive ballroom, a billiard parlor, an apothecary shop, and a gentlemen's saloon. Located on the site of today's Poinsett Hotel on Main Street, the Mansion House provided the finest dining and hotel accommodations in the area.[58] Collectively the resort hotels in the Upcountry added to the region's economic prosperity and diversity and provided an escape for Lowcountry residents, Jews included.

In the early 1850s, another cotton boom occurred in the Upcountry contributing to higher cotton prices and greater grower profits.[59] According to Ford, "with a second cotton boom and the expansion of railroads into the Upcountry the volume of business transacted in upcountry towns increased tremendously."[60] Manufacturing also increased in the region as paper mills, cotton mills, gun factories, carriage works, tinworks, and flour mills provided employment for the growing population.[61]

Greenville flourished in the mid-nineteenth century during which time several Jewish merchants relocated to Greenville from other southern locations. Jews sought out new opportunities in promising, growing communities.

Greenville's business community was still small with very few retail stores which created a need for more and varied businesses. In 1855 Samuel Brafman opened the doors to the Baltimore Clothing Store, the name of the business emphasizing Brafman's connections to his hometown.

Abraham Isaacs, who was born in New York, made his way to Greenville in the 1850s and became a "merchant retailer."[62] He entered a business partnership with A. Nicholl and they operated a men's clothing store until the outbreak of the Civil War. Simon Einstein and Joseph Sonenberg opened Einstein Company, a dry goods store in 1857, and Abigail and L. L. Levy from Charleston opened a dry-goods establishment in 1859. It did not last long, however. Tragically, the Levys appear to be the first-known victims of anti-Semitism in the Upcountry.

ANTI-SEMITIC EPISODES IN THE UPCOUNTRY

According to the 1860 journal of a young Furman University graduate, there were several incidents involving a group called the "Invisibles" who harassed and mistreated several Jewish businesspeople in Greenville. The hostility was directed toward L. L. Levy, his business, and a "negro boy named Vol." While it is unclear what happened, the Invisibles were determined to run the Levys out of Greenville. On a cold December night, they went to Levy's store, "seized him rode him on a rail up the river shaved half his head and beard and made him promise to leave in one week." The diary's author, Belton Mauldin, lamented that "I did not get to see the fun; should have enjoyed it."[63]

The dry goods store closed and the Levys disappeared from Greenville, but they were not the only Jewish businesspeople who were persecuted. The Invisibles targeted several other Jewish merchants. In a December journal entry Mauldin noted: "We determined to take Joe Lowenberg out on a ride; failing this however, we seized Samuels, and carried him across the bridge at the upper ford riding him a short distance on a rail; carried him over in the woods and there I shaved half his head as close as I c'd with a pair of shears and trimmed his beard also then turned him loose ordering him to leave town by to-morrow morning w'h he said he w'd do, he cried like a baby the whole time and the whole occurrence was quite amusing."[64]

In a city where Jews prospered and appeared to be part of the fabric of southern society, it is unsettling to discover examples of anti-Jewish violence. Within the context of other journal entries Mauldin penned in 1860, it is clear there was a growing sense of southern nationalism and exclusion against "others" during the period leading to secession. This combined with a fundamentalist Baptist Christian belief in the Southern cause may help explain his and others' hostility toward Jews.

Another journal entry suggests possible bitterness toward Jewish businessmen and their relationships with Black people. On January 23, 1860, Mauldin confided in his journal: "Got some harnesses . . . and hurried the negroes off as they were disposed to hang around these Jew stores here, detestable places that they are."[65]

Anti-Jewish prejudice was a characteristic expression of the age. Bertram Korn maintains that social, economic, and political factors brought latent prejudices against Jews into the open.[66] These tendencies appeared in the years before the Civil War and were amplified during the war when prejudice against Jews occurred most frequently in connection with the economic life of the Confederacy.

In another Georgia incident, disgruntled citizens met in 1862 to protest Jewish traders. Colonel J. L. Seward blamed "foreign counterfeiters and profiteers" who were demanding exorbitant and ruinous prices for food and supplies on Thomasville's German Jews who were (supposedly) conspiring with Jewish peddlers. Local citizens believed that Jewish businessmen were "buying up particular localities, articles of prime necessity, thereby producing a scarcity and transferring such articles to other localities"[67] A Committee of Vigilance decided that German Jews would be given ten days to leave town.[68] In a time of severe economic crisis, the "foreign Jew" was perceived as contributing to the worsening calamity.

However, later episodes of anti-Semitism occurred in the South as well. In 1926, Sam Davidson was chased out of Hahira, Georgia, by the Ku Klux Klan (KKK). Fortunately, Davidson found a friendly environment in Chesnee in northern Spartanburg County, where he established Davidson's Department Store. Davidson had received a threatening letter from the Klan warning him: "we command that you be absent from this town, with your belongings . . . as you are not a desirable citizen in this community."[69] Davidson did not wait for the promised second warning. He packed up his possessions and relocated to the South Carolina Upcountry, where his brothers and mother were living.[70] Davidson opened a clothing store in the small community of Chesnee and when he retired, his daughter, Jeanette Davidson Finkelstein, continued to operate the business until 2009 when she was in her early nineties.[71]

PEDDLING IN THE UPCOUNTRY

On a sweltering summer morning in July 1903, Abraham Surasky, a well-known and respected peddler, was murdered in Aiken, South Carolina, by a client's husband who maintained that he walked in on the peddler trying to seduce his wife. Surasky, a 35-year-old immigrant from the Polish shtetl of Knyshin, had an excellent reputation among the many non-Jews in and around Aiken.

According to historian Patrick Q. Mason, the husband, Lee Green, "had long held a grudge against Jewish peddlers in general and Surasky in particular. . . . Chronic indebtedness," maintains Mason, was common "between the rural people and the peddlers who sold them goods."[72] After the bloody murder, Green ripped the pages out of Surasky's account book detailing his debt to the peddler. Mrs. Green made frequent purchases from Surasky and had not always been able to pay what she owed.[73]

Fortunately, violence toward peddlers did not occur with any frequency in South Carolina, but Surasky's murder illustrates the risks and dangers encountered by Jewish peddlers in nineteenth and early twentieth century America.

Based on existing documentation, it appears that Jewish peddlers were welcomed in Upcountry South Carolina, especially in the period after the Civil War when commodities were scarce. Even though most peddlers struggled with the English language as newly arrived immigrants, their status as whites gained them entry into southern homes where a strict racial divide existed.[74] For Jews, the shifting boundaries of race that defined American society in the nineteenth and early twentieth century was more clearly differentiated in the South where "the other" in white southern society was associated with Black people. Diner maintains that their whiteness meant that Jews could sell to Black customers, while at the same time, retain the rights and respect accorded to whiteness.[75]

The desperate need for goods in remote areas of the South worked in favor of Jewish peddlers, as "South Carolina was the consummate backwater, in retreat from the currents of modern life," according to historians Dale Rosengarten and Theodore Rosengarten, who assert that but for "immigrant men willing to put a pack on their backs and peddle their wares . . . South Carolina was a virtual frontier."[76]

The number of Jews engaged in peddling might be considered a group characteristic fashioned by hundreds of years of itinerant peddling in Europe.

Historian Hasia Diner writes that peddling was often the first occupation many Jewish males entered when they arrived in America. It offered several incentives to immigrants starting out: "independence and self–employment, the prospect of advancement through hard work, and the promise of eventually owning a store."[77]

Peddling was an attractive option for immigrants because it required little command of the English language, or the capital needed to purchase goods for peddling.[78] However, Jewish peddlers often had to overcome obstacles before they took to the road.

Prior to the Civil War, fearing that abolitionists might pose as peddlers or that peddlers would trade with enslaved people, South Carolina enacted stringent assessments on peddling licenses. In 1825, peddlers paid fifty dollars for a license while in 1835 the cost skyrocketed to $1,000.[79] The licensing requirements also reflect what Mendelsohn states as "the attitude of many southerners who believed that Jewish peddlers were dishonest, a combination of American prejudices against itinerant traders with older ideas about Jewish commercial practices."[80]

Several state legislatures had raised licensing fees for peddlers to unaffordable levels in the decades before the Civil War, although in the postbellum period, licenses were once again affordable, and goods were usually provided on consignment from wholesalers.[81] In mid-nineteenth century Massachusetts, a Hawkers and Peddlers Act assessed fees according to "morals and citizenship," while in North Carolina citizenship was a prerequisite to obtaining a peddling license.[82] The exorbitant price of a license, no doubt, accounts for the absence of peddlers in the Upcountry before the Civil War.

The numbers of Jews engaged in peddling increased in the late nineteenth century with the arrival of East Europeans—nearly 2.25 million Jews from the regions of Ukraine, Belarus, Lithuania, Poland, Romania, and Galicia between 1890 and 1924. Many immigrants had peddled in Central Europe before emigrating and drew on familiar experiences in the Old World upon arriving in America.[83]

Israel From, a native of Lithuania, began peddling in Union in 1879 after a cousin settled there. Polish-born George Visanska followed a family member to Charleston and left the Lowcountry to join his uncle in Abbeville. He became an upcountry peddler, eventually opening a peddler supply business providing goods to itinerant merchants.[84] Visanska later became a business partner in the Rosenberg Mercantile Company in Abbeville, which sold clothing, hardware, farm machinery, guns, and ammunition to local farmers and townspeople.[85]

Russian-born David Poliakoff left Worcester, Massachusetts, during the 1890s to be near his sister in Abbeville. Years later, his cousin, Rosa From Poliakoff recalled, "He [David] started peddling—they all started out as peddlers, my father did too—he started peddling and followed the Savannah River. Each day he'd go a little bit further, establishing a clientele."[86] Russian-born Sam Davidson joined his uncle in Anderson upon arriving in the Upcountry in 1903 and with the encouragement of his uncle commenced peddling.[87]

More is known about the peddler Nathan Shapiro than any other peddler in the Upcountry because of a lengthy interview of Shapiro conducted by a Works Progress Administration (WPA) writer in 1939. Shapiro left Russia in 1896 to join a cousin working as a peddler in Baltimore. The day after Shapiro arrived in the port city, his cousin bought him a tin of ware-buckets, dippers, and pans. He then commenced peddling with his cousin. A year later, the two headed for the South Carolina Upcountry, where they became established as peddlers in Union County.[88] In 1906, Nathan Shapiro bought a round-trip ticket to Baltimore and selected the stock he would peddle in Union County from the Baltimore Bargain House.[89]

Many southern peddlers obtained goods and credit from Jacob Epstein, a Lithuanian Jew who started as a peddler and eventually established the Baltimore Bargain House in Maryland in 1882.[90] Epstein and a friend settled in Baltimore in 1879 where they had relatives. According to Epstein's biographer, the young immigrants obtained credit from a wholesale house and began to peddle merchandise needed by country housewives. Epstein filled his pack and was soon peddling throughout the upper South.[91] In early 1881, Epstein left peddling to start a wholesale house that burgeoned into a giant enterprise. Trusting the peddlers, he willingly sold them goods on credit.[92] By 1890 customers were coming from all over the South.[93]

Epstein used creative marketing strategies to lure peddlers and merchants to Baltimore. In January 1909, he chartered seven ships from Jacksonville, Florida, and Savannah, Georgia, bringing peddlers and merchants to Baltimore without charge.[94] Supposedly Epstein even paid peddlers' railroad fares to Baltimore to restock their merchandise.[95] The significance of Jewish networks and their ties to Epstein is noted by historian Deborah Weiner who maintains that Epstein "was the individual most responsible for the creation of Jewish communities" in central Appalachia.[96] Epstein was not the only merchandise house that provisioned peddler Jews. Jews peddled in all regions of the United States and obtained goods and credit from merchandising houses in Chicago, New York, and Philadelphia.[97]

Years later, Shapiro ended his trips to Baltimore and began purchasing his goods from Jay Cohen, a Jewish merchant who had established a dry goods business in Union and extended Shapiro credit for his peddling supplies. According to Shapiro: "I settled with Mr. Cohen by paying him up on Saturday night for the pack of goods that I had taken out Monday morning. Then I refilled my wagon before I left the store on Saturday night so that I could get an early start on the next Monday morning."[98]

Peddlers were especially welcome in Union, located south of Spartanburg and dominated by cotton plantations in the southern part of the county. While merchants sold dry goods on Union's Main Street, the county was large and spread out with peddlers supplying goods to the rural dwellers living in its far reaches. Shapiro sold "notions, needles, pins, buttons, belts, suspenders, hair pins, linens, and piece goods."[99]

Caroline Coleman, in her reminiscences of growing up in Greenville County at the turn of the twentieth century, recalls how thrilling it was when she and other children playing in the yard noted a "familiar stooped figure toiling up the lane." She yelled to her grandmother, "Grandma, there's a peddler a-coming." Coleman reminisces, "Into the big living room the peddler would come. We watched in wide-eyed wonder as the inner covering was unfastened and all the riches of Araby lay before us."[100] Another southerner in the 1880s remarked that ". . . Jewish peddlers . . . gave us something to look forward to. It was almost like having Santa Claus come . . . . We loved to see the big bundle opened up, for we seldom saw new things."[101]

Shapiro recollects of his days as a peddler in Union County and the significance of his visits for farm women: "Farmers never came to town over twice a month. Their wives hardly came more than twice a year."[102] According to one upcountry farm wife in the 1870s, her husband "would go to Spartanburg to buy the things he wanted;" adding that "it was hard to buy things during Reconstruction. Those old carpetbaggers and scalawags were hanging out all around Spartanburg, but I never went there a single time."[103] In his study of southern country stores, southern writer Thomas Clark also notes that women approached these centers of commerce with reluctance and uneasiness.[104]

Shapiro described the relationships he forged with his customers: "Farmers depended on the peddlers. When they got to know you well, they bought all the things that they needed from you. If a farmer wanted something you did not have, you got it and brought it on your next visit to his house." Peddlers created warm relationships with their customers who were loyal to specific peddlers and would buy only from them. According to Shapiro, "some of my good customers would not buy from any of the other four peddlers in the county at all. The other four had their exclusive customers as well."[105]

The historian Lu Ann Jones writes that Jewish peddlers "extended the market reach into the South" and "turned farm households into sites of consumption."[106] Southern rural farm households were places of consumption made possible in large part by the appearance of itinerant merchants.[107] Farm women bargained, bartered, and purchased goods from the peddler and could make their purchases in the privacy of their backyards or front porches.[108] By selling manufactured goods to farm women and Black people, peddlers offered an alternative source for consumerism for people "often limited by constraints on their travel and by their discomfort in commercial places where white men gathered."[109]

While there are no existing records of peddlers who sold goods to Black people in the Upcountry, historians have found evidence of business relationships that existed between Jewish peddlers and formerly enslaved people in other areas of the South. In his study of Jews in Atlanta, Steven Hertzberg asserts that "Jewish peddlers . . . who filtered south after the war, eagerly courted the patronage of Blacks, willingly bargained over prices, showed infinite patience in dealing with simple people in small business affairs, and treated their customers with a civility that the latter rarely received from white southerners."[110] The historian Clive Webb theorizes that as strangers to the South, immigrant peddlers did not share the region's racist notions.[111] Thus, Black people were open and hospitable to Jewish peddlers, and the peddlers were kindly and attentive toward their Black customers.[112]

Black individuals who purchased goods from a peddler could avoid the distance and difficulty of reaching a country store as well as southern country storekeepers whose racist assumptions shaped access to credit and goods.[113]

Upcountry peddlers often found lodging in the homes of gentiles. Shapiro, who generally carried his pack about seven miles a day in Union County, spent the night for little or no money at the homes of "friendly farm families."[114] Shapiro recalled the first time he spent the night in a farmhouse: "My pack was heavy and my feet ached for I had peddled all day. I could not tell them [the Humphries] in English that I wanted to spend the night, but I made signs and they made signs back. Well, they gave me my supper, a comfortable bed, and a nice breakfast. The next morning when I offered money, they shook their heads and waved the offer away."[115] Shapiro also spent nights in the Governor Gist Mansion in Union County. The Gilliam family occupied the governor's home at that time, and Shapiro stayed in what was known as the ball room, furnished with antiques, where he slept in a heavy mahogany four-poster bed.[116]

All five peddlers in Union County, four Jews and one Frenchman, often lodged at the Porters, described by Shapiro as "kind-hearted people," who provided the peddlers with room and board.[117] In Greenville County, Caroline Coleman's grandmother refused any compensation after giving the peddler a place to sleep.[118]

In addition to lodging with farmers, Jewish peddlers often boarded in local hotels as did Abraham Mayer, who peddled in the rural Upcountry and boarded in Spartanburg's Windsor Hotel during the 1890s.[119] Louis Switzer and Sam Bloom were Greenville-based peddlers both of whom returned to their families in Greenville for the Sabbath after being on the road all week.

Jewish peddlers faced many hardships on the road. Abraham Kohn, who began peddling in New York, reported loneliness and isolation as did many peddlers who were on the road much of the year.[120] They also experienced fear, traveling into unfamiliar territory, not knowing how they would be accepted by the locals. Observing the Sabbath was a hardship Jews faced on the road; however, often Jews throughout the South provided accommodations for peddlers to observe together. In Natchez, Mississippi, for example, former peddlers turned shopkeepers hosted Jewish peddlers who were unable to return home for the Sabbath meal.[121] Other Jews who peddled closer to home returned in time to celebrate the Sabbath with their families, as did Louis Switzer and Sam Bloom.

Jewish peddlers contributed to the economic revival of the South in the late nineteenth century,[122] and provided goods to needy customers across the country from the bourgeoning cities of the Northeast to the frontier where they traded with pioneer farmers and Native Americans. Peddlers' routes spread out from the Northeast to the Deep South, into the Mississippi Delta and across the Midwest. The California Gold Rush attracted Jewish peddlers who frequented the mining camps,[123] while others peddled in Upstate New York, Cincinnati, and Nashville, becoming part of what Diner calls "a transcontinental Jewish economy."[124]

Jewish peddlers also contributed to the growth of Jewish communities. By utilizing kin and social networking, Jews enticed other family members and friends to join them, eventually growing a community where many Jews moved from peddler to merchant.

The work ethic and perseverance of peddlers was rewarded as many of them became merchants in the towns and cities of the Upcountry. A successful peddler-turned-businessman David Poliakoff, who emigrated from Kamen (a shtetl northeast of Minsk, Belarus), established a dry-goods store in Abbeville in 1900 after peddling first on foot and then by wagon in the Upcountry.[125] Israel From peddled for more than twenty years before opening a dry-goods store in Union that operated for nearly a century by his descendants. Sam Davidson started peddling not long after emigrating from Russia to South Carolina before establishing a dress shop in Chesnee that remained a family business until 2009.[126]

After years of peddling, Nathan Shapiro saved enough money to start a business in Union. Similarly, Sam Bloom, who emigrated from Russia, started a successful business in Greenville after years of selling goods on the road. Blooms was a popular department store in Greenville for nearly one hundred years.

Jewish merchants lived in the same communities where they conducted business, and for the most part knew their customers. Collectively, Jewish merchants and peddlers contributed considerably to consumerism and business expansion in the Upcountry in the years before and after the Civil War. But in the 1860s, with war on the horizon, Jewish entrepreneurial activities would be stalled for several years.

JEWS AND THE CIVIL WAR

In the tension-ridden years that preceded the Civil War, the controversy over slavery engulfed the Southern states. In South Carolina, secessionists called for the state to withdraw from the Union. Even though there were a few dissenting voices in the Upcountry, every newspaper in South Carolina supported secession.[127] In a letter addressed to his son, Greenville's McBee wrote, "these Abolition Fanaticks have set themselves never to cease until the Negroes are all free . . . and . . . never reflect on the consequence."[128]

When South Carolinians received the news that Abraham Lincoln had been elected president, the state legislature called for the election of a secession convention. The legislature directed the governor to call for volunteers from the militia and to resort to a draft if necessary. Once the Confederate

States of America was established and the fighting began, the state troops were mustered into the Confederate forces.[129]

By May 1861, two companies of volunteers departed Greenville. The 16th Regiment was mustered into Confederate Service in December 1861, and The Butler Guards left for Virginia on May 6 and became Company K of the Second Regiment, South Carolina Volunteers.[130] The volunteers who made up the Butler Guards included several Jews from Greenville. The merchant, Abraham Isaacs, swiftly closed his store in downtown Greenville and joined the Butler Guards, proud to serve in the Confederate forces. Even though Isaacs was a native New Yorker, he almost certainly felt like many other Jews who fought for the Confederacy, believing it was their duty as Southern residents to do so. As Robert Rosen explains in his study of Jewish Confederates, Southern Jews fought for the South to prove they were loyal and worthy citizens.[131] A commissioned lieutenant, Isaacs was captured five times but managed to escape each time. Wounded at Gettysburg,[132] Isaacs returned to Greenville and went into the clothing business with Simon Swandale. Isaacs was known to be generous in settling accounts with Confederate veterans and others who were experiencing economic difficulties following the Civil War.[133] When Isaacs died in Greenville at the age of sixty-seven in 1889, his obituary noted that "he was a good soldier . . . and relieved many a man of a [financial] burden. He was a good businessman and one of high personal integrity."[134]

Isaac W. Hirsch was only seventeen years old when he enlisted with the Butler Guards. He had been living with and working for the Prussian-born merchant Lewis Carr of Greenville.[135] Hirsch served the Confederate cause for two years and after being wounded in 1862 in the battle at Seven Pines in Henrico County, Virginia,[136] he returned to his family's home in Charleston where he worked as a clerk in a clothing store and several years later was listed as a "clothier."[137]

Life changed dramatically in the Upcountry as young males departed to fight for the Confederate cause. So many students volunteered for the army from the all-male Furman University in Greenville that commencement was cancelled in 1861. When the college reopened in the fall, no students enrolled, and Furman closed until the war was over.[138]

By the end of 1863, the rate of inflation was terrifically high in Upcountry South Carolina and suffering great throughout the entire South. Furthermore, the Union invasion of South Carolina brought refugees flooding into the Upcountry as they struggled to escape the destruction wrought by Sherman's troops. Many of the refugees escaping the fires of Columbia made their way into the Upcountry but found transportation difficult as Sherman's men had destroyed railroad tracks as well.[139]

The end of the Civil War in 1865 and its impact on South Carolina was devastating and resulted in the loss of more than 23,000 lives and the economic loss of 400,000 enslaved people, for whom the war's end meant freedom.[140] For Spartanburg and Greenville Counties as a whole, the Civil War and emancipation not surprisingly produced a substantial economic loss. John William DeForest, chief of the Freedmen's Bureau in Greenville from 1866 to 1868, wrote of the "suffering people" in the Upcountry. According to DeForest, "local poverty . . . resulted from the leanness of the soil, the imperfection of agriculture, the loss of hundreds of young men in battle, the exhaustion of stock and capital during the war and . . . the thriftless habits incident on slavery."[141]

Reconstruction brought a brief period of military occupation and the establishment of the Freedmen's Bureau. In 1876 Reconstruction in South Carolina ended, and the state returned to conservative Democratic rule.

ECONOMIC DEVELOPMENT IN THE POST–CIVIL WAR ERA

In the quarter century following the Civil War, southerners tried to catch up to the North in manufacturing. With the aid of northern investments, new railroad systems continued to create growing urban centers in major upcountry cities. The historian Howard Rabinowitz writes that "railroad penetration and industrial development went hand in hand" in the South."[142] Several railroads including the Charleston and Western Carolina, the Southern, the Piedmont, and the Northern made stops in Spartanburg providing easy access in and out of the city.

Although cotton production collapsed in the Upcountry during the war, it grew sharply in the next few decades. After producing 2,851 bales of cotton in 1870 "Spartanburg County rebounded with the production of 24,188 bales in 1880 and 35,383 bales in 1890."[143] In 1860, Greenville County had only produced 2,682 bales of cotton, but by 1880 cotton production had risen to 17,064 bales and further increased to 28,482 bales in 1890.[144] Between 1880 and 1900, the number of acres planted in cotton in the Upcountry increased by 30.3 percent.[145] As O'Neill remarked, "Cotton like a great white wave flooded through the Midlands (of South Carolina) into the [Upcountry]."[146]

The five counties of Oconee, Pickens, Anderson, Greenville, and Spartanburg quintupled their cotton production during this period. Spartanburg and Anderson, each of which had raised only a few thousand bales a year in the 1850s, vaulted into the ranks of the state's leading cotton-producing counties. "The increase in cotton output," according to historian David Carlton, "involved a precipitous shift from a diversified small farming economy in which foodstuffs played a major role to one specializing heavily in production of an inedible crop for the international market."[147]

Carlton considers why this occurred but concedes that the reason remains unclear. "Some economic historians," he notes, "view it as a simple response to comparative advantage; specialization in cotton, they argue, was more profitable than diversified farming. Others argue that white farmers were locked into production of the cash crop in a futile effort to repay the debts they began to incur in the 1860s."[148]

Regardless, Carlton asserts that "the result was a striking enhancement of the role of the merchant, especially in upcountry counties destined to become the heartland of South Carolina's textile industry."[149] Thus "the rise of cotton made possible the accumulation of capital by a new class of potential entrepreneurs in a part of the state endowed with waterpower and a heritage of small-scale manufacturing."[150]

Jewish immigrants as well as native-born Jews piggybacked off the economic developments occurring in the Upcountry and the emerging textile industry to establish an economic niche as merchants and entrepreneurs. As will be seen throughout this study, Jews positioned themselves to take advantage of the opportunities made possible by growing centers of trade and a burgeoning textile industry to become purveyors of clothing and dry goods, thus playing, as historian Adam Mendelsohn describes, "a pivotal role in refashioning Americans into mass consumers."[151]

In the last quarter of the nineteenth century, the number of trading centers in the Upcountry increased. New towns came into existence while older ones like Greenville and Spartanburg expanded. Poised at the precipice of major economic development, Greenville was officially designated a city in 1869 and resumed its position as the mercantile center of the county.[152] In 1881 Spartanburg became a city and in 1885, a board of trade, forerunner of the chamber of commerce, was organized by Spartanburg businessmen.[153]

Anderson, just south of Greenville, had been incorporated in 1833, and the growth of the community accelerated with the arrival of the Greenville and Columbia Railroad in 1856. The first Jews in Anderson were Michael and Martha Lesser who emigrated from Prussia by way of New York and Georgia. In Anderson, the Lessers established a mercantile store on the city's main square. In 1871, their daughter, Carrie, married Oscar Geisberg, a former Union soldier and followed the family's mercantile interests by opening a dry goods business.[154] Michael and Martha's son Morris A. eventually took over the business while the rest of their children initiated other entrepreneurial ventures. Years later, the Lessers's daughter Dora (Geisberg) owned Geisberg's Millinery shop; their son Harry opened a shoe store, and his wife, Sadie, owned The Vogue Shop; while Leo, another son, sold general merchandise.[155]

Hieke notes that the post-Reconstruction years witnessed a "small-scale population exchange between the regions of the United States." Jews crossed the regional boundaries of the American South and moved within the North and into the West as well.[156] Hieke refers to these movements as "trans-regional migrations."[157] Such trans-regional migrations became a common occurrence as Jewish migrants moved in and out of upcountry locations from elsewhere in the South resulting in a growing number of Jewish concerns in Greenville and Spartanburg. Joseph Sonenberg opened shops in Greenville specializing in men's clothing.

Isaac Weil, a Baltimore native, established the Great London Clothing House on Greenville's Main Street in 1877 and opened another store on the opposite side of the street in 1883. Weil operated the two stores until he consolidated the business which made it the largest establishment in Greenville. Merchandise, located on three floors, included clothing for men, boys, and children. It was reported that "the trade extends throughout this and the adjacent counties, where the goods enjoy a reputation for uniform excellence that has led to a constantly increasing demand.[158] Weil was described as "an energetic and experienced merchant, knowing when and how to buy at the lowest figures, and consequently attracts hordes of customers by the marvelous cheapness at which his goods are offered for sale."[159]

Harris Mark had engaged in business in Union, as well as Columbia before the Civil War. Mark later relocated to Greenville and partnered briefly in a clothing store with Hyman Endel (Hzrman), who became an eminent member of the Greenville community for the fifty-six years he was in business.[160]

Born in Richmond, Virginia, Endel was the son of German Jewish immigrants. When the Civil War broke out, his father, Moses, enlisted in the Confederate army and was later arrested by Union troops for blockade-running.

Endel left Richmond and followed his uncle, Harry Mark, to Greenville in 1870 where the two men initially resided together. Uncle and nephew became business partners in 1877. They opened two stores, one near the intersection of Washington and Main Streets and the other at the intersection of River and Pendleton Streets. The stores specialized in men's ready-to-wear clothing manufactured by the Schloss Brothers of Baltimore.[161] Endel likely met his future wife, Frances Gruber, in Baltimore while he was purchasing goods for his Greenville businesses.

Mark and Endel were extremely successful merchants. After his uncle retired from the firm in the 1890s, Endel continued managing the business. Subsequently he opened the Globe Clothing House on South Main Street and used his business profits to build an imposing mansion on North Main Street where he and his wife employed a live-in cook and servant.[162]

Endel served as a prominent member of the Greenville business community. In March 1911 he represented South Carolina as a delegate at the Southern Commercial Congress in Atlanta. The gathering was composed of business and professional men for the furtherance of the South's business and commercial interests.[163] Endel's business acumen was particularly beneficial to the local economy as he later helped establish cotton mills in Greenville.[164]

Endel was deeply involved in Greenville and shared his financial success by contributing generously to local as well as national charities and foundations. In addition to substantial contributions to the City Hospital Fund, he was a supporter of Furman University and the Greenville Women's College, where his sister, Fannie, enrolled as a student. In his will, Endel established a fund for the purpose of providing three academic medals known as the "Endel Memorial Medals" to be awarded to graduating seniors at Furman. Deeply committed to Jewish philanthropic societies, he bequeathed $1,000 to the Hebrew Orphan Home of Atlanta and the Jewish Consumptive Relief Society of Denver, Colorado.[165]

Endel was a Reform Jew and a founding member of the Temple of Israel, a Reform synagogue in Greenville, and served as its first vice president.[166] His 1925 obituary reveals his depth of involvement in Greenville: "During his stay in this city, [Endel] has taken an active interest in all community enterprises and built up a circle of friendships that included practically every home in this county. His kind and charitable disposition has endeared his memory to many whose lives have been touched by it. Appeals for worthy charity got his eager attention and he was always ready to give of his time

Greenewalds in the 1920s, Main St., Spartanburg, courtesy of James D. Cobb

and means to enterprises that meant development in Greenville."[167] Endel's upward mobility and economic success helped him embrace American culture and paved the way for his strong identification with Greenville's civic life.[168] His story of success and inclusion in the South would be replicated by many other Jews who made successful lives for themselves and their families in the Upcountry.

Between 1876 and 1899, several other Jewish merchants opened businesses in Greenville. Israel Gittleson, Isaac Weil, Abraham Rosenthal, and Aaron Schraibman were merchants who hired other Jewish men—often family members—to clerk in their stores.[169] Switzer, Simon Iseman, and Abe Goldberg were all clothing merchants. In 1886 Moses Greenewald opened M. Greenewald, Outfitter of Men and Boys. The son of German Jewish immigrants who settled first in Philadelphia and subsequently Americus, Georgia, Moses followed his father in the retail clothing business. He forged a familial network of migration and business opportunity when he arranged for his three brothers, David, Max, and Isaac, to join him in Spartanburg. Greenewalds soon became the largest men's store in town, and the civic-minded Greenewald brothers contributed significantly to the life of the city. At the turn of the twentieth century, they also became involved in founding Temple B'nai Israel (discussed in chapter 3).

By the late nineteenth century, the growing prosperity of the Upcountry became evident in the elegant Victorian homes lining Magnolia, Main, and Pine Streets in Spartanburg. In 1881 a massive statue of Daniel Morgan, the Revolutionary War hero, was placed in Morgan Square, and electric street-lamps lit downtown. A new street railway system connected all major parts of Spartanburg with many of the outlying villages.[170] In addition to the all-male Wofford College, the city also boasted of Converse College, a woman's institution of higher learning. By the late 1890s Spartanburg's business section had grown to one hundred stores, which was significantly more than the thirty-four that existed in 1854 when the first Jewish families made Spartanburg their home.[171]

CONCLUSION

While the Jewish population in the Upcountry never equaled the number of Jews in Charleston, the mid-nineteenth century signaled the beginning of a slow but steady Jewish migration to the cities and small communities in the area. The pioneer Jewish merchants who established retail trade establishments in the Upcountry during the last half of the nineteenth century were the precursors to a larger number of Jews who would settle in the region during the next century. Some were successful, others were not. Several pioneer Jews disappeared after a few years suggesting that they had failed in their business endeavors or sought better opportunities elsewhere. This was not unique or exclusive to Upcountry Jews. As Hieke noted in his study of Jews in South Carolina and Georgia, Jewish settlement was not always stable or permanent, and "Jews came to and departed from America's cities and small towns frequently."[172] It often took decades for Jews to establish themselves in communities where they prospered.

Conversely, Jewish merchants and businesspeople such as Abraham Isaacs, Simon Swandale, and Hyman Endel of Greenville, achieved considerable success in business and flourished for decades after their arrival. Not only did they prosper in their business endeavors, but they became respected citizens who contributed immeasurably to their new communities, reflecting what Bauman discovered of most southern Jewish businessmen which was that "as they rose economically and enjoyed relative tolerance, they contributed to civic affairs."[173]

Often, as we have seen, Jewish merchants who established businesses in the Upcountry had links to New York and Baltimore wholesalers. These wholesalers provided goods to peddlers and merchants in the South and offered them reasonable terms for paying on credit. In fact, Goldstein and Wiener confirm that Baltimore's Jewish merchants had sent representatives to southern cities even before the Civil War, and the number of these agents increased dramatically when the war ended.[174]

As transportation routes improved in the South, Jewish economic networks expanded. Baltimore wholesalers more efficiently supplied clothing, dry goods, and other consumer goods to merchants throughout the southern states. The commercial and ethnic networks forged between Baltimore and the Upcountry became more pronounced as Jewish peddlers purchased goods from Baltimore wholesalers.

By the end of the nineteenth century, Jewish contributions to the economic and civic life of the Upcountry were apparent. Because of their scant numbers, however, Jewish religious and organizational life had barely developed. Jewish worship would not be formalized until after the turn of the twentieth century when financially successful Jews established synagogues in Greenville and Spartanburg. In the meantime Jews made do with informal minyans that met in the backrooms of local Jewish businesses and traveled farther afield when a rabbi was needed. Occasionally Jewish wills stipulated that upon death their bodies should be returned for burial in their original American residence, as Hyman and Francis Endel instructed.[175] Other Jews, however, were given permission to be buried in separate sections of Christian cemeteries.[176]

On the threshold of a massive textile revolution that would change the future of South Carolina, the Upcountry found itself transitioning from a cotton-producing region to the center of the South's textile industry. In the early years of the twentieth century, Jews would become part of the impending industrial revolution that would transform the economy of the Upcountry.

CHAPTER 2

Foundations of Jewish Enterprise in the Upcountry

Jewish migration to Upcountry South Carolina in the early twentieth century was a result of growing business and industrial developments particularly in textile manufacturing. The rise of the textile industry resulted in larger populations and an increased number of Jews seeking economic opportunity in South Carolina.

The foundations for a southern textile industry had started to take shape during the antebellum period. During the next several decades textile manufacturing slowly shifted from New England to the South. In South Carolina, the textile mill boom was centered in its two largest cities, Spartanburg and Greenville, and scattered throughout smaller towns in the Upcountry.

Many of the early mills in South Carolina were established by northern manufacturers. New Englanders Thomas Hutchings and William Bates built the first mills located near the Spartanburg County line in Greenville in 1820. Several more mills soon followed, built by Rhode Island investors who laid the foundation for the mill boom that followed the Civil War.

The distribution of manufactured products of Spartanburg's early mills remained primarily local until the coming of the railroads in the 1850s.[1] As the historian Walter Edgar notes, "The development of a railroad network brought economic benefits to towns across the state."[2] Continuous railroad development such as the Carolina Clinchfield and Ohio Line in 1909 made it possible for Spartanburg to ship and receive goods to a wider market.[3] According to Edgar, as the nation's railroads consolidated, South Carolina merchants began to deal directly with wholesalers and exporters in northern cities such as Baltimore, Philadelphia, and New York. Greenville and Spartanburg were on the main line of the Southern Railroad that linked to Charlotte, Atlanta, and other southeastern cities.[4]

In the years following the Civil War "the political climate in upcountry South Carolina was receptive to local entrepreneurs who helped the region transition to a more fully capitalistic New South economy."[5] Bankers and merchants tended to be the leading business organizers of towns and cities, while newspapers and newspaper editors were inclined to fervently endorse a pro-business position to the community. The textile industry's expansion grew rapidly in the postwar period, supported by leading voices in the upcountry, who endorsed the cotton-mill building that had begun in the antebellum period. Gradually, millions of dollars of New England capital went into South Carolina mill investments, as a result of the crisis northern manufacturers faced with their labor force. South Carolina's low wages and tractable labor made the South a profitable site for textile manufacturing.

By the late nineteenth century, mill building reached a fever high in the Upcountry, strengthened by a spirit of boosterism flaunted in newspapers and supported by the community's business elite. The 1880s and 1890s marked a dramatic expansion of the textile industry in the South. According to Carlton, "in 1880 South Carolina's textile industry consisted of fourteen firms employing 2,000 operatives; by 1910, 147 corporations were producing yarn and cloth with a workforce of 45,000. The typical 1880 mill had fewer than 6,000 spindles, but by 1910 it had more than 25,000."[6]

While most of the antebellum mill builders in South Carolina had been New Englanders, most late nineteenth- and twentieth-century mills were built by South Carolinians. Only twenty mill builders had lived outside the state. Carlton notes "while northern aid was essential to the development of the industry" the industrialization of the South Carolina Piedmont was "largely the product of southern brains."[7]

Mill development evolved with the establishment of the Arkwright Mill, Inman Mill, Saxon Mill, Lawson's Fork Creek Mill, and the Whitney Mill, all located in Spartanburg County.[8] Other mills soon followed: Pacolet, Tucapau, Converse, Drayton, and Arcadia, among others. The number of spindles in Spartanburg also grew from about 8,000 in 1880 to 500,000 by the turn of the century and surpassed New England in the total number of spindles in 1925.[9]

By 1882, Greenville boasted seven textile mills in operation, the largest being the Piedmont Manufacturing Company, Camperdown Mills, and the Huguenot Mill. Smaller mills such as Reedy River, Fork Shoals, Pelham, and Batesville were also established in the late 1880s.[10] One of the most significant developments in Greenville County's cotton textile history was the founding of Piedmont Manufacturing Company, which increased the value of manufactured goods in the county from $350,000 in 1870 to nearly $1.5 million by 1880.[11]

Greenville's textile industry accelerated its growth in 1895 with 60,000 spindles and nearly 1,000 employees.[12] Mills Manufacturing organized in 1895, followed by Monaghan Mill. In the same period, Lewis W. Parker and John Woodside became the masters of mill consolidation. Parker organized several mills and in 1910 created the Parker Cotton Mills Company, which owned sixteen mills with a combined capital of $15 million and more than a million spindles.[13]

Carlton calls the rise of the textile industry in the South Carolina Upcountry "one of the more striking developments in postbellum southern social history."[14] In 1900, Spartanburg and Greenville were the leading textile regions of the state. In 1910 South Carolina was home to 167 mills that employed 47,000 operatives.[15]

Southern textile mills were given a further boost following World War I. New England mills had declined as a result of wage hikes, laws establishing maximum hours, the prohibition of child labor, and the halting of the exploitation of women workers. Many New England textile companies were forced to declare bankruptcy because of a rash of textile strikes immediately after World War I. Faced with declining profits, many New England textile manufacturers looked to the South to establish their business.[16] South Carolina had a pool of workers who "worked longer hours for less pay than New England workers and were not inclined toward organization."[17]

As a result of the expanding textile industry, the populations of Spartanburg and Greenville, as well as other mill towns in the Upcountry, grew substantially. In addition to mill hands, the number of upper-level mill management grew as town and city business and professional people believed that in addition to profit, mill development would increase the local population and that successful cotton mills would attract other enterprises to the region.[18]

A board of trade and cotton exchange were established in Greenville to promote the city business center. The aim of the board of trade, renamed the chamber of commerce, was to make Greenville a "big city."[19] In May 1870 business leaders established the Greenville City Club for the "promotion of sociability and good feeling" for newcomers. The Jewish merchant, Abraham Isaacs, a Greenville businessman, was elected vice president.[20]

Real estate companies were established, and warehouses were built to accommodate the new trade in fertilizer and cotton.[21] Greenville developed as businesses proliferated. A small, but growing Greek community began to form in the 1890s, and by the early twentieth century, Greek restaurants and confectionaries multiplied.[22]

In Spartanburg, the heart of the commercial district was centered around Morgan Square. Banks, jewelry shops, drug stores, photographers, furniture stores, and variety stores surrounded the square, crossed Church Street, and moved into East Main Street. A thriving fruit stand and ice cream parlor were operated by the first Greek immigrants in the community.[23] An Irish immigrant, who first worked at Macy's in New York, relocated to Spartanburg where he opened the Carolina Cash stores in the 1880s, and Joe Whot, a Chinese immigrant, operated a laundry.[24]

Black-owned businesses also developed in both Greenville and Spartanburg, revealing a growing entrepreneurship among the cities' Black communities.[25] In the late 1880s, Black citizens created business districts in the Black section of town with grocery stores, funeral parlors, hotels, real estate firms, small restaurants, theaters, and barber and beauty shops.

By the early years of the twentieth century, the transformation of Upcountry South Carolina from a cotton-producing agricultural area to a major hub of textile manufacturing had major ramifications for the people of the Upcountry. The spur to the local economy as a result of textile factories accelerated the mercantile and commercial activities of the region. Textile manufacturing created jobs, which meant an increase in the number of workers and the proliferation of business enterprises to serve them.

In addition to a steadily growing number of Jewish migrants, business opportunities beckoned Greeks and Italians who became entrepreneurs in the food industry and established restaurants, lunch counters, confectionary stores, and fruit markets. More than any other immigrant group, however, Jews were the most numerous. Their entrepreneurial contributions changed the character of merchandising and had a major impact on the availability of consumer goods in the Upcountry.

IMMIGRANT ENTREPRENEURIAL ACTIVITIES

Entrepreneurship has emerged as a topic of increasing interest among immigration, business, and economic historians. In recent years, scholars have recognized the significance of factors such as ethnicity and social group affiliation on entrepreneurship.[26] Social scientists have defined immigrant entrepreneurial success according to three interactive components: opportunity structures, group characteristics, and strategies. Opportunity structures consist of market conditions in a particular region; group characteristics may be cultural or traditional working patterns developed in a homeland country. and strategies utilize selective migration tactics and include the mobilization of resources and social networks.[27] All three components intersected for Jews who migrated to South Carolina.

Opportunity structures, or market conditions, were plentiful in the Upcountry as textile manufacturing created ample opportunities for business enterprise. As the beginning of this chapter reveals, the growth and consolidation of the textile industry created a large market for labor, and consequently thousands of people flooded into the area for work. Mill laborers needed work clothes, and the managerial class required business attire. Upcountry cities grew, and the number of manufacturing firms supporting businesses and suppliers multiplied.

The historian Michael R. Cohen describes American Jewish entrepreneurs and other ethnic minorities as "at the forefront of entrepreneurship, clustering in narrow sectors of the economy."[28] Migrant Jews in the Upcountry clustered in retail merchandising, chiefly in men's and women's clothing. "The clothing trade, characterized by continuous innovation among retailers and wholesalers," writes Adam Mendelsohn, "ensured a depth of Jewish participation . . . and "the fastest path to advancement" in the United States."[29] The trajectory that an overwhelming majority of Jews followed in America reflected a combination of economic niches that helped shape economic outcomes[30] as well as group characteristics.

Group characteristics, the second component, is a topic that has been explored by many scholars. Friedrich A. Hayek, an economist and philosopher, proposed a connection between capitalism and Jews. Hayek argued that "in a capitalist society everyone becomes in some measure an entrepreneur, on the lookout for the more effective use of resources."[31] Hayek "conceived of capitalism as dynamic and that dynamism was due to the discovery of new needs and new ways of fulfilling them by entrepreneurs possessed with resourcefulness."[32] According to Hayek, the link between Jews and capitalism is a positive one; the Jews are valued "for demonstrating the cultural trait of resourcefulness, the intellectual act of discovering new opportunities for the use of resources."[33]

Jerry Muller, a leading historian of capitalism also writes compellingly about the relationship of Jews to capitalism.[34] He argues that: "The development of modern capitalism created new economic opportunities in Europe and its colonial offshoots. Jews were disproportionately successful at seizing them. . . . Their experience and the cultural propensities it engendered, predisposed them toward commerce and finance and toward the free professions."[35]

Strategies, the third component, reveals how Jews took advantage of selective migration tactics and mobilized resources and social networks.[36] This becomes evident as the lives of Jewish migrants in the Upcountry are deconstructed and networks of migration, credit, housing, and employment are revealed.

A close examination of Jewish businesses in Spartanburg, Greenville, and other Upcountry communities provides examples of how Jews created familial and social networks that brought them to South Carolina. Analysis of Jewish settlement in the Upcountry reveals several overall patterns of migration: First, a majority of Jews who settled in the Upcountry were transplants from other US locations. Many Jews were European immigrants who initially settled in New York or other locations in the South, such as Virginia and Georgia. Other secondary migrants were sons and daughters of immigrant Jewish parents who were chiefly from the German states and the Russian Empire, and some were Jews who emigrated directly from Europe to the South. Jews moved into regions where market conditions were promising and profitable. Whether in the cities and towns of North Carolina discussed by historian Leonard Rogoff,[37] or the coalfields of Appalachia explored by Deborah Weiner, Jewish entrepreneurs thrived in the consumer goods sector.[38] By 1900 almost every Jewish resident of Greenville was a merchant. Furthermore, every Jewish male living in Greenville in 1900, according to the Federal Census, was born in the Russian Empire or the German states. Russian-born Morris Switzer operated a clothing store and German-born Samuel Dreifus was a grocer. Aaron Schraebman, who emigrated from Russia in 1899, was the proprietor of a dry goods store, and Prussian-born Levi Rothschild and Harry Marsh were clothing merchants. German-born Isaac Jacobi was a clothing salesman and Polish-born Louie Fayonsky started out as a shoemaker. Mark Cohen, Louis Copel, and Louis Switzer, all Russianborn immigrants, were peddlers.[39] Fayonsky and Cohen, who were recorded as peddlers in 1890, achieved upward mobility when they became retail merchants in 1910.

Several new faces appeared in Greenville in the early twentieth century as Jewish merchants hired highly trained Russian-born tailors and Jewish clerks for their growing businesses. By 1920 Jewish merchants were clustered primarily on South Main Street in the heart of downtown and provided clothing, shoes, jewelry, dry goods, and optical services to the Greenville community. The increase in Jewish merchants corresponds to the growing

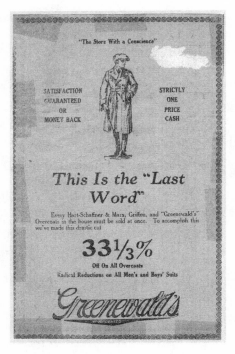

Greenewalds advertisement, 1922, Main St., Spartanburg, courtesy of
Spartanburg Herald

population of the city of Greenville, which increased to 23,127 in 1920 from
15,741 in 1910.[40]

Paralleling the increasing number of Jewish businesses in Greenville was
the growth of the Jewish community in nearby Spartanburg. Forty Jewish-
owned businesses lined downtown Spartanburg during the first three decades
of the twentieth century. In addition to men's clothing stores, Jewish businesses sold dry goods, women's clothing, hats, shoes, and jewelry. German-
born Abraham Goldberg sold men's clothing, furnishings, and shoes, and
Greenewalds was the largest department store in the city. Abraham Meyerson, who hailed from Russia and owned and operated the Carolina Mercantile Company, and Russian-born Hyman August (Ougust) was the proprietor
of the New York Loan Office. Harry Price (Preis), the son of Lithuanian
parents living in New York, launched a men's clothing establishment in
Spartanburg in 1903 called the New York Bazaar.

Greenewalds, 1911, sales staff, courtesy of James D. Cobb

SECONDARY MIGRATIONS

Upcountry Jews followed familial and social networks to South Carolina typically in a chain-migration pattern. These networks were so interconnected that through the 1960s, large numbers of Upcountry Jews were related to one another.

For many immigrant Jews, the Upcountry was a secondary destination that came after initial settlement elsewhere in the United States. Having resided previously in another American location, many immigrant Jews learned English and acquired knowledge of American ways before moving to the Upcountry.

The Blooms emigrated from Poland and followed family members to Columbia. Unlike many Jews who initially settled in New York, the Blooms and their kin were drawn to South Carolina. Working first as a peddler, Harris Bloom moved to Greenville in 1910 and several years later established Bloom's Department Store that thrived for nearly one hundred years.

Morris Lurey, a native of Bialystock, Poland, initially immigrated to Providence, Rhode Island. He and his brother, Samuel, came to the South and settled in Greenville in 1910, where they started a dry goods store.[41] Hyman August took up residence on Manhattan's Lower East Side in 1900, and ten years later he emerged as a successful businessman in Spartanburg where he owned and operated the New York Loan Office, a pawn shop, and a shoe store.[42] Likewise, Russian-born Max Cohen initially took a job in Manhattan as a cloak maker but several years later was the proprietor of Spartanburg's Dixie Shirt Company.[43] Abraham Morris of Russia came to Spartanburg in 1914 after working at Bloomingdale's in New York and bought into Joseph Miller's business, the Standard Cloak Company, a women's wear store.[44] Russian-born Joseph Goldstein had been a salesman in a New York clothing store before becoming owner of Goldberg's Clothing Spartanburg. Samuel Loef was a native of Germany who lived in Columbia before relocating to Spartanburg where he operated Loef's Pressing and Hat Blocking Parlors, and with German-born Philip Weintraub was co-owner of a junk dealership. Morris Bobrow initially lived in New York after emigrating from Russia. In Spartanburg he was a self-employed shoemaker. Finally, Bernard Berlin was born in Russia and started out as a peddler in Union before becoming proprietor of a dry goods store in Spartanburg. A number of these Jewish immigrants started out in New York, worked in a variety of jobs—particularly the garment industry—accumulated capital, and then moved to the South where they took advantage of growing cities such as Spartanburg and Greenville to invest in business opportunities.

CREATING BUSINESS STRATEGIES

Theorizing migration as a process that connects people in social networks with personal and economic motives helps explain the Jewish experience in the South. Jews were drawn to the South by family and friends, and these personal connections were one of the most important factors determining the specific communities in which they settled. As they sought economic opportunities, they developed an intricate system of social networks. According to Muller, these personal connections were fostered by Jews, who, because of their religion and "otherness," were subject to prejudice and exclusion by the larger, non-Jewish society, "and who felt a sense of community and commonality with other Jews." Muller maintains that "the obligation to look after fellow Jews was deeply embedded in Jewish law and culture, and it existed not just in theory but in practice."[45] The following examples reflect migration strategies utilized by Jews.

One of the first and most successful Jewish businesses in Spartanburg was Greenewalds Outfitter of Men and Boys. The store closing in 1991 brought an end to 105 years as one of the leading retailers of men's clothing in the city. Moses Greenewald was the son of German Jews and the first of five siblings to make his home in Spartanburg, a secondary destination after residing in Wilmington, North Carolina. His brothers David, Jacob, and Isaac eventually joined him and entered managerial roles in the business. Their sister, Hannah, soon followed her brothers to Spartanburg, where she lived with Isaac and Max. For nearly one hundred years, the management of Greenewalds passed from one family member to the next.[46]

There were many other Jewish businesses in the Upcountry that operated for several generations such as Prices' Store for Men and Kosch and Gray in Spartanburg; Bloom's Department Store, Lureys, Davis Auto Supply, and Zaglins in Greenville; Rosenbergs and Poliakoffs in Abbeville and Greenwood; Froms in Union; and Davidson's in Chesnee. Family ties, however, didn't always guarantee that a business would survive in the Upcountry, nor throughout the South for that matter.

Two of the oldest Jewish enterprises in Spartanburg are Prices' Store for Men, which is still in operation, and Kosch and Gray Jewelers, which closed in August 2019. Harry Price was the son of Lithuanian Jews who had settled on Mott Street on the Lower East Side of New York. In the 1890s he visited a sister who married a man from Georgia. Inquiring about business opportunities, Price took the advice of his brother-in-law, who told him that Spartanburg "was a good place for business."[47] Price relocated to Spartanburg in 1900 and opened a men's store, the New York Bazaar. By 1903 Harry Price had married Dora Mann of nearby Newberry and changed the name of the business to Harry Prices' Store for Men. A fine men's store, it provided good quality clothing to the growing numbers of millowners and upper management who became regular customers. Students and faculty at nearby Wofford College also became his steady consumers. Descendent Harry Price, the third generation of the family in the men's clothing business, is still operating the downtown store, under the name Price's Store for Men, the oldest Jewish-owned establishment in Spartanburg. The business is more than 120 years old and still provides the best quality men's merchandise in the city.[48]

Meyers-Arnold Co., 1890s, Main St., Greenville, courtesy of the Coxe Collection, Greenville County Historical Society

Many of the Jews who followed Harry Price to the Upcountry were related, reflecting a chain migration of family members, all of whom engaged in business. Harry Jr. followed his father into the business while his daughter, Anne, married Seymour Gray, the proprietor of Kosch and Gray Jewelers.[49] Gray's family were Russian Jews who immigrated to Richmond, Virginia. Gray decided to follow a relative to Spartanburg and ultimately went into business with a jeweler, establishing Kosch and Gray. The business was passed down from father to son and survived for nearly one hundred years.[50]

Similar instances of familial networks of migration and settlement characterize Jewish life in Greenville as well. Alex and Manus Meyers were born into a business family in Virginia. Their immigrant grandfather, German-born Ben Myers, whose initial job in the antebellum United States was peddling, eventually became the proprietor of a department store. Brothers Alex and Manus, who inherited the firm of Meyers Brothers in Newport News, subsequently purchased a business in Greenville in 1903. Upon leaving Newport News they left the management of the business to two other brothers, Lewis and Noland.[51] Alex and Manus purchased the J. Thomas Arnold Company and changed the name to the Meyers-Arnold Company. A few years later the small dry goods establishment had grown to such an extent that the other two brothers, Lewis and Noland, joined the company and together the four brothers made the Meyers-Arnold Company the largest department store in South Carolina.[52]

These patterns were replicated in every small town in the Upcountry. In 1872, Polish-born Wolf Rosenberg established Rosenberg & Company in Abbeville after moving there from Chester, South Carolina. Within three years, Rosenberg relocated the business to a larger store and brought his brothers and nephew, George Visanska, the former peddler, into the business. They opened a second store in 1882 and by 1895 the local newspaper boasted: "Rosenberg & Co. has attained greater financial success than any other firm in town. They own more bank stock, more town property than any other firm in Abbeville County."[53] This pattern of starting a retail business and then using the profits to invest in real estate and banking was again typical of the southern Jewish business trajectory.

One of the most successful and most veteran Jewish merchants in Union was Lithuanian-born Israel From (Fram), who started peddling goods in the northern part of Union County in 1901. From and his wife, Bertha, were beckoned to Union by her cousins, Hyman and Philip Berlin (Berlinsky). After immigrating to the United States and settling in Baltimore, the Berlin brothers left Baltimore in the 1890s and started peddling in the South. Several years later, they settled in Union where they opened a dry goods store.

Israel From purchased a horse and wagon, and in 1904 opened another dry goods store down the street from their cousins, the Berlins. The From family conducted business on Main Street in Union for more than a century. Other members of the family followed From in a chain-migration network. Israel's brother, Solomon, who retained the original family name of Fram, also made his way to Union, where he too opened a store across the street from his brother's business.[54]

Several other Jewish merchants operated businesses in Union, including Myer B. Friedberger, a German immigrant, and Philip M. Cohen, a dry goods merchant from Hamburg, Germany. Cohen eventually operated a dry goods store in Union after gaining merchandising experience working as a clerk.[55] Nathan Shapiro, the well-known Union peddler, eventually started his own merchandising business in Union as well. Considering the population of Union, which was only 5,400 in 1901,[56] the presence of four Jewish merchants in the community was noteworthy.

Morris (Mojzek) Drucker, born in Kartoz Breza, Russia, worked in Union as a clerk and then moved on to Denmark, South Carolina, where he became the proprietor of a dry goods store. He later opened another dry goods store in the small village of Fountain Inn, near Greenville.[57] Israel Gittleson,

Isaac Weil, Samuel Dreifus, Isaac Goldwater, and Samuel Levinson were all Russian- and German-born Jewish merchants specializing in the men's clothing business in Greenville during the 1880s and 1890s. They were joined by several other Jewish merchants including Morris Samuel and David Lowenburg. Another early Jewish settler was Levy Rothschild, manager of the clothing store he established with Samuel Brafman.[58] In 1886, Rothschild was awarded a contract by Greenville to furnish police uniforms for city policemen.[59] Rothschild's business continued to prosper well into the 1920s after he established his own clothing and men's furnishings store on South Main Street.

Perhaps because it was a small Jewish community, German-born Jews and East European Jews (primarily Russian) got along well and cooperated with one another. Unlike larger cities such as New York or Baltimore, for example, where large numbers of acculturated German Jews resented East European Jews who arrived later and did not readily assimilate, those conflicts did not seem to exist in the Upcountry. As discussed in the next chapter, Jews, regardless of where they came from, belonged to the same synagogues and participated in the same civic events and fraternal organizations.

OBTAINING CREDIT

One of the more formidable obstacles facing entrepreneurial Jews in the late nineteenth and early twentieth century was the ability to obtain credit. As Michael Cohen explains in his study of Jewish economic growth in the Gulf South, "Jews and gentiles operated in separate social spheres. Elite Protestant organizations and establishments often discriminated against Jews;"[60] thus, Jews looked to other Jews to provide credit. David Gerber adds, "The stereotypical Shylock image gave rise to certain hesitations to recommend Jews for credit."[61] Consequently, "these prejudices led Jews to turn to family and friends as an alternative network for their businesses."[62] Cohen explains that "southern Jews were connected to their fellow Jews through deep economic ties, fostered by family and ethnic networks. . . . Close-knit networks provided individual businesses with access to the capital and goods of larger markets, and once this access was established, these businesses could then extend their networks to share that access with other Jewish firms."[63]

While major Jewish firms such as Lehman Brothers helped large southern Jewish businesses grow in the Gulf South, Baltimore's Jacob Epstein extended credit to Jewish peddlers and merchants throughout the rural South through his Baltimore Bargain House. Nathan Shapiro, for example, received credit from Epstein in order to procure the goods he needed to peddle in Union County.[64] Leonard Rogoff relates the story of Jacob and Abe D'Lugin, Lithuanian immigrants who received credit from Epstein to start a store in Wilmington, North Carolina. Before he sent them on their way Epstein told them, "I want you to pay me back a little bit every week, whatever you can afford, and I'll send you more merchandise." As Rogoff remarked, "He was giving them the opportunity to be successful."[65]

Historian Deborah Cohen offers another explanation for Jewish credit networks rooted in the Judaic concept of tzedekah, the communal obligation to help others. "By enabling a young man to get a start in life, they were performing a mitzvah, often translated as a good deed; that their good deed advanced their own business goals and strengthened the economic condition of the Jewish community as a whole simply confirmed the relationship between communal and individual good."[66]

Cohen maintains that Jews "set each other up in business by making small loans."[67] Jews also supported each other in times of need. According to Marsha Poliakoff, a member of the Jewish community in Spartanburg, "in times of financial loss," fellow Jews supplied funds to help restore the business or pay off a mortgage.[68] She noted that "even those [Jewish businesses] in competition with one another were friends. If there was illness or when someone suffered a loss, many of them were immediately present. They would fill in for a sick merchant by working in shifts, even for weeks at a time to operate the business until the person recovered."[69] In Spartanburg, Jewish businessmen formed an investment club they called "Lucky Seven" that advanced loans to other Jewish merchants in need.[70] Jews were duty bound to one another by a shared religious and cultural solidarity, another example of the significance of ethnic networking. Family networks were equally important for establishing business enterprises. Family members pooled their resources to establish a business that might have been impossible without the help of others. Brothers brought brothers into the business as did the Greenewalds in Spartanburg and the Manus brothers in Greenville. In 1910, brothers Harris and Mendel Kantor (Kantorovitz) opened the Kantor Company, and in the 1920s, the Davis brothers opened a used-tire and automotive shop in Greenville that eventually employed all their children. Nathan Fleishman and his wife's brother-in-law, Phillip Klyne, operated Fleishman and Klyne, a dry goods business in 1926.

JEWISH SOCIAL NETWORKS AND
HIRING PRACTICES

Jewish businesses were most often family enterprises formed by familial and ethnic networks. Brothers, sisters, wives, sons, daughters, and nephews helped in the daily business operations. Abraham Morris's wife worked side by side with her husband in the Standard Cloak Company in Spartanburg while his daughter, Sylvia, regularly accompanied him to New York to purchase goods for the store.[71] In Greenville, Ida and Israel Switzer and three other siblings worked as clerks in their father's (Tsale Reyzilovich) dry goods store.[72] Harry and Freida Zaglin were employed in their father's kosher butcher shop.[73] In 1910, Louis Goldstein clerked in his brother's clothing store,[74] and Jeanette Davidson Finkelstein worked in her father's Chesnee dry goods store. Charles Kline was a tailor at Lagerholm where his daughter, Sarah, was also employed as a seamstress. Henry, Julius, and Sam Bloom worked together in Bloom's Department Store in 1912, and by 1919 after continued growth, five members of the family ran the business, including daughters Louisa and Minnie who worked as clerks.[75]

Solomon Knigoff left Russia in 1903 and put down roots in Greenville. He opened the Manhattan Pawn Shop and was determined to make enough money to bring his brothers and sister to America. By 1915, his brother Adolph joined him in the Greenville Pawn Shop and several family members shared his living quarters.[76] Pawn shops were typical Jewish professions and, like the scrap business, required little initial capital.

While Jewish merchants usually hired family members, that did not preclude them from hiring nonrelated Jews. Levy Rothschild employed several Jews in his men's store. In 1907 Isaac Jacobi worked at Rothschild's as a bookkeeper and Harris Kanorovitz was a cutter. Arnold Schonwetter was a tailor, Siegfried Schwartz was employed in sales, and Rosa Kline was a seamstress.[77] Harry Goldstein was employed as a clerk in Morris Glickman's Broadway Shoe Store, and Minnie Fayonsky was a clerk at The Vogue, all Greenville establishments.[78]

Jewish enterprises reveal the important roles of women in business establishments. In 1941 Lou Freedman started the Peggy Hale store in Spartanburg. He soon married Sylvia Morris, a divorced woman who worked with her father, Abe Morris, proprietor of the Standard Cloak Company. Abe Morris asked Lou and Sylvia to join him in managing the company after their marriage. Henry Jacobs, Sylvia's son from her first marriage, was eventually invited to join the family business. Lou became his stepson's mentor. In the following years, Henry Jacobs opened more than 600 stores nationwide, known as "One-Price Clothing" modeled on the Standard.[79]

Marian Feinstein, the daughter of East European Jews, grew up in New York City and came to Spartanburg when she was twelve years old. Her father, who worked in ladies ready-to-wear clothing in New York, came to Spartanburg and opened The Fashion in the late 1930s. After studying dance in New York, Marian returned to Spartanburg and launched Miss Marian's Dance Studio. After her death her daughters and a granddaughter took over the dance studio and continue providing dance lessons in jazz and tap to their Spartanburg students.[80]

In Greenville, Victor Davis (Piha) was one of the few Sephardic Jews in the Upcountry who had immigrated from Rhodes, a small Greek island near Italy. He met and married Molly Kaufman, a Romanian immigrant, in 1919 in Montgomery, Alabama. In 1922 they relocated to Greenville to assist Molly's brother, Harry Kaufman, in the auto parts business. They were some of the few Jewish businesspeople who offered consumer products for automobiles that were being introduced into the American markets in the 1920s and 1930s. Within four years, Victor had his own auto-parts establishment. The business remained in operation for fifty-five years and was eventually taken over by Victor's sons after they returned from serving in World War II.[81] In the Davis family, daughters and sisters were trained to work in the auto-parts business as salespersons and bookkeepers.[82] Women, especially daughters, helped in the daily operations of a family business, such as Freida Zaglin, who worked for her father in his Greenville kosher meat market, and Louisa and Minnie Bloom who were clerks in their father's department store. Jeanette Davidson Finkelstein worked with her father for decades in his clothing business, and eventually took over the Chesnee operation after his death.[83]

Jewish women who participated in business activities, for the most part, tended to be the daughters of immigrant Jews or the American-born wives of American-born Jews. Growing up, the children of Jewish parents contributed significantly to the family business and often took over the reins of the business when parents became older or passed away.

BRINGING QUALITY CLOTHING AND SERVICES TO THE UPCOUNTRY

In addition to carrying an extensive array of good-quality clothing and accessories, Jewish merchants hired tailors who made gentlemen's suits by hand.

Greenville merchants often sought skilled Jewish tailors from New York. Levy Rothschild, a Greenville "clothier and haberdasher," (and nephew of I. W. Jacobi and brother-in-law of Hyman Endel) frequently contacted the Industrial Removal Society[84] for skilled workers. In 1907, Rothschild wrote the Industrial Removal Society stating, "We would be very much pleased if you could furnish us with two first class coat makers for merchant tailoring work." A later request asked for "a good coat maker who is Americanized." Arnold Schonwetter, a Greenville "maker of fine clothes," requested "two tailors no matter if they are green." In 1911, the Industrial Removal Society wrote to the owner of Greenville's Kantor Company that in response to his request it could send "Jacob Sherman, 21 years of age, unmarried, who is in this country two years and speaks English" to fill the position of a men's and ladies' tailor.[85]

Jewish merchants were best known for bringing fashionable New York clothing to the South. The names of some Jewish establishments reflected the predisposition of Jewish merchants to market their businesses with names that could be identified with New York City, the American capital of fashion. For example, the name of Harry Price's s first men's store was known as The New York Bazaar in Spartanburg, and in Anderson, Benjamin Poliakoff's New York Pawn Shop.

Upcountry South Carolinians had access to the latest fashions at Abe Goldbergs, Prices', the Standard Cloak Company, Max Cohens, and many others. Greenewalds was touted as "the style center of the Piedmont" and carried "practical gifts" for men from house robes to Dobbs Hats, cigarette cases, and golf apparel. In Greenville, Jewish clothing merchants dotted Main Street with stylish stores such as the Vogue, advertised as "exclusive but not expensive."

Jewish merchants stocked their stores with the latest fashions they purchased from their buying trips to New York and Baltimore, fashions that appealed to women and men.

CONCLUSION

The renowned southern historian, C. Vann Woodward, writing on the textile boom, posited that the "public zeal that accompanied mill building can be likened to a 'crusade' . . . [that] has enshrined the cotton mill in a somewhat exalted place in Southern history . . . [and] has been made a symbol of the New South, its origins, and its promise of salvation."[86] South Carolinians embraced the changes that were taking place in the Upcountry as it transformed from a predominately agricultural region to a landscape covered with mills and smokestacks. Local newspaper editors and city boosters welcomed the mills and their workforce as a symbol of the industrial progress that established their place in the New South.

As mill building swelled in Spartanburg, Greenville, and other regions of the Upcountry, the population increased sharply and the need for products and services multiplied. Jewish merchants, along with a small but growing number of southern Europeans, particularly Greeks, discovered business opportunities to accommodate the growing number of working- and middle-class residents.

As the Jewish community grew, peddlers-turned-businessmen and Jewish merchants dotted various Main Streets throughout the Upcountry. Drawn to the region by market conditions, as well as social and familial networks, Jews employed strategies for establishing businesses. They relied on credit networks and often pooled their resources to start a business and employed family members as clerks, cashiers, and secretaries. While many business establishments did not survive the next generation, there were many that did. Jewish business establishments in Spartanburg, such as Prices, Greenewalds, and Kosch and Gray, survived for one hundred years or more. Similarly, the legacy of several Jewish businesses in Chesnee, Union, Anderson, Abbeville, and Greenville continued for three generations. Jeff Zaglin, whose great-grandfather was Greenville's rabbi and shochet in the early twentieth century, still operates the business his father started in the 1940s.

As Jews put down roots in southern soil, they steadily entered the ranks of the American middle class. Along the way they established religious institutions and self-help organizations and became involved in the civic life of communities, topics explored in the next chapter.

CHAPTER 3

Creating Community

Businesspeople drove the economic engine of the small Jewish communities in Upcountry South Carolina. They also spearheaded the creation of religious organizations and self-help associations. While establishing temples and synagogues to satisfy their religious needs, Upcountry Jews engaged with the non-Jewish world by participating in fraternal organizations and civic life.

The growth of formal religious organizations took place slowly in Upcountry South Carolina, primarily because of the small number of Jews. But as the Jewish population grew,[1] and became geographically and economically settled, Jews established synagogues and self-help associations that enriched their religious and social lives.

The Jews of Spartanburg were the first to organize a religious congregation in the Upcountry. In 1905 several Jewish businessmen formed a minyan (prayer quorum) and began meeting regularly in the back of various businesses for morning prayers. Although this date is cited as the beginning of Spartanburg's "active Jewish community," the *Carolina Spartan* made note of the city's "Hebrew friends" meeting for Yom Kippur in its September 1888 issue.[2] In 1912 this same group met in a tailor shop owned by Abraham Levin to organize a house of worship, and Levin was elected the first president.[3] For several years—until a facility was built—services were held in a hired hall and a rabbi was brought in from elsewhere in the state to conduct High Holy Day services.[4]

Rabbi Jacob Raisin of Charleston came to Spartanburg in 1915 to promote a fundraising drive to which local Jews responded by making donations ranging from fifty cents to $1,000.[5] Having raised adequate funding, Temple B'nai Israel opened its doors in the summer of 1917 as a Reform temple. At its founding, the congregation only numbered approximately twenty-seven families. There is no evidence available that suggests rancor among members over establishing the temple as a Reform congregation, even though many of the founders hailed from Orthodox East European families. However, compromises between the Orthodox and Reform members were necessary because Spartanburg lacked the critical mass to sustain more than one congregation. One of these compromises was to follow the laws of kashrut in the temple kitchen and for the food that was prepared.[6]

It was not unusual for small Jewish communities to make similar compromises. Weissbach found that "Jews living in small towns often overcame their ideological and liturgical divisions so that they would be able to sustain some kind of local congregational life."[7]

Founding members of the temple were merchants and businesspeople, which reflected the occupational demography of Jews in Spartanburg. Nearly all the founders, as well as the initial male members, were born in East Europe, (most from Russia, except for two German Jews), and several were American-born Jews from Russian-Jewish families. Whether native-born or immigrant, they were all transplants from other places in the United States.

The founding members of Temple B'nai Israel reflect the business character of the Jewish community and their place in the commercial life of the city. They included Joseph Spigel, a native of Ukraine, and proprietor of Spigel Brothers Jewelers and Spigel Brothers Real Estate; Russian-born Hyman August, owner of a pawn shop, shoe store, and the New York Loan Office; clothiers Harry Price .and the Greenewald brothers (David, Max, Isaac, and Moses), American-born transplants from Georgia. Other founding members were the merchant/tailor German-born Abraham Levin; Russian-born Julius Schwartz, proprietor of the Carolina Mercantile Company; American-born Louis Meyerson, manager of A. Goldbergs; and Russian-born Max Cohen of the Dixie Shirt Company.

Members of the temple included Joseph Jacobs from Russia who organized the first Sunday School; Samuel Hecklin, a Russian immigrant who owned the Sample Shoe Store; and Samuel's brother, Barney, a shoemaker, and co-owner in the shoe business. Abraham Blotcky, born in Russia in 1874, operated a sales and advertising agency in Spartanburg by 1910. American-born Harry Brill owned and operated the Brill Electric Company, while Russian-born Joseph Goldstein had been a salesman in a New York clothing store before operating Goldberg's Clothing in Spartanburg. Meyer Levite had lived in Ohio before migrating to Spartanburg, where he owned the Globe Sample Company and managed an Asheville firm known as Pollacks Shoes. Samuel Loef, a native of Germany lived in Columbia, South Carolina, before relocating to Spartanburg where he operated Loef's Pressing and Hat Blocking Parlors, and with German-born Philip Weintraub was co-owner

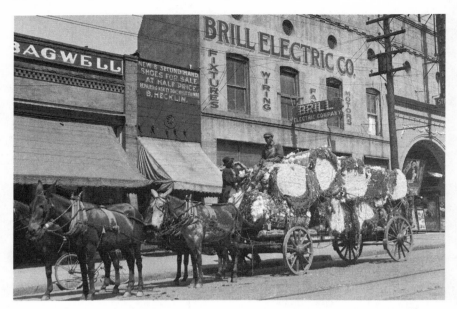

Cotton transport down Main Street, undated photograph, Spartanburg. Passing Brill Electric and B. Hecklin Shoes. Courtesy of Herald-Journal Willis Collection.

of a junk dealership. In Spartanburg he was a self-employed shoemaker. Abe Myerson was born on the Lower East Side of New York City and came to Spartanburg via family connections; he owned the Carolina Mercantile Company. Myerson's cousin, Jerome Pero, also left New York where he had worked as a salesman and became a buyer for Abraham Goldberg's business. Benjamin Burnstein relocated to Spartanburg from Chicago and became the owner-manager of a junk dealership. Finally, Bernard Berlin, a native of Russia, started out as a peddler in Union County before becoming proprietor of a dry goods store in Spartanburg.[8]

The litany of initial founders and members of Temple B'nai Israel and their occupations reveals several important points regarding the Spartanburg Jewish community. Namely, that Russian and German Jews worked together to create religious organizations. Unlike large cities where religious affiliation was factionalized by ethnic origin, the Jewish communities in the Upcountry were simply too small to split according to national background.

In large cities across the nation, there existed a great deal of ambivalence between German Jews and Russian-born Jews. German Jews who had immigrated earlier in the twentieth century and were highly assimilated into American society commonly looked down upon the East European Jews who arrived later in the century. These were generally poor, uneducated, Yiddish-speaking, Orthodox Jews who relished the traditional practices associated with their ancestral home. German Jews, many of whom were highly successful in business and banking, associated largely with the Reform movement and had attained a "level of wealth and social prominence that brought them into closer contact with non-Jews."[9] Fearful that the influx of East European Jews would weaken their hard-won acceptance in American society, German Jews frequently separated themselves from the newcomers.[10]

These attitudes were common in large cities. Mark Bauman notes that East European Jews in Atlanta were not accepted into German-Jewish social organizations, and states that "although their separation from German Jews was partly voluntary, it was also due to the recognition that the Germans wished to have little to do with them."[11] Historian Gerald Sorin discerns that "German Jews . . . were discomfited by the class and cultural differences of their East European coreligionists, and they feared that visible concentrations of new immigrants would generate or intensify Jew-hatred."[12] In Baltimore, Goldstein and Weiner remark that "the massive size of the migratory wave" [of East Europeans in the post 1880s] . . . created fear among the city's acculturated Jews that "newcomers might imperil their social standing and deplete the resources of their charitable institutions."[13]

Unlike settlement patterns in large American cities, where German Jews had settled earlier, and were economically successful as well as significantly acculturated into American society, German and East European Jews had arrived in Spartanburg at about the same time, and were, therefore, starting out on equal footing.

Another important factor worth noting is the remarkable entrepreneurial spirit among the Jews of Spartanburg. Most of the founders and members of the temple were foreign-born with little education under their belts. And yet, East European Jews as well as German Jews achieved commercial success in business. The social gulf that frequently separated immigrant Jews from the local Christian elite seemed nonexistent in Spartanburg and other communities throughout Upcountry South Carolina. Jews in the Upcountry did not work in factories and sweat shops that were common in large, urban areas. Thus, their prevalence in business and commerce created a positive response among native South Carolinians who associated business with progress and the New South.

Temple B'nai Israel, located on Dean Street in downtown Spartanburg, hired Rabbi Samuel Cohen as the first leader to serve the newly formed congregation. The temple, designed in Greek Revival style, commemorated the event with a marble tablet on the main wall of the temple foyer.[14] A common choice for temples and synagogues during the early twentieth century, these Greek Revival architectural designs reflected a Jewish desire to demonstrate their rising social and material success.[15] The location of the temple in downtown Spartanburg attested to Jews' prominent place in the heart of the business district.

Although male congregants formally led the congregation, the women of Temple B'nai Israel "expressed their Judaism by working within the Jewish community, particularly in charitable and educational endeavors," according to Pamela Nadell and Jonathan Sarna in *Women and American Judaism*.[16]

The women of B'nai Israel founded a Women's Auxiliary in 1916 and in 1922 changed its name to Temple Sisterhood. Members raised funds for pews and stained-glass windows for the new temple and even finished the basement floors by hand to create an area where children could study.[17] The Women's Auxiliary was an organization of Jewish women who served the temple and the community and provided fundraising activities and community services. Leonard Rogoff explains that Jewish ladies aid societies blended traditional roles in American ways: The women functioned in a similar way to Christian women who raised funds for "Sunday schools, missionaries, or their own poor."[18]

Dr. Rosa Hirschmann Gantt founded and became the first president of B'nai Israel's Women's Auxiliary.[19] Gantt traveled to Charleston with other delegates to consider the advisability of establishing a state federation Temple Sisterhood. The federation assembled, and the Spartanburg sisterhood served as one of four charter members, along with Charleston, Columbia, and Camden.[20]

Gantt led the fundraising activities that solicited funds from Jewish and non-Jewish businesses for the stained-glass windows for the temple. Women of the auxiliary sold cakes that they baked, held rummage sales, and hosted bridge games to raise money.

In 1924 in a somewhat unusual role for women, Gantt negotiated with Oakwood Cemetery for a Jewish section and Jewish burials were made possible locally. Prior to 1924 Jewish funerals were held in Columbia or in other parts of the state.[21] In the early years of the temple's existence, in another action not typically associated with women, the sisterhood secured a rabbi and paid his salary for several months. In the 1920s the women raised funds for a furnace and contributed to the scholarship and dormitory fund for the Hebrew Union College.[22] Women provided important services by raising funds for their congregations, providing succor and aid for needy members, and sponsoring social events.

As previously indicated, many of the Jews living in Spartanburg in the early twentieth century were European immigrants or the children of immigrants, and several of these families tried to follow the laws of kashrut. In 1919 Rose Hecklin, the daughter of devout Russian Jewish parents, moved with her family to Spartanburg from Providence, Rhode Island. After attending local schools, she married Harry Smiley (Smilowitz) in 1928.[23] Rose and Harry kept a kosher home with the help of a shochet who frequently came to Spartanburg from nearby Asheville, North Carolina.[24] Like several other Orthodox Jews in the Upcountry, the Smileys fought to retain tradition even as they moved for economic opportunity to an area with few Jews. As discussed below, Jews in Greenville also struggled but successfully continued to observe the regulations of kashrut.

The temple became the center of Jewish life in Spartanburg. It served as a place for meetings, charity socials, and even plays and musical performances. Friendships among the close-knit group were cemented through temple activities. According to B'nai Israel's historian, Marcia Poliakoff, "Sunday night was the high spot of the weekend. Jewish couples got together for dinner where they routinely ate fried chicken and the men played poker."[25] Jewish families in Spartanburg maintained their own social circles and remained deeply cohesive and interconnected with other Jews reflecting their determination to retain an ethnic-religious identity while participating in the larger Christian community as members of secular organizations.

Two Jewish congregations in nearby Greenville started in the early twentieth century: Beth Israel, an Orthodox synagogue, and the Temple of Israel, which followed the Reform tradition. Unlike the Jews of Spartanburg, the Jews of Greenville did split according to religious affiliation. This is somewhat surprising given the small number of Jews in Greenville at the time.

In 1911 twenty-five Jewish businessmen met, elected officers, and adopted the name Beth Israel for their Orthodox congregation. On June 17, 1916, they received a certificate of incorporation from the secretary of state designating their synagogue as a "place of worship."[26] The congregation hired a resident rabbi and members held services in their homes and businesses. Rabbi Charles (Tzemach). Zaglin was ordained in Lithuania, immigrated to

Rabbi Charles Zaglin and family, undated photograph, first Orthodox rabbi in Greenville and proprietor of a kosher butcher shop, courtesy of Jeffrey Zaglin

New York City in 1907, and initially served as a rabbi in Wilmington, North Carolina. He was summoned to Greenville where he served as the community's rabbi, shochet, and mohel.[27]

After generous contributions from members and several years of raising funds, Beth Israel was completed in 1930. Located on Townes Street, in an established neighborhood that included many Jewish families, synagogue members chose a classical revival style that resembled the Jewish temple in Spartanburg.[28]

Because it was established as an Orthodox synagogue, men and women were seated separately in the sanctuary. Anne Lurey, a member of Beth Israel, recalled that there had been a balcony above the main entrance that separated women from male members of the congregation. Later, however, women sat on the left side of the sanctuary and men on the right.[29] The synagogue building included an auditorium on the second floor with a seating capacity of 275 and downstairs religious school rooms and another auditorium where entertainment and special programs were held.

The women of the congregation promptly organized a Ladies Auxiliary with Mrs. Harry Lee, president; Mrs. Leon Shain, vice president; Mrs. Nathan Stotsky, secretary; and Mrs. Julius Bloom, treasurer. Like other Orthodox Jews belonging to Beth Israel, Amelia Bloom kept a kosher home with separate meat and dairy dishes, utensils, and silverware for both Passover and non-Passover food. Because it was not always possible to obtain kosher meat, the family ate local nonmeat items such as greens, okra, grits, turnips, cornbread, biscuits, beans, and sweet potatoes. On religious holidays they celebrated with traditional Jewish foods such as matzoh and latkes.[30]

Amelia Bloom had a chicken coop in the backyard where she kept chickens, and Rabbi Zaglin regularly came to the Blooms's home to slaughter their poultry. Amelia's son, Jack, described the food they ate as "kosher southern-country cooking, embellished with pot roast, fried chicken, chicken soup, chopped liver and sweet and sour meatballs. . . ."[31]

In an interview with Jack Bloom in his Greenville home, he recalled that his mother relied on two gentile "farmer ladies," Mrs. Butler and Mrs. Waddell, who supplied the family with hand-churned country butter and fresh vegetables and fruits in season.[32] They came each week and brought fresh fruits that were eaten immediately or preserved. In summer, a farmer from the mountains near Greenville delivered blueberries and huckleberries.[33]

Gradually, Orthodox traditions launched in Greenville, including a mikvah for ritual cleansing. Rabbi Zaglin dug the mikvah himself for his wife, who refused to relocate to Greenville until one was available. Later, the congregation built a mikvah in the synagogue where women cleansed themselves in the ceremonial bath located on the backend of the building near a stream that flowed behind the synagogue. Frieda Selma Zaglin-Kaplan, the rabbi's oldest daughter, recalled the difficulty getting to the mikvah: "they built a mikvah . . . [with] a trap door and they had to go down under the office in the ground to get [there]."[34]

Eventually, Zaglin stepped down as rabbi to dedicate himself full-time to his business in downtown Greenville, where he sold both kosher and nonkosher meats and other groceries. He expanded his business with an abattoir and added delivery trucks to his enterprise. According to his grandson, Jeffrey Zaglin, he bought refrigerated coolers and a freezer and distributed meats to small towns throughout the Upcountry.[35]

Rabbi Zaglin's brother, Morris, followed him to Greenville in a typical family migration pattern and became active in the synagogue. He founded the Young Men's Hebrew Association (YMHA) and developed Jewish educational facilities for the youth. In 1927 he was instrumental in forming a Zionist organization in Greenville and served five years as president.[36] In 1938 Morris Zaglin served as the first chairman of the Beth Israel Cemetery Association, an organization founded by members of Beth Israel Synagogue and Temple of Israel, Greenville's Reform temple.

In 1911, a rival faction of Jews, who desired to follow the Reform tradition, started meeting informally in private homes and in the rooms over Efrid's Department Store where they prayed and began plans to organize a congregation. The organizers included many local and well-known businessmen such as Levy Rothschild, Hyman Endel, Isaac Jacobi, and the industrialist David Kohn. Other charter members were Morris Levy, Alex Meyers, Manos Meyers, George Reisenfeld, and Phil Weinberger.[37] Similar to the members who founded Temple B'nai Israel in Spartanburg, the organizers of the Reform congregation were both East European and German Jews, but unquestionably, there were more Jews of German descent who established the temple. However, this was a result of identification with the Reform movement rather than conflict within the Jewish community. Although the Jewish community in Greenville was larger than the Spartanburg Jewish community, there were only approximately ninety-five Jews in the early 1900s.[38] The large number of German-Jewish founders reflect the national tendency of German Jews to identify with Reform Judaism.

In 1917 they established Children of Israel congregation. Land for the temple was donated by the merchant Manos Meyers and was dedicated on April 12, 1929, as Temple of Israel. Soon thereafter, the Ladies Temple Sisterhood organized with Mrs. Isaac Jacobi serving as president; Mrs. Louis Fayonski, vice president; Mrs. Alexander Volpin, treasurer; and Mrs. Abraham Blumberg, corresponding secretary.[39]

Various male congregants led services until a full-time rabbi was secured. Maurice Mazure, who served as the first rabbi from 1936 until his death in 1951, remarked that the "hospitality of the town had a great deal to do with his decision to come to Greenville."[40] Rabbi Mazure, a frequent speaker before clubs and civic organizations in the city held a visible position in the community. He reorganized the religious school where Jewish religion, history, and ethics were taught, and provided instruction in Hebrew.[41] Isaac Jacobi helped establish a Sunday school that was operated by the women of the congregation, thus fulfilling traditional female roles.[42]

The synagogue became the heart of the Jewish community. It was a center for worship, learning, philanthropy, and socialization. It provided security and a sense of identity for Jews who became friends with other members. Initially, at least, Jews socialized with other Jews, but gradually Jews became involved in nonreligious communal activities that strengthened their position within secular society.

All three synagogues in Upcountry South Carolina served the Jewish community for several decades. By the mid-twentieth century all three congregations had outgrown their original buildings and eventually built new ones to accommodate the growing needs and numbers of Jews in Upcountry South Carolina.

JEWISH WOMEN'S ACTIVISM

Outside of religious associations connected to local temples and synagogues, Upcountry Jewish women in the early twentieth century generally remained on the sidelines when it came to political and civic events. In large part, this was a result of the many Upcountry Jewish women born in Europe who did not speak English. However, American-born Jewish women were more likely to get involved in activities outside of their religious gatherings. They joined women's clubs and actively campaigned for progressive reforms, such as public health initiatives and votes for women during the early twentieth century.[43] The most prominent, educated and progressive Jewish activist in the Upcountry during the early twentieth century was Dr. Rosa Hirschmann Gantt of Spartanburg. Born in Camden in 1874, Rosa Hirschmann moved with her family to Charleston from Cades, South Carolina, where her father, Solomon, an immigrant from the Austro-Hungarian Empire, started out peddling until he accumulated enough money to open a general store, first in Cades, and later, a second one in Gourdin. Because no high schools existed at this time in the rural regions of the state, Solomon moved his family to Charleston and opened a wholesale grocery store on King Street.[44]

Rosa's mother, Lena Nachman Hirschmann, died when Rosa was fourteen years old, leaving Rosa to care for her father and younger siblings. Her numerous responsibilities, however, did not deter her from excelling in her studies.

After completing high school, Rosa enrolled in the school today known as the Medical University of South Carolina and in 1901 became one of the first two women to obtain an MD from that institution. After postgraduate training at the Aural and Ophthalmic Institute and the New York Ear and Eye Hospital, Dr. Hirschmann was appointed resident physician at Winthrop College in Rock Hill, South Carolina.[45]

In 1905 she married Spartanburg attorney Robert Gantt and established a practice in that city as an ear, nose, and throat specialist. Along with her medical practice, Dr. Gantt pioneered work in public health by dispatching mobile health clinics to rural areas of South Carolina lacking physicians. One of her greatest achievements was her innovation of a "health mobile" hailed for "bringing health to the country," staffed with physicians, nurses, and nutrition workers who offered immunizations, examinations, and pre-natal and dental care.[46]

A highly respected doctor, she served as an officer for the otherwise all-male Spartanburg County Medical Society and was one of the first female members of the Southern Medical Association. She also served as president of the American Medical Women's Association. During World War I, Gantt organized local women to serve in the Red Cross, sell Liberty Loans, and engage in hospital work for soldiers. She was the only woman to serve on a draft board in the United States and hold a commission from the Department of Commerce as a medical examiner of air force pilots. As noted above, Dr. Gantt was the first president of the Women's Auxiliary of Temple B'nai Israel, instrumental in securing a Jewish burial site at Oakwood Cemetery and elected president of the South Carolina Federation Temple Sisterhood.

Through her temple responsibilities and her work as a suffragist, Gantt illustrates how Jewish women of her era blended traditional Jewish values with prevailing American social and religious concerns. In 1914, Gantt stood on the cutting edge of suffragist activity when she joined the first suffrage organization in the state, the South Carolina Equal Suffrage League. Serving as the league's legislative chair while still practicing medicine, Gantt was one of the few educated women who became both professionally and politically active.

After decades of devoted service to Spartanburg, Dr. Gantt died in 1935 following surgery for uterine cancer. Reflecting the high esteem in which she was held by residents of the city, an obituary published in the *Spartanburg Herald* praised her for her many accomplishments: "She was one of the outstanding women of this section, not only a shining example of a physician standing for the highest and best in ethics, but a leading worker in social service."[47]

Gantt's death was a loss to the medical community and to the synagogue where she devoted much of her time. A New South progressive, Gantt served her synagogue while challenging gender barriers as a doctor and suffragist.

FITTING IN: JEWS AND SOUTHERN COMMUNAL LIFE

Throughout America in the early twentieth century, progressive middle-class business leaders committed themselves to improving society. In the South, according to A. V. Huff, "progressives tended to be business and professional people imbued with the 'New South' spirit."[48] A manifestation of the progressive New South spirit was the rise of civic clubs. Business leaders established clubs and service organizations devoted to improving community life by supporting education, growing the local economy, fighting disease, and improving the lives of children.

Jewish businessmen joined with other local leaders in development and enhancement projects. Their participation in civic activities gave them a stake in their local communities, illustrating what the writer Eli Evans observed about southern Jews: "They were not insular but rather believed ardently in participating in the civic and organizational life of the community."[49]

Jews in Upcountry South Carolina were deeply engaged in community life. The Greenewald brothers of Spartanburg exemplify Jewish men, who, after establishing a successful business, became active in civic activities and benevolent associations. In 1881 an opera house was built on the western end of Morgan Square. Max and later, his brother, Isaac, co-managed the venue. At the beginning of the twentieth century, Max was the local impresario selecting productions to play in Spartanburg. A talented musician and a lover of the arts, he seemed naturally drawn to the theater.[50] Jewish involvement in theater circuits was not unusual at this time and precedes their rise to prominence in theater, popular music, and motion pictures.[51]

Before arriving in Spartanburg in the early 1900s, Isaac had studied piano at the New England Conservatory of Music and served as musical director for a vaudeville company performing in the northeast.[52] Often referred to as the "Greenewald" Opera House, the local entertainment palace proved an economic boon to the growing city. Actors and company personnel stayed at nearby hotels and ate at downtown cafés.[53] The opera house was replaced in 1907 by a new and much larger theater, and Isaac continued working with the new facility for many years.

Another member of the Jewish community who contributed to the cultural life of Spartanburg was Annae Kramer Blotcky, a Swedish-born Jew, who married Abraham G. Blotcky in 1904 in Des Moines, Iowa. Several years later, she and her husband moved to Spartanburg where Abraham owned and operated an advertising agency.[54] Abraham and Annae were members of Temple B'nai Israel, and Annae taught music and voice. She also served as the choir director for the First Presbyterian Church and was the director of the Men's Glee Club at Wofford College. Annae became a famous opera singer and performed in concerts and for Jewish groups in many towns and cities. In 1911 she sang Scandinavian and Norwegian music with the Russian Symphony Orchestra at Madison Square Garden in New York City, and in 1914 she performed with members of New York's Metropolitan Opera at Converse College in Spartanburg.[55]

Cultural life and participation in civic life were common among a number of Spartanburg Jews. Take, for example, the Greenewald brothers. Max served as captain of the volunteer Spartan Fire Engine Company and was a member of the Improved Order of Red Men, the nation's oldest fraternal patriotic association "devoted to inspiring love for the United States and principles of liberty."[56] Isaac rose to the rank of Exalted Ruler of the Benevolent and Protective Order of Elks. Another brother, David, served as a director of the Spartanburg Music Festival and was a member of the board of directors of the Spartanburg Chamber of Commerce and the Elks Club.[57]

During the late nineteenth and early twentieth centuries—the golden age of fraternal associations—Jews were attracted to the mystic brotherhoods for many of the same reasons as their gentile neighbors. The lodges offered opportunities for personal relationships with members of the predominate group.[58] Amy Hill Shevitz writes that "often in small towns, almost all Jewish men belonged to lodges such as the Masons."[59] This was certainly true in the Upcountry where Jews joined civic and fraternal organizations, which were a crucial means for Jews to fit into southern communal life.

Some of the earliest Jewish businessmen participated in numerous and diverse fraternal orders. Isaac Weil was a Mason and a member of the Odd Fellows in Greenville. Hyman Endel joined the Masons, Odd Fellows, and Knights of Pythias, an organization devoted to friendship, charity, and benevolence. Alex Davis was a Mason, a Shriner, and a charter member of Sertoma, a nationwide organization devoted to hearing health.

Spartanburg's Harry Price participated in the Loyal Order of the Moose as did Meyer Mallinow, who was also a Shriner and a member of the Elks Club. Abraham Simon was a member of the Shriners, the Elks Club, the Scottish Rite (part of Freemasonry), and the Knights of Pythias. Southern Jews, like Jews across the country, joined fraternal and service organizations that were dominated by Protestants but were also clearly associations that were crucial for fitting into secular society. Members from both German-Jewish and East European-Jewish background "became fixtures in their communities," and in some instances their "families remained locally prominent over many decades."[60]

WORLD WAR I AND JEWISH INTEGRATION

Jews experienced a greater sense of community with their participation in World War I. The outbreak of war and, ultimately, American participation in the hostilities, provided an opportunity for Jewish Americans to integrate more fully into American society.

National events (such as wars), according to historian Christopher Sterba, "have a broader integrating effect, providing experiences that ethnic groups could share with the larger American public."[61] Nearly 200,000 Jews were recruited and drafted nationwide, illustrating their feelings of patriotism toward their adopted country.[62]

Like their brethren throughout America, Upcountry Jews responded to the demands of World War I in a variety of ways, reflecting their loyalty to the United States and commitment to the larger Jewish global community. Many Jewish boys enlisted, like the foreign-born Abraham Blumberg, who emigrated from Kovno, part of the Russian Empire, in 1902. Blumberg served with the US Army while stationed at Camp Sevier in Greenville. While posted at the camp, Blumberg filed papers to become a citizen. By the time he returned from the war, he was an American citizen and settled in the small town of Dillon in eastern South Carolina, becoming a successful merchant and dry goods salesman.[63]

Before settling in the Upcountry, Abraham (Scheiman), known as Simon, emigrated from Russia in 1911. In 1917 he attempted to enlist in the army to fight in the war but was turned down because he was only sixteen years old. A committed Zionist, he later signed up in Manhattan to become a member of the Jewish Legion: five battalions of the British Army that consisted of Jewish volunteers from the United States, Palestine, Great Britain, Canada, and other countries who served in Palestine and fought against the Turkish Army during World War I. When he returned to the United States after the war, he married Lottie Geffen of Atlanta, moved to Spartanburg, and operated women's clothing stores in Spartanburg and Greenville.[64]

Although he did not fight in the war, Isaac Greenewald of Spartanburg served on the Jewish Welfare Board. The board was established three days after the United States declared war on Germany for the purpose of supporting Jewish soldiers in the US military during the war.[65]

Greenville's Julius Bloom, a native of Bialystok, Poland, entered military service on October 9, 1917, with the 118th Infantry Regiment, known as the Butler Guards. Bloom was stationed at Camp Sevier in Greenville until his division shipped out for Europe, where they engaged in heavy combat against Germany in northern France and Belgium. Bloom was injured with severe shrapnel wounds in October 1918.[66] When he returned to Greenville, he resumed his career as the proprietor of Bloom's Department Store.

Upcountry South Carolina had the good fortune of being selected as a location for two army training camps that were constructed during the summer of 1917. Camp Sevier in Greenville had the capacity to house 46,000 men and Camp Wadsworth in Spartanburg housed 30,000 troops, all from New York. Both cities accommodated Jewish soldiers stationed locally. On September 17, 1917, *The Greenville News* announced that the Jewish New Year would be observed in Greenville with a service held by Rabbi Zaglin for Jewish soldiers stationed at Camp Sevier.[67]

In Spartanburg, Jewish soldiers had the option of worshipping at Temple B'nai Israel and they regularly dined with temple members at their homes. Local Jewish women opened their homes to Jewish soldiers and provided them with Sabbath meals and a warm, friendly, family environment. The late Bill Price (of Prices' Store for Men) recalled soldiers tying up their horses at the hitching post in front of his parents' house when they came for Sabbath dinners with his family. His parents, Dora Mann Price and Harry Price, frequently invited soldiers for dinner from the New York Calvary Regiment stationed at Camp Wadsworth.[68] Northern soldiers made friends and even courted sweethearts while training in the South and returned after the war to marry local Jewish girls and put down roots in the Upcountry. A local historian noted that the soldiers "helped to boost the local Catholic and Jewish populations."[69]

Jewish women became involved in a myriad of charitable activities to aid the soldiers by volunteering for the Red Cross and raising money for the War Bond campaign. Dr. Gantt was involved in the war effort in numerous and diverse ways. She helped arrange religious services and entertainment for soldiers at the camp and welcomed soldiers to her home for Sabbath dinners. Dr. Gantt organized 500 women volunteers to work in medical services and headed drives for household utensils that could be donated for scrap metal.[70]

Spartanburg transformed into a booming city as 30,000 soldiers from New York descended upon Camp Wadsworth. The city profited from the training camp as it attracted money and business to the city. Sergeant Kenneth Gow observed, "If an enterprising merchant would open a store here, he would make his fortune."[71] Needless to say, business was booming in downtown Spartanburg where Jewish and gentile businesses catered to the needs of the soldiers. Relations between Spartanburg civilians and soldiers from New York remained relatively pleasant throughout Camp Wadsworth's existence, although several complaints concerning price gouging were received. A commonly expressed grievance was that Spartanburg's prices were "higher than Broadway's."[72]

Jewish-owned business enterprises dotted the main streets of Spartanburg, Greenville, Anderson, Union, Abbeville, and small towns throughout the Upcountry, providing the local population with a sense of pride in the growing, commercial enterprises in their communities. Jewish merchants worked long hours, often opening their stores between five and six o'clock in the morning to accommodate farmers and mill workers.[73] They provided a wide variety of merchandise to eager buyers: dry goods, men's and women's ready-to-wear clothing, jewelry, shoes and boots, eyeglasses, and plumbing and electrical supplies. Dry goods stores outfitted mill workers with inexpensive clothing while the better men's stores dressed the mill owners and professionals with suits and crisp white shirts. Jewish businessmen were among the first to introduce department stores to the Upcountry with Meyers-Arnold and Bloom's Department Stores in Greenville, thus giving the residents in these areas a taste of big city fashions and large-scale merchandising.

Successful businesses meant that Jews were achieving upward mobility that helped them acquire attractive homes in the better residential sections of town. Initially there had been a small Jewish enclave on Townes Street in Greenville,[74] and one in Spartanburg, but generally Jews did not settle in ethnic enclaves as they did in larger, northern cities. Simply, there were too few of them.

If local newspapers are any indication of the community's views toward their Jewish neighbors, it was very favorable for Jews were seen as contributing extensively to the economic life of the community. The activities of Jewish merchants appeared frequently in local newspapers anxious to underscore the commercial growth of Spartanburg, Greenville, and other Upcountry communities.

In 1919, the *Spartanburg Herald* showcased two Jewish businessmen, Harry Brill, the owner of an electrical supply business, and Abraham Goldberg, the owner of The Battery, a men's department store. Brill was described as "one of the most progressive citizens of the city, and a booster for Spartanburg every day of the year." Goldberg, who also served as president of a skirt company in New York City, was defined as "a live wire [who] believes in Spartanburg's big future . . . ready . . . to make of Spartanburg a greater city."[75] That Jewish businessmen, especially transplants from New York City and Baltimore, had opened businesses in the Upcountry was for many community leaders testimony to the progress they were making and their future place in the New South.

Local newspapers regularly highlighted Jewish businessmen and lamented the community's loss when they passed away. Obituaries reveal how an individual was viewed by the community. Upon the death of Jacob Cohen, a businessman with firms in Union and Spartanburg, a writer for the *Spartanburg Herald* wrote, "Mr. Cohen was a deep thinker, and a man of a vast fund of knowledge. [His death] . . . has caused wide-spread sorrow and regret. Mr. Cohen was prominent in civic matters."[76]

When David Greenewald passed away in 1919, the *Spartanburg Herald* reported [his] "clothing store was destined to become one of the model mercantile establishments of the city of Spartanburg. Greenewald achieved a distinct chapter in Spartanburg's history and his life work added dignity to the title 'A Merchant.'"[77] The board of directors of the chamber of commerce then passed a resolution stating, "Spartanburg has lost an esteemed citizen who ever worked for the progress of the city."[78]

Moses Greenewald died in 1926, and the *Spartanburg Journal* informed readers that "his progressiveness, liberal-minded nature and unselfish contribution to his city's growth . . . and his sterling worth and sound character were acknowledged and admired by all."[79] Similarly, when Israel From of Union passed away, the editor of the local newspaper wrote that "he has lost a true and worthy friend and the county one of its best citizens."[80]

When Rebecca Winstock Rosenberg died at the age of ninety-one, she was touted for her many contributions to the community.[81] Rosenberg, who had moved to Greenwood with her husband, Abraham, in 1885, was "active in civic and cultural life, aided in establishing the towns first library, and served as Vice President of the Greenwood Hospital Association." The editor of the local paper added that, "no other community can boast of a hospital such as Greenwood's due to the work of a small group of civic-minded women."[82]

CONCLUSION

Jewish business leaders spearheaded the establishment of synagogues in Upcountry South Carolina, which was crucial for the Jewish community. Synagogues brought the Jewish people together for worship and socialization with other Jews. Jewish religious institutions in the Upcountry also confirmed the place of Judaism in the religious mosaic of American society. Newspaper editors reported on Jewish religious events and wrote complimentary obituaries when a Jewish businessman passed away, providing community members with favorable impressions of their Jewish neighbors. This chapter also demonstrates that Jewish women, like Rosa Hirschmann Gantt, became activists for progressive reforms such as women suffrage and providing health services to the underserved. In addition, she played an important role in her synagogue and in the Spartanburg community.

Joining communal and fraternal organizations with largely Protestant memberships helped Jews blend into the predominately Christian world of the Upcountry, "reinforcing the shared interests of Jews and non-Jews."[83] Jewish soldiers who fought for their country in World War I reaffirmed their loyalty to the United States, while experiencing a camaraderie with non-Jewish soldiers in a collective experience. All of these efforts ultimately helped Jews acculturate to life in the South Carolina Upcountry.

CHAPTER 4

Jewish Business and Industry in the Interwar Years

Significant agricultural and industrial changes occurred in the Upcountry in the years following World War I. Cotton growers experienced tough times with plummeting cotton prices and damage caused when the boll weevil infested the cotton fields of the state beginning in 1917. During the war, cotton had sold for fifty cents or more per pound, but by the end of 1920, the price dropped to 13.5 cents a pound.[1] The collapse of cotton and tobacco prices in 1920, according to historian Walter Edgar, "was the result of overproduction and the loss of overseas markets."[2] Spartanburg and Greenville were the hardest hit as they ranked high among cotton producing counties.[3] Historian Kathy Cann writes that "the textile industry thus entered a period of fluctuation, a hint of what was to come with the Great Depression of the 1930s."[4]

The decline of cotton, however, was a blessing in disguise for some of Spartanburg's visionary farmers who realized the potential of peaches as a crop that could grow profitably in the Upcountry. In the early 1920s the Spartanburg peach industry "had grown to such proportions that 245 carloads valued at more than $250,000 had left local orchards destined for markets in the North and Midwest."[5] Eventually peaches became one of Spartanburg County's leading cash crops. In fact, the county produced more peaches than Georgia, which promoted itself as the "peach state."[6]

As the region became more agriculturally diverse, industrial development also grew as New England's textile industry became increasingly invested in the Upcountry. In the 1920s, New England's textile manufacturing suffered from competition with southern mills, overproduction, and labor unrest.[7] Violent labor strikes and pressure from mill workers led New England state legislatures to establish maximum working hours, pass laws to end child labor, and halt the exploitation of women workers. In the wake of declining profits, New England companies looked to the South where labor costs were lower and protective legislation did not exist.

This chapter examines Jewish manufacturers and merchants in the Upcountry in the interwar years, from 1923 through 1941. These years launched the beginning of immigrant and northern Jewish manufacturing companies in the region. It also examines foreign-born Jewish women who earned extra income by providing boarding services to their compatriots and their American-born daughters who took jobs as salesclerks and secretaries in business offices.

TEXTILE MANUFACTURING MOVES SOUTH

In early 1923, Pacific Mills of Lawrence, Massachusetts, constructed a massive textile plant in Spartanburg County and hired 2,500 workers.[8] Only a part of the company's textile print works had been transferred to its Spartanburg location, while the rest remained in Massachusetts. Seven years later, following a long and bitter strike in Lawrence, the company moved the remainder of its printing operations from Massachusetts to Spartanburg County.[9]

Other Northern textile and textile-related firms relocated to the Upcountry in the 1920s. These included the Draper Textile Machinery Company of Hopedale, Massachusetts, and the Fairforest Finishing Company of New York.[10] Samuel Slaters and Son of Massachusetts began building a cotton mill north of Travelers Rest in Greenville County, and Hampshire Underwear and Hosiery established there in 1928.

Northern industries also bought out existing cotton mills in Greenville and Spartanburg, such as Judson Mills, purchased by Deering-Milliken of New York; while New Englanders bought out Tacapau Mills, Valley Falls, and Arcadia Mills.[11] However, mill expansion during the 1920s "created a deceptively rosy picture of economic conditions in the textile industry."[12] Southern workers labored longer hours for less pay than New England workers,[13] and for the time being, at least, were not inclined toward organization. However, that would change, as the not-so-docile southern workers began to organize in the late 1920s and 1930s.

For more than a century, textile and cotton mills founded by New Englanders and forward-thinking South Carolinians dominated Upcountry manufacturing. In the early to mid-twentieth century, a new wave of entrepreneurs established companies in South Carolina. This second wave was composed of foreign-born and American-born Jews, transplants from the mid-Atlantic states who introduced clothing manufacturing to the South. This second wave began in the 1920s and resurfaced again after World War II.

A third wave of manufacturing followed in the latter part of the twentieth century, characterized by international investments.

JEWS IN TEXTILES

There are excellent studies of the history of textile manufacturing in Upcountry South Carolina and its role in the making of the New South.[14] These studies naturally focus on the evolution of cotton mills dating from the late eighteenth century to the apex of textile manufacturing in the mid-twentieth century. As previously noted, New Englanders owned and operated most cotton mills in the Upcountry.

In the early twentieth century, Jewish entrepreneurs played an increasingly significant role in textiles and clothing manufacturing in the Upcountry. The presence of Jewish textile manufacturers appeared in the 1890s in neighboring North Carolina, where Moses and Caesar Cone invested in southern mills.[15] At one time the Cone brothers were the world's leading producers of denim and corduroy cloth especially for Levi's jeans[16] and "became one of the South's largest textile empires."[17] In the Upcountry, another Cohn, spelled *Kohn,* paved the way for other Jewish textile manufacturers.

David Kohn played an essential role in bringing attention to Greenville as a textile center. David's father, Theodore, had emigrated from Bavaria in 1850 and settled in Orangeburg, South Carolina. In 1862, he enlisted with the Edisto Rifles and, like other southern Jews, fought for the Confederacy. Wounded, and released before the war's end, he married Rosa Wald, and opened a dry goods store in Orangeburg.[18]

David was one of six children born to this immigrant couple in the 1880s. He graduated from high school and attended Clemson College where he studied textile engineering, graduating in 1902. One of his brothers, August Kohn, became a South Carolina legend in his own right. After investigating and publishing studies of South Carolina mills, he published a book still read today by students of cotton mill history, *The Cotton Mills of South Carolina* (1902).[19]

While a student at Clemson, David Kohn spent his summer vacations working in various textile plants, erecting, and overhauling machinery and learning every aspect of the business. "When the young textile engineer arrived in Greenville," writes local Greenville historian, Judith Bainbridge, "he was already an experienced cotton mill man. He had spent four years at Olympic and Granby Mills in Columbia, a year as assistant superintendent at an Alabama factory, and another as superintendent of a mill in Georgia."[20]

Kohn was recruited by the Parker Cotton Mills in Greenville and became head of the statistical department in 1908 where he supervised production. While at Parker Mills, he taught designing and textile engineering at the Monaghan YMCA Night School, the first school that offered such classes in the South.[21]

In 1912 Kohn married Camille Jacobs, heiress of Lansburgs Department Stores of Washington, DC.[22] In 1913 he became general manager of Judson Mill in Greenville, and two years later he opened a commission business with longtime resident R. C. Hudson.[23] With this move, he left the manufacturing side of textiles and entered the finishing, converting, and selling of cotton goods with the firm of Hudson and Kohn, where he served as vice president, general manager, and eventually president.

Kohn is known for his leadership role in the founding of the first Southern Textile Exposition in Greenville in 1915, a trade fair for textile manufacturers. Textile representatives exhibited their machinery, products, and services at this fair attended by thousands of people associated with textile manufacturing. With 160 exhibitors and more than 40,000 people attending, the exposition attracted more people than local hotels could accommodate.[24]

With the exposition's overwhelming success, Textile Hall, built in Greenville in 1917, served as the site for future expositions as Greenville became the permanent home of the biennial event.[25] Aided by the influx of northern textile companies, the southern textile exposition soon became an international symbol of South Carolina's growing industrial economy. At the 1920 exhibit, for example, a group of Chinese financiers and manufacturers contracted to buy $50 million worth of machinery for Shanghai factories.[26]

In addition to his professional accomplishments as a textile engineer, *The Greenville News* characterized Kohn as "a public-spirited man who has wielded influence over a considerable period in the textile, historical and civic fields in South Carolina."[27]

Kohn was deeply involved with Greenville and his religious community. In 1911, he helped establish Greenville's Reformed Jewish Congregation, the Temple of Israel, and was also a member of B'nai B'rith. During World War I, he led the Liberty Bond drive and chaired the Jewish relief drive.[28] An outgoing and active community member, he was a 32nd degree Mason, a lifelong Shriner, a member of the Elks, and secretary of the local chapter of the Clemson Alumni Association.[29]

David Kohn's rise in the textile industry was even more significant because he was a Jew in a field dominated at this time by New Englanders and leading South Carolinians.

NEW YORK MANUFACTURERS MOVE SOUTH

In the 1920s, a second wave of manufacturing began to sweep the Upcountry: garment making. Jewish-owned apparel manufacturers relocated to the Upcountry for the same reason as textile manufacturers—namely state incentives encouraging investment, lower labor costs, and nonunionized workers.

Jews dominated clothing manufacturing in New York City where they worked every aspect of clothing from supply to retail. The historian Adam Mendelsohn reports that in New York in 1910 "more than 50% of immigrant Jewish men born in Russia were employed in the production, retail, or wholesale of clothing as were 44% of Jewish men born in America."[30] By 1913, "almost all the factories and workshops were owned by Russian Jews and three-fourths of the workforce remained Jewish."[31]

Eventually, Jewish firms proliferated in other areas of the country including Chicago, Philadelphia, Baltimore, Rochester, and Cincinnati.[32] The trend of manufacturing clothing in smaller cities also developed among Jewish entrepreneurs associated with the New York clothing industry. As Weissbach notes, manufacturers "wanted to go into business for themselves in places where they might escape the strike activities and the difficult conditions they had encountered in the metropolis."[33] Other Jewish garment factories relocated in nearby North Carolina, including two firms that opened in Asheville: Highland Manufacturing, operated by Harold Goldbloom, and the Vanderbilt Shirt Factory owned by Milton Lurey.[34]

In the Upcountry, two clothing companies had a major impact on South Carolina manufacturing: the Dixie ShirtCompany of Spartanburgand the Piedmont Shirt Company of Greenville. The Dixie Shirt Company and the Piedmont Shirt Company provided work to thousands of South Carolina women and established additional companies throughout the South and beyond.

The earliest clothing manufacturing company founded in Spartanburg was the Dixie Shirt Company, owned and operated by a Russian-Jewish immigrant who migrated to Spartanburg around 1910 from New York City. Max Cohen initially operated a clothing store in Spartanburg, and in the early 1930s, founded the Dixie Shirt Company, manufacturer of men's and women's clothing. Two branches of the company operated in the Upcountry, one in Spartanburg and the other in Greenville. Max's son, Jack, later became the manager of the Spartanburg firm that employed approximately 600 needleworkers at its peak during World War II. The company ramped up production

Piedmont Shirt Company, ca. 1941, courtesy of the Coxe Collection, Greenville County Historical Society

during the war years starting in 1941, when the War Department contracted the company to make 105,000 khaki cotton shirts.[35]

The Dixie Shirt Company expanded throughout the South, and included companies in Baltimore, Asheville, and Paducah, Kentucky. The company also employed salesmen throughout the South to sell its goods. In 1932, for example, an advertisement appeared in the *Chattanooga Daily Times:* "Wanted: a salesman to carry men's and boys' popular priced dress shirts manufactured by the Dixie Shirt Company in Spartanburg."[36]

During the war years, the Spartanburg plant produced 7,000 shirts a day for the army and employed 600 people.[37] In 1945, the Greenville company with several hundred workers fulfilled government contracts and hired an additional one hundred women between the ages of "16 and 40 with power sewing machine experience for the shirt making trade for the war effort."[38] Women were employed as dress-shirt collar setters, while men were hired as knife cutters, die press operators, and salesmen.[39]

Piedmont Shirt Company, 1942. The physical plant was expanded as the company grew. Courtesy of the Coxe Collection, Greenville County Historical Society.

As a young child, Max Trout, whose family lived near the Dixie Shirt Company in the 1930s, recalls a lunch wagon appearing at the factory every day at noon and the workers filing out to purchase sandwiches and other food items.[40] Those workers were primarily women, who reached the Dixie Shirt Company, located on the far west end of Spartanburg at the former Camp Wadsworth grounds, by trolley car. In late August 1945, the War Department cancelled its contracts with several area clothing manufacturing companies.[41] With the cessation of war apparel, the Spartanburg company suspended operations in the late 1940s.[42]

Greenville was the site of another major clothing manufacturing company established in 1928 by Shepard Saltzman who came to South Carolina from New York. Saltzman, born in 1901, was the son of Nathan Saltzman, a New York garment worker, who, with his wife, Jennie, emigrated from Minsk. In 1926, young Saltzman married Shirley Friedman of Rumania and together they had three children.

Saltzman came to Greenville enticed by the tax breaks and the state's support for manufacturing. With seven years of experience in the shirt business in New York as a salesman, piece goods buyer, and factory manager, the twenty-five-year-old Saltzman explained his move to the South thusly, "In the early days, a retail merchant had to go to Baltimore, Philadelphia, or New York if he wanted shirts to sell. Railroads were slow and it took almost two weeks to get a shipment of goods . . . this fact was one of the dominant reasons for my decision to locate in a Southern state. Why not locate right among the mills and bleacheries, save freight on the cloth, and at the same time be able to give quick service to all the stores in the Carolinas and Georgia?"[43]

Saltzman must have made a convincing case for his proposed business plan as he appealed to the local Greenville community for credit. To supplement his own $5,000 investment, he achieved the backing of ten leading Greenville citizens for $1,000 each.[44] With their financial support, Saltzman opened a shop in a second-story loft on an obscure side street in Greenville. The financial support of leading Greenville businessmen to invest in an unknown entity attests to the tolerant, progressive attitudes of leading civic members in the Upcountry. It was no secret that Saltzman was Jewish, but that did not hinder their support for the stranger from New York City. "The Piedmont Shirt Company opened for business in 1928, the first of its kind in the state of South Carolina. In a few short years it expanded to a larger building of 30,000 square feet. Initially, Saltzman worked as a designer, stylist, piece goods buyer, bookkeeper, and salesman. The business took off quickly, the sales force increased, and the area of distribution eventually expanded beyond the local territory and into the surrounding Southern states."[45]

Saltzman immediately turned to his Jewish connections in New York and hired Jewish friends and family members to fill his management positions. Harry Abrams was one of the first men he brought on board. Abrams, the son of Russian immigrants, had managed skirt factories in Manhattan and Troy, New York, before Saltzman recruited him to Greenville to run the main plant where he supervised between 300 and 400 employees.[46] Later, Saltzman hired Abrams's daughter, Anita, to work as a stenographer at the company.

Saltzman hired his cousin, Morris Leffert, a Russian immigrant living in New York City, to work as division supervisor.[47] Saltzman even recruited his father, Nathan, who had been working in a shirt factory in New York, thus settling his parents in the community as well.[48] Soon, in a typical pattern of chain migration, his sisters, Anna and Dorothy, joined the rest of the family in Greenville.[49]

By 1938, Saltzman was operating four factories, one each in Greenville, Greenwood, Greer, and Tampa, Florida.[50] By the early 1950s, his workforce had risen to 1,700, after buying out the Kaynee Company, founded in 1888, producing boys' wear.[51] Hundreds of local women found jobs at the Piedmont Shirt Company in the cutting department as "bundle girls," "pin girls," and "number girls." The company hired women for jobs as cuff setters, button sewers, single-needle operators, and first-band collar workers. However, the company hired only African American women (until the late 1960s) as shirt pressers.[52] A 1950 advertisement for "Young Colored Women to train as shirt pressers," offered Black women an opportunity for a job that white women in South Carolina traditionally refused. White high school and business school graduates qualified for jobs in the personnel office and worked as secretaries and bookkeepers. Though Saltzman could not have known it at the time, one individual he hired would become the most esteemed Jew in Upcountry South Carolina. One of the greatest Jewish success stories to emerge from Greenville was Max Heller, a refugee from Austria who came to Greenville in the late 1930s under Saltzman's sponsorship. Heller worked for the Piedmont Shirt Company, as did his father, also brought to America by Saltzman. Heller's experiences as a refugee, his rise in clothing manufacturing, and, finally, his incredible career as mayor of Greenville, is the topic of future chapters.

In the early years of the Piedmont Shirt Company, Saltzman serviced retailers in nearby areas. He then broadened out to include Tennessee, Kentucky, Florida, Virginia, and then Texas, Louisiana, and Missouri. "As the business grew because of the expansion of the national market for ready-made clothing, Saltzman began to envision an operation that covered thirty states, including New York, New England, and the Midwest. Finally, he set his sights on national distribution,"[53] where he sold to Jewish and non-Jewish retail businesses.

Saltzman achieved enormous success. In 1938 he established the Wings Shirt Company, and in 1952, he established Wings Boyswear, Inc. By 1953 Piedmont Shirt was the number one brand in the popular price field.[54] In the early 1950s, his companies were exceeding $10 million in yearly sales.

Saltzman divided his time between his homes in Greenville and New York City, rejoining his family in New York on weekends. According to his granddaughter, Victoria Morrow, Saltzman's wife, Shirley, could not tolerate living in the South and moved the children back to New York "where they could grow up in an atmosphere of culture."[55] Apparently, she had become acculturated to life in an American metropolis and living in Greenville was like living in the southern Backcountry.

In 1955, at the height of his business success, Saltzman passed away. His son-in-law, Martin Morrow, took over the business and eventually purchased the company from the Saltzman family. He operated the company until 1986, when it then passed to his brother, the final proprietor of Piedmont Shirts, Wings, and Wings Boyswear.[56]

Shepard Saltzman exemplifies many sons who followed their fathers into the world of the garment industry, and recruited Jewish immigrants and American-born Jews into the industry, "typical in the formation of ethnic niches."[57] His reliance on fellow Russian Jews from New York whom he likely knew from his previous experiences also suggests an internal chain-migration pattern typically associated with immigrants who hailed from the same communities in Europe. He felt comfortable with these landsmen whom he could trust, and they, in turn, benefited from the ability to move into secure positions with people with whom they felt at home. Saltzman and the Piedmont Shirt Company figure prominently in subsequent chapters that examine clothing manufacturers, unions, and race relations.

Jewish migrants continued to establish clothing factories in the Upcountry in the 1920s and 1930s. These were smaller plants with local, as opposed to regional and national, impact. Similar to the aforementioned garment manufacturers, these too, were secondary migrants from the northeast who came South to establish garment manufacturing companies. The Kaplans's odyssey to Anderson began in New York City, where Gustave, a Russian immigrant who arrived in New York in 1901, operated a shirt manufacturing company. He moved the family to Harrisburg, Pennsylvania, where he managed another company; but in the 1930s, the Kaplans relocated to Anderson, a "location that was inhospitable to unions."[58] There they established Shirtmaster. The eldest son, Julius, became president of the company, and his younger brother, Joseph, secretary-treasurer. The company grew to nearly 400 employees and received government contracts during the war years.[59]

The once successful company closed after a scandal destroyed the business. Joseph Kaplan, secretary-treasurer of Shirtmaster, pleaded guilty in a US District Court in Greenville in 1959 to a check-switching scheme that he manipulated between two small Abbeville banks. Unable to meet the payroll of his 150 employees at the Abbeville location, he began the check manipulations in early 1957.[60]

The presiding judge, C. C. Wyche, told Kaplan he would "consider reducing the sentence, and might even consider probation, if Kaplan can find some honorable means of repaying the two banks."[61] Kaplan must have been well-liked in the community because the chief of police, the mayor, and the sheriff of Abbeville, wrote character witness letters on his behalf.[62] However, Kaplan never raised the approximately $100,000, and he was sentenced to a five-year prison term.[63]

Harry Abrams, initially hired by Shepard Saltzman to fill the position of superintendent at the Piedmont Shirt Company in 1938, left the company for a job as general manager of the Dixie Shirt Company in Spartanburg, owned and operated by the Cohen Family. Abrams had started his career in apparel manufacturing in Troy, New York. In 1944, Abrams organized the Raycord Company in Spartanburg that initially manufactured tire cord fabric, before converting to men's shirts, women's blouses, and pajamas. Raycord became one of the largest apparel manufacturers in Spartanburg County with 1,200 employees.[64]

Abrams started training his son, Irving, in the clothing business at the age of fourteen. The young man worked after school and during the summers in the shipping department and spread fabrics for the cutters. When World War II broke out, Irving joined the army, rising to the rank of lieutenant colonel. Upon returning from the war, he completed a degree at Clemson College in textile engineering.[65]

Under Irving's leadership, Raycord constructed a new building to house its shirt assembling operations, using automated equipment designed to increase efficiency.[66] Raycord operated a plant in nearby Gaffney as well. The company expanded to manufacturing women's blouses and suits and operated a factory outlet store in Greenville.[67]

These companies provide examples of the clothing manufacturing companies established in the Upcountry in the early decades of the twentieth century. Jewish clothing manufacturing companies continued organizing in South Carolina during the next four decades.

JEWISH MERCHANTS

Business was at the heart of Jewish life in Upcountry South Carolina as it was throughout the South.[68] Jews continued to find the small towns of the

Upcountry welcoming, and secondary migrations from other regions sustained throughout the 1920s and beyond. However, as Weissbach discovered in his study of Jews in small town America, "the peopling of America's small Jewish communities . . . was not simply a story of initial settlement followed by stability and continuity, but rather one of fluidity and change."[69] This statement is especially true for Jews in South Carolina.

While many members of the Jewish business community remained in the Upcountry for decades, others departed because of business volatility. Thus the pattern for Jewish-owned businesses was one of stability or failure, adaptability or relocation.

The 1920s were good years for Upcountry Jews, as they were for the country at large. Between 1922 and 1929, expanded production, heightened consumerism, and an upward trend of wages led to unbridled economic optimism in the United States.[70]

Business continued to be at the heart of Jewish life in the Upcountry, and most businesses remained steady with substantial profits. Shopkeepers adapted to the times reflecting patterns of consumption and the demand for luxury goods. The few businesses that could not compete packed up their goods and moved to other locations to start over again.

The economic prosperity that defined America in the 1920s ended with the crash of 1929. Every community, large or small, was affected by the stock market crash. While some Jewish businesses struggled, many others flourished in the Upcountry. Generally, however, business continuity characterized most Jewish establishments as they remained firmly planted in Upcountry communities, most of them passing from father to son, and often, from brother to brother, or father to daughter. Such intergenerational family business succession was common among Jews in the Upcountry, contrary to Eli Evans's pronouncement that "the story of Jews in the South is the story of fathers who built businesses to give to their sons who didn't want them."[71] While this may apply to some Jewish families, it does not represent the typical story of many Upcountry Jews.

Continuity is apparent in the pattern of Upcountry Jews who remained wedded to their communities. Unlike their northern urban kin who moved to the suburbs beginning in the 1920s,[72] South Carolina Jews did not move to suburbs because they did not exist. Cities like Greenville and Spartanburg, the largest in the Upcountry, were medium-sized communities where the Jewish business class worked, often within walking distance of their homes, These businesses changed or adapted as storekeepers expanded their merchandise, and new establishments surfaced to provide the latest consumer goods during a decade famous for consumerism.

One of the most successful family-run businesses in the Upcountry at this time had its roots in the small village of Woodruff, located south of Spartanburg and near the colonial-era Walnut Grove Plantation. The quiet village of cotton farmers witnessed a population surge when the Woodruff Cotton Mill opened its doors in 1898. By 1910, the mill doubled in size and the population of Woodruff tripled to approximately 1,600. About the time Woodruff was expanding from the growing numbers of mill workers, Max Cohen, opened a dry goods store in the heart of the small village. His timing was impeccable, as it "corresponded with the development of Woodruff as a trading center for the nearby rural communities,"[73] and the influx of hundreds of mill workers.

Max and Fannie Cohen had six children, and their two eldest sons, Jacob (Jack) and Elija (Eli) started collaborating with their father when they were young boys. At the age of seventeen, Jack struck out on his own and went to Anderson, after linking up with a Jewish junk dealer. After learning the business, Jack returned to Woodruff, bought a mule and wagon for fifty dollars, and canvassed ten counties in the Upcountry, buying and selling junk. By 1919 he had saved $6,000, which he invested into a business that grew to a series of stores known as Cohen's Chain Stores. He appointed his father to head the company, and Jack served as vice president and his brother Eli as secretary-treasurer. The company organized in Laurens (where according to Jack, "the business became the talk of the town because of the low prices." Jack worked night and day to build the business, opened more stores, bought in larger quantities, and undersold the big stores. As he stated in one of his full-page ads in *The Greenville News,* "I spent five cents of every dollar I took in for advertising."[74] By 1930 Jack Cohen had opened twenty-seven stores throughout the South and Cohen's was touted as the "fastest growing chain store in South Carolina."[75]

During the 1920s, Greenewalds, the oldest Jewish mercantile operation in Spartanburg (1886) expanded its merchandise from men's wardrobes and accessories to women's clothing. When its founder, Moses Greenewald, passed away in 1919his brother, David, became manager.[76] Harry Price, who initially founded his store as The New York Bazaar in 1903, "became known for his gracious and courteous manner and was friends with Mayor John Floyd, who owned the neighboring dry goods store and sold caskets from his back door."[77] In the 1920s, when more young people attended college than

Cohen's Chain Store, 1925, Main St., Greenville, courtesy of the Coxe Collection, Greenville County Historical Society

ever before, the Price family forged an alliance with Wofford College, and carried sportswear, specialty Wofford mascot merchandise, employed Wofford students, and outfitted Wofford's faculty.[78]

During the 1920s, Samuel Hecklin's business, the Sample Shoe Store, was doing so well that his brother, Barney, who collaborated with him in the business, opened his own retail shop, the Family Shoe Store. When Samuel Hecklin retired, his son, Simon, turned down a coaching job at Georgia Tech to continue his father's business in Spartanburg.[79]

Abraham Rosenberg, a Polish immigrant who opened a dry goods store in Greenwood in 1884, passed the business to his son, Ernest, when he retired in 1920. Ernest renamed it the Rosenberg Clothing and Shoe Company and transformed it into a specialized clothing and personal accessory store. Ernest kept the firm operating until 1996.[80] In Greenville, Morris Lurey, who was born in Bialystock, emigrated to the United States in 1902, where he opened the New York Shoe Store that operated for decades, passing from one family member to the next.[81] Polish-born Hyman August settled in Spartanburg in 1902 and initially opened the Battery Clothing Store, where his wife, Sadie, worked as a clerk. His next business venture was a pawn shop. During the 1920s he branched out into leather goods, then operated a beauty shop, and finally opened the Cinderella Shoe Shop.[82] Similarly, Russian-born Sam Bicoff operated a delicatessen in Greenville, and ten years later became the owner of a dry goods store, known as the Chicago Bargain House.[83] Jewish businesses were constantly updating their enterprises to meet the consumer demands of any given era, even if it meant reinventing themselves every few years.

Many other Spartanburg businesses established earlier in the century continued to thrive during the 1920s and beyond. Among these were the Globe Textile Store, Siegel Brothers Jewelry Store, Abe Goldberg's Clothing, and Brill's Electric. New Jewish businesses opened during the 1920s as well, among them was Abe Smith's Pawnshop and Music Store. Smith had emigrated from Lithuania to New York City before settling in Spartanburg.[84] His brother, Julius, joined him, and together they were partners in a loan company.[85]

Max Siegel left Russia in 1900, and settled in Anderson, where he earned his living as a peddler. Later, he established a livestock business, supplying meat to local markets. He and his wife Bessie, had four sons, Sam, Abe, Reuben, and Sol, who branched into other areas of business in Anderson in the late 1930s including a liquor store, a service station, and a wholesale grocery store.[86]

Greenville's long-established Jewish businesses like Harris Bloom and Sons, Fayonsky's clothing store, Knigoff's Pawn Shop, L. Rothschild's Men's Clothing, Goldstein's Shoe Store, Glickman's, Broadway Shoes, Jacobi Electric, and Cohen's Department Store, among others, continued to do a brisk business during the decade of the 1920s.

Jewish businesses stayed open on Saturdays, the biggest shopping day of the week to accommodate their non-Jewish clientele. Like other Jewish merchants across the nation, Upcountry Jews often forsook their Sabbath to accommodate their clientele. In contrast, Spartanburg "sidewalks were rolled up on Wednesday afternoons,"[87] as downtown stores closed so Baptists could attend Wednesday night church services.

JEWISH MERCHANTS IN AN ERA OF CONSUMERISM

Major cultural changes occurred in the 1920s because of consumerism. The historian Michael Flamm demonstrates that consumerism was deeply

Davidson's Department Store, undated photograph, Chesnee, courtesy of
Pauline Davidson

intertwined with identity, how people defined themselves. A new mantra
emerged in the 1920s: "You are what you wear."

Shoe stores began appearing in the 1920s during a time when footwear was
becoming stylish and inexpensive because of mass production. Specialized
shops emerged to manage the growing demand for fancy and high-quality
footwear, fitting consumers with the perfectly sized shoe. These included
Samuel Hecklin's Sample Shoe Store, Hyman August's Cinderella Shoe Shop,
and Barney Hecklin's Family Shoe Store in Spartanburg. Goldstein's Shoe
Store, Broadway Shoe Store, and Pollock's Shoe Store were a few of the many
shoe retailers that lined Main Street in Greenville. Pollock's Shoe Store was
a much-loved business in Greenville. Russian-born Lou Pollock started a chain
of shoe stores in Asheville, Greenville, and Palm Beach, Florida, and generously sponsored a shoe giveaway for needy children each year at Christmas.[88]

Jewelry stores also became more numerous, again, reflecting the growing
consumer culture in luxury items during the 1920s. In that decade, some of

Pauline Davidson, proprietor of Davidson's in her late eighties, Diane C. Vecchio photograph

the Jewish-owned jewelry stores included Spiegel Brothers, Zalenskys, and Elliott's, owned by Joseph Wachter in Spartanburg. Hale's Jewelers opened in Greenville, and D. M. Spiegel opened a jewelry and optical business in Greenwood. Jewish proclivity to expand and diversify attests to their business acumen and ubiquity in clothing and fashion. Jewish immigrants had the skills to match the market's needs.

New Jewish-owned businesses joined well-established Greenville enterprises in the 1920s. More than a few of these firms were suppliers for the nationwide boom in automobile manufacturing, such as Kaufman Brothers, the Davis Auto Parts Company, and Zaglin's Auto Store.[89] The Davis Auto Parts Company passed from father to son, and even daughters and granddaughters managed the company, worked as bookkeepers, or in the sale of auto parts.[90]

Countless Upcountry Jewish businesses remained intact well beyond the 1920s passing from generation to generation. However, various businesses disappeared from Upcountry towns. Success was far from guaranteed. These businesses no longer appeared in city directories or enumerated in the federal censuses. Consequently, like other enterprises that faltered, the proprietors moved to other communities for better business opportunities. Examples include the Abraham Bobrow family, who had emigrated from Belarus and settled in Spartanburg in 1913, after living in Philadelphia; Meridian, Mississippi; Uniontown, Alabama; and Chicago. After operating a shoe repair business in Spartanburg for ten years, the family of five relocated again, this time to Newark, New Jersey, where Abraham Bobrow became a candymaker.[91] Frequent relocations were common among Jewish businesspeople, but other business enterprises ended abruptly because of illness or death.

Levy Rothschild's clothing business prospered in Greenville beginning in the 1880s. With no children to carry on the business, Rothschild's disappeared from downtown Greenville when he died in 1927.[92] Abraham Silverman, who initially emigrated from England to Charleston, managed the Ladies Fur Shop in Greenville, but it disappeared by the 1920s, as did L. Schonwetter's Clothing Store, and Allen Brothers & Arcus, a ladies' ready-to-wear shop owned by Russian immigrants who had moved to Greenville from New York.[93]

Even with some storefronts changing, continuity, adaptation, and stability exemplified the experiences of most Jewish businesspeople in the Upcountry.

GENDER AND ECONOMIC OPPORTUNITIES

Married, immigrant Jewish women typically did not work outside the home. Jewish women, like married Italian immigrant women, constituted the largest percentages of immigrant women between 1870 and 1920. However, "they had among the lowest employment rates counted by census takers."[94]

To understand such trends, it is necessary to recognize, as the historian Riv-Ellen Prell notes, the "significance and power of relationships within households and the market where women act but are often invisible in certain analytic frameworks."[95]

In previous analysis of Italian immigrant women, it was found that women in Endicott, New York and Milwaukee, Wisconsin, functioned in a wide range of female work experiences. Women's intersection with the economy was defined by local opportunities as well as the impact of the life cycle of women's lives. A comparative study of women workers in these two cities, revealed that women earned money by providing boarding services to their kinsmen, their role in family businesses and other wage-earning experiences, like midwifery, typically invisible occupations.[96] Similar trends occurred in Upcountry South Carolina where married Jewish women, like Italians, worked in family-owned businesses and earned income by taking in boarders. Prell argues that while "feminist historians integrated women into historical narratives as actors capable of agency," [Jewish] women are disappearing from the narrative in recent studies of Jews in America. She attributes this to the "economic turn" in American Jewish history, where Jewish men emerge as the norm and primary actors in economic history.[97]

There is no doubt that Jewish men led in entrepreneurial ventures in the late nineteenth and early twentieth centuries, but that should not diminish Jewish women's economic activities as producers. Indeed, ample evidence exists of Jewish women's business undertakings in the Upcountry beginning primarily in the 1920s and growing stronger throughout the twentieth century. These include women who started businesses or took over their husband's or father's businesses after their retirement or death.

TAKING IN BOARDERS

Boarding provided newly arrived immigrants a supportive environment. Surrounded by compatriots and conversing in their native language while eating familiar foods helped ease immigrants' transition to American life and the loneliness they undoubtedly faced.[98] Providing services to boarders was a way immigrant wives could earn money while remaining at home, thus combining economic, household, and child-rearing tasks. Taking in boarders was a business like any other where currency was exchanged for services.[99]

In every Upcountry town and city, Jewish wives provided boarding services to newly arrived immigrants. For example, Fannie Rothschilds had two boarders living in her Greenville home in 1900, and in 1910 two German boarders were living with Abe and Esther Goldberg and working in Goldberg's clothing store as salesmen.[100] Bessie Switzer raised four children while providing services to two boarders,[101] as did Ella Bloom who had six children and a boarder.[102]

German-born Rosa Fleishman, who was living in Anderson with her husband, provided a room for a boarder and a home for her sister-in-law as well.[103] In 1920, August and Sadie Hyman owned a home on Elford Terrace in Spartanburg, where they resided with their four children and a boarder by the name of Maurice Switzer.[104]

Multiple extended family members often lived under one roof. In 1910, for example, Samuel Hecklin, his wife, and their four children shared an apartment with his brother and sister-in-law and their six children. At the age of thirteen, Samuel Davidson emigrated from Russia and took up residence with an uncle in Anderson who provided him with a job in his dry goods store.[105] Harry Schahub lived with his uncle, Nathan Shapiro and his wife in Union in 1920, while twenty-one year old German-born Erwin Hertz lived with his uncle, Harry Brill, where he secured a position as a salesman in a local jewelry store in Spartanburg.[106]

Obtaining a place with an already established relative, an important link in the migration chain, was the most common way new immigrants established themselves in America. Other migrants, whether from abroad or secondary migrants from other American locations, were often boarders who typically lived in compatriots' homes.

Weissbach suggests that boarding and/or renting were also indicative of economic uncertainty. In his analysis of small communities, he notes that "nowhere did homeowners leave their small towns with any greater frequency than renters did."[107] Single men, in particular, had a high rate of geographic mobility, suggesting that "the search for better economic circumstances was the consideration most likely to prompt individuals to move out of small towns."[108]

Extrapolating household information from the Federal Census reveals boarding patterns, homeownership, and household structure. In the Upcountry, these data reveal that Jewish immigrants either lived with kin or were boarders before establishing their own households.

In addition to taking in boarders, Upcountry Jewish women assisted their husbands in mercantile enterprises. One of the earliest women found working in a family business was German-born Kate Goldberg, who, in 1905, clerked in her husband's Spartanburg clothing store, K. Goldberg & Co.[109]

OUT TO WORK

Major changes occurred among the younger generation of American-born Jewish women, a reflection of nationwide trends. In the 1920s and 1930s, the daughters of Jewish immigrants in the Upcountry entered the workforce after completing secondary education or attending a business school. High school training often prepared young women with typing, arithmetic, and stenography—skills needed to meet the demands of office work. Historian Julia Kirk Blackwelder notes that "reformers introduced business courses into high schools and colleges at the end of the century and these courses had expanded widely by 1920."[110]

Changing patterns of women's employment created opportunities for white-collar occupations. The number of women holding clerical jobs tripled between 1910 and 1920.[111] Women's white-collar work accelerated as women took jobs as typists, clerical workers, secretaries, and stenographers.

These jobs required skills that became common among American-born Jewish women: command of spoken and written English and training as filers, typists, and stenographers. Jewish women acquired these skills in high school business classes or in secretarial schools. In fact, both Spartanburg and Greenville had business schools that taught these skills.

Unlike their sisters in urban areas employed in garment factories in the late nineteenth and early twentieth centuries, Jewish daughters in Upcountry South Carolina came from business-class families. Unlike large cities such as New York, Chicago, and Philadelphia, a Jewish working class never developed in the Upcountry. This is borne out in studies of smaller Jewish communities like Indianapolis and Knoxville, among others.[112] In these cities, as well as those of the Upcountry, a Jewish working class did not exist, and Jews identified with middle-class values. Thus when unmarried Jewish women worked outside the home, they worked in white-collar jobs and in the business establishments of family members or friends.

In 1930, Alice Hecklin worked for her father in his Spartanburg shoe store. Lena From worked as a saleswoman in her father's dry goods store in Union, and Greenwald's in Spartanburg hired Ida Hecklin and other young Jewish women to work in their Ladies Department.[113]

Louisa, Minnie, Anna, and Clara, first cousins and daughters of Harris and Julius Bloom, worked as clerks in the family-operated dry goods store, H. Bloom and Son in Greenville. Helen Abrams was a buyer for the Belk Department Store in Greenville, a chain store founded in the late 1880s in North Carolina,[114] while Vivian Cohen maintained the books for her father's firm, Carolina Hide and Junk in Spartanburg.[115]

Sarah Hecklin, the daughter of Russian immigrants, was employed as a secretary for Dr. C. William Bailey and her sister, Rosie, was a stenographer. Anita Abrams of Greenville worked as a stenographer at the Piedmont Shirt factory where her father was also employed.[116] Florie Geisberg was a saleslady at a dry goods store, and her sister-in-law, Sadie, sold women's clothing at a shop in Anderson.[117] Dora Price, the wife of Harry Price, the proprietor of Prices' Store for Men, worked as a cashier at the clothing store for thirty years after her husband's death in 1937.[118]

The numbers of Jewish women in the workforce increased exponentially after World War I when greater opportunities emerged for women workers. These and other examples testify to the important roles of immigrant women in the workforce. While revenue from boarders provided married women with an income during the years mothers were homebound with child-care responsibilities, single women had more opportunities to enter the work-force with the expansion of white-collar jobs. William Toll maintains that "patterns of female employment from 1900 through 1930 suggests that East European Jewish families used the tradition of mutual responsibility to gain economic security."[119] This was equally true for the young, Jewish women working outside the home in the Upcountry. These single women lived at home and helped the family through their earnings or labor in a family enterprise.

THE GREAT DEPRESSION HITS THE UPCOUNTRY

The economic prosperity that defined the country in the 1920s ended with the Crash of 1929. Banking was the first affected by the economic downturn. Throughout the Upcountry, banks closed their doors.

Mill workers suffered the most during the Depression. The economic decline hit textile manufacturing and customer demand for textile goods declined, decreasing production. Textile mills cut back their workforce to three or four days a week as orders for goods fell sharply.[120] Labor unrest had been escalating throughout the 1920s in textile communities across the South. In 1929, strikes occurred at several mills in Spartanburg and Greenville and often grew violent during the lean years of the Depression. The stretch-out and accompanying wage cuts led to strikes beginning in 1929 in North Carolina while strikes in mills in Greenville and Spartanburg soon followed. In the 1930s, the "work of organizing Spartanburg County to strike began in August 1933 and continued until the General Strike a year later."[121] None of the textile millowners were Jewish, but Jewish businesses felt the hardships experienced by mill workers and others, as businesses and consumer spending declined in every sector. In October 1930 the American Cigar Company, operated by Jewish immigrants, closed its factory and 200 employees lost their jobs. Numerous cigar makers left Greenville and found employment at the Charleston plant.

While several Jewish businesses failed, leading them to seek opportunities elsewhere, other Jewish businesspeople migrated to the Upcountry after experiencing business failures in previous locations. Morris Chaplin (Tschaplinsky) moved his family from Columbia to Greenville in the early 1930s after his business in the state's capital failed. Once in Greenville he opened a "hole in the wall pawn shop" that was successful, and soon he began loaning money as well.[122] Pawnbroker firms were one of the businesses that withstood the Depression, as Eric Goldstein and Deborah Weiner note, "and even saw increased demand."[123]

In 1932, Harry Tanenbaum, of Kobrin, Russia, and his family abandoned their failing businesses in Augusta, Georgia, including a general store and a jewelry store, and moved to Spartanburg, where he was hired at Skalowsky's Jewelry Store.[124] The Abelkops had emigrated from Odessa, Russia, to Wilmington, North Carolina, and operated a general store; however, business was so slow that they decided to move to Greenville. The family's clothing store did moderately well in Greenville, but Abelkop sought better prospects. In 1932, he opened another clothing business in Spartanburg that succeeded.[125]

William Rosenfeld and his wife, Cyvia, relocated to Greenville from Asheville in the early 1930s. William had worked in the insurance business in Asheville and relocated to Greenville after learning that no Jewish insurance agents existed in the Upcountry. In 1933, he started the William Rosenfeld Insurance Company. His son and grandsons, upon graduating from college, joined him in the insurance business forming the Rosenfeld-Einstein and Associates Insurance Agency. The firm, established eighty-seven years ago, is still in operation today by Rosenfeld family members.[126]

The Depression hit Jews in the Upcountry unevenly. While some Jewish merchants migrated from other areas in the South to the Upcountry and did well, other Jewish enterprises failed. Rosa From Poliakoff shared her memories of the Great Depression and its impact on Jewish businesses. "There were a lot of Jewish merchants who just didn't make it . . . and they had to go through this bankruptcy thing." However, she maintained that "it was wonderful at that time how the Jewish people stuck together . . . if there was a bankruptcy, the Jewish people would always go and they would '*Allee den kommen zusammen*,'" meaning they (the Jewish men) all came together.' They'd go off in the back room and make their plans. They would buy this stock, and if this little Jewish merchant would want to retrieve it somehow, they would help him keep his business. Somehow or other, they would put their money together to buy [his stock]."[127]

Jewish-owned businesses that survived the Great Depression had to adjust to challenging times. In the 1920s, Nathan Fleishman and his brother-in-law, Phillip Klyne, opened a dry goods business in Anderson, with a branch in Greenville and one in Georgia. The Depression forced them to close the Georgia branch while the Greenville and Anderson branch continued to operate.[128]

Bloom's Department Store in Greenville scaled back the size of its operation and moved to a smaller building.[129] Jewish businesses in Spartanburg slashed prices on their merchandise. As an example, Greenewalds offered men's suits worth $35.00 to $45.00 each at $24.50.[130] Furthermore, Greenewalds, according to a grandson, "went from a tremendous profit to zero during the Depression, lost lots of money, remained open but had to take huge salary cuts."[131]

CONCLUSION

This chapter sought to demonstrate the role of Jewish entrepreneurs in the industrial development of the Upcountry in textiles and clothing manufacturing, a phenomenon that has gone unnoticed in the economic history of Upcountry South Carolina.

Moreover, it reveals how gender and the economy are intertwined. Jewish wives and mothers were contributors to a hidden economy, providing boarding services to their fellow landsmen, while their daughters entered white-collar occupations and worked in the family business.

Notwithstanding the hardships of the Depression years and the fact that some Jewish businesses failed, most Jewish businesses weathered the storm well. Their enterprises expanded and modernized to fit the consumer culture of the 1920s. Although not everyone succeeded, Jews moved to the right place at the right time with the appropriate skill sets and contacts.

In all their endeavors, from small shops to large manufacturing enterprises, Jews relied on family members and close friends to grow their enterprises. These kinship networks reached South Carolina from Europe, New York, and other East Coast cities.

CHAPTER 5

The Promise of American Life

Rosa From, the 1932 valedictorian of her Union high school class, attended Agnes Scott College, a private, liberal arts school in Georgia. Her roommate was Eva Poliakoff, whose brother she eventually married.[1] Rosa's three sisters attended Winthrop College in Rock Hill, South Carolina, and her brother attended Georgia Tech.[2] Several other Upcountry Jewish women in the 1930s attended Winthrop, including the sisters Norma and Irene Kassler from Gaffney, and Lena, Mary, and Sarah From of Union.[3]

After Jews established successful businesses in the Upcountry, they turned their attention to long-term stability and upward mobility. This chapter examines how Jews acculturated into American society through homeownership, citizenship, and education, while retaining a strong sense of Jewish identity through culture, religion, and foodways. Homeownership in the Upcountry helped Jews acculturate and intermingle with non-Jews in middle-class neighborhoods. For the immigrant generation of Jews, greater integration also occurred by obtaining US citizenship. Upcountry Jews endorsed education for their children as a means of acculturation and sought citizenship to attain "100% Americanism."

HOMEOWNERSHIP

Upcountry Jewish families invested in homeownership quickly, often within ten years of settling. This was typical of Jewish life in the South as elsewhere outside of the industrial cities of the Northeast. Home buying can also be viewed as a necessity in the local housing market of the Upcountry and the South in general, where apartments were scant and single-family dwellings were the norm. Home-owning families represented not only success in the competitive world of business, but a commitment to remaining in the Upcountry.

As discussed in chapter 4, Jewish immigrants initially provided boarding services for kin or acquaintances from their hometown in the old country.

"In so doing," writes historian Samuel Baily, "migrants were tied by bonds of shared residence and mutual assistance."[4] Upcountry communities quickly became populated by men and women related to one another.[5] The recreated community of Jewish businesspeople helped newly arrived immigrants establish business connections and adjust to their unfamiliar environment.[6]

Starting around 1910, several Jewish families purchased homes in Harris Place, located two blocks from Morgan Square, in the heart of the business center in Spartanburg. In Greenville, Jewish families initially lived near the Orthodox synagogue. Whereas this marked the initial home-owning stage, most Jewish families, beginning in the 1920s, dispersed throughout the two cities and purchased homes in middle- and upper-middle-class neighborhoods surrounded by non-Jews. As Judith Endelmann observed in Indianapolis, as Jews moved up economically, "they changed their residence to match their rising fortunes."[7]

Homeownership became the norm for Jews in the Upcountry. Samuel and Gussie Hecklin, who owned the Sample Shoe Store on East Main Street, purchased a two-story brick home on Otis Boulevard, a charming tree-lined street with spacious front yards in Spartanburg. After sharing a rental with Sam's brother, sister-in-law, and six children, the Hecklins enjoyed ample space in their new home. Located in the middle-class community of Converse Heights, the four Hecklin children grew up playing and attending school with their non-Jewish neighbors. Harry and Dora Price of Prices' Store for Men, purchased a spacious home on North Converse Street, also located in Converse Heights. Hyman August, who had emigrated from Poland in 1890 had lived in Spartanburg since 1902. In 1920, he and his family, who owned the Cinderella Shoe Store, moved into a two-story brick home with his wife, Sadie, and children in a very desirable Spartanburg location on Elford Terrace.[8]

Max Cohen, who founded the Dixie Shirt Company, and his wife Fanny, purchased a home on Swinn Drive in 1920 large enough to house their eldest son, his wife, and five other children.[9] Harry Fayonsky, a Russian immigrant, World War I veteran, and proprietor of a dry goods store in Greenville, purchased a bungalow-style home in a residential area near downtown. Harris Bloom, the proprietor of Bloom's Department Store and his wife, owned a home next door to their son Julius and his wife, Amelia, in Greenville.[10] Two of the most prominent Jewish families in Abbeville, the Visanskas and Rosenbergs, were wealthy merchants and highly respected citizens. G. A. Visanska owned a large, 1882 Steamboat Gothic-style home, and Solomon Rosenberg acquired a stately home on North Main Street in Abbeville.[11]

Following this pattern in Spartanburg, the Greenewalds, Spigels, Smiths, Skalowskis, Shapiros, and Goldbergs purchased homes in the 1920s.[12] Likewise, this pattern was replicated in Greenville, where the Lurey, Davis, Zaglin, and Switzer families became successful businesspeople and homeowners. In the small towns of Anderson, Easley, Gaffney, Greenwood, Union, and Fountain Inn, local Jewish residents including the Geisburgs, Sarlins, Sheftalls, Rosenblums, and the Karditz families, business proprietors all, purchased homes located in middle-class neighborhoods.[13] Jews moved freely throughout the Upcountry, purchasing homes wherever they chose with no restrictive clauses prohibiting them from doing so.

The transition from boarding to homeownership reflected the accumulation of financial resources and rise in status. Furthermore, homeownership in integrated neighborhoods helped advance acculturation as Jewish children grew up alongside non-Jewish children. Young people played together in neighborhood-organized activities such as baseball, football, street hockey on roller skates,[14] hopscotch and jump rope. Alex Davis recalled growing up in the late 1920s and early 1930s in Greenville. "We had a small Jewish community here, so, most of my playmates were the gentile boys in the neighborhood.[15] We used to play with the Blacks just like they were best friends of ours." Davis recalled that he had "rich playmates, who lived in average homes, and went to school with us." "In fact, from the first grade . . . and through high school, one of my best friends (a non-Jew) took me on a lot of trips when they went to the mountains. It was nice and at that time there was no anti-Semitism at all. Mother and Dad had their gentile friends, too."[16] Jack Bloom, who grew up in Greenville at the same time as Davis, commented that he "grew up in a community where there were no Jews . . . in my neighborhood . . . the boys I played with . . . there was never any indication of anti-Semitism."[17]

Jewish integration occurred more swiftly in the Upcountry where Jews made up a small minority of the population compared to Jews living in densely populated urban areas. Apart from the small early settler neighborhoods in Greenville and Spartanburg, Jews never lived in ethnic enclaves dominated by Jewish groceries and delis, businesses, and shuls. Rather, Jewish-owned businesses were located on every main street in towns and cities throughout the region. Jewish businesses interspersed with non-Jewish retail establishments, and Jews bought homes in non-Jewish neighborhoods, all of which led to greater acculturation of Jews in the Upcountry.

The custom of home buying signaled Jewish stability, continuity, and mobility as well as acculturation. It also represented a dramatic shift from the boarding and extended family living patterns depicted in chapter 4. Studies of economic mobility have placed considerable emphasis on the importance of homeownership.[18] Unlike their compatriots in urban areas who were less likely to become homeowners, Jews in the South pursued home-ownership for a variety of reasons. Jewish populations grew around merchants and their businesses creating an anchor for their lives in the Upcountry.

CITIZENSHIP

Another sign of acculturation among the Jews of the Upcountry was the frequency and rapidity with which immigrants became naturalized citizens. Nationwide, Jews pursued citizenship much more readily than other immigrant groups, in part, because they did not have the desire to return to their country of origin. In addition, Jews of the Upcountry sought citizenship as a further means of acceptance in their communities. With their status as citizens, Jews could not be accused of not wanting to become "real Americans." The historian Maddalena Marinari notes that Jewish immigrants' "lack of ties with their homelands and their history of persecution in Europe persuaded them of the importance of acquiring US citizenship."[19] In this respect they acted much differently than Italians, for example, who frequently engaged in circular or return migration and retained strong connections with their homeland.[20] "Return migration inflamed popular opinion" against immigrants, writes historian Nancy Foner.[21] She asserts that "at the time, a common concern was that the new arrivals were not making serious efforts to become citizens and real Americans."[22]

The Americanization movement that commenced with World War I and continued through the postwar era, "accelerated the rate of naturalization as immigrants felt tremendous pressure to prove their loyalty to the nation and to conform to the credo of 100 percent Americanism that dominated wartime and the postwar era."[23] The Americanization movement, often and unfortunately, coupled with the resurgence of the Ku Klux Klan in the 1920s, targeted eastern and southern European immigrants, and labeled Jews and Catholics as alien subversives. Subsequently, a deluge of petitions for naturalization soared in the United States.

Between 1907 and 1911, immigrants filed an average of 41,000 petitions for naturalization per year, whereas in the 1920s, the annual average climbed to 188,430."[24] Among those becoming naturalized citizens were the Jews of South Carolina. A surge of naturalization petitions occurred among Jews in the Upcountry. They frequently became citizens within a decade or two after arriving in the United States. Sarah Fayonsky, who collaborated with her husband Louis in their dry goods store in Greenville, moved quickly to apply for naturalization. After arriving in the Upcountry in 1900 she made her declaration in 1905. Louis Fayonsky, who immigrated to the United States in 1882, became a naturalized citizen in 1910.[25]

A famous Upcountry Jewish sculptor who escaped Russia during the revolution, Abraham Davidson, along with Israel From, a Union dry goods merchant, and Hyman August, a Spartanburg storekeeper, were all naturalized in the 1920s. Abe Blumberg, a merchant in Dillon, who immigrated in 1902 and served in World War I, became naturalized in the 1920s, as did his wife, Minnie.[26] Abraham Shain, a tailor, arrived in the United States in 1909 and gained citizenship by 1925. The Spartanburg merchant Abe Goldberg became naturalized in 1920, followed by Abe Levin who earned citizenship in the 1930s. Sam Lurey, proprietor of a dry goods and grocery store in Greenville also became a citizen in the 1930s.[27] Samuel Fleishman of Germany, the owner of a "Gents Merchandise Store" in Greenville had already obtained citizenship by 1920, and Esther Goldberg and Rosa Fleishman became citizens in 1920, the same year as their husbands.[28]

The only other significant group of immigrants in the Upcountry were Greeks, who settled there beginning at the turn of the twentieth century. In a random sampling comparing Jewish and Greek naturalizations in the Upcountry, Jewish immigrants naturalized a little more quickly than Greeks. Out of twenty-five immigrants from each group studied, eight Greeks had been in the United States for more than twenty years before naturalizing; four had been in the country for more than ten years before applying for citizenship, and ten Greeks naturalized within ten years of immigrating to America. One individual had lived in the United States forty-five years before he became a naturalized citizen, and two remained aliens after living in the United States for more than twenty years.[29] Jewish naturalization on the other hand, averaged ten to twelve years between arrival and naturalization.[30]

Naturalization marked a further step toward integration into American life. It signaled the desire of Jews for civic inclusion, political participation, and recognition as American citizens.

AMERICAN-BORN JEWS AND EDUCATION

One of the most important means of assimilation for the children of Jewish immigrants was education, a vocation they pursued with passion. In the 1920s and 1930s, more students nationwide remained in school and graduated than ever before. As the children of businesspeople, young Jews in the Upcountry were among those completing their high school educations. Often, this was not possible for poor, urban Jews who relied on their children's paycheck to help provide support for the family. In New York City, for example, the Immigration Commission reported that in the early twentieth century "only about twenty percent of Jewish husbands were financially able to support an entire household without the help of other family members."[31]

The assumption that education was a successful means of assimilation and upward mobility has been voiced by many scholars studying the immigrant experience in America. Historian Alan Kraut notes that "schools have been regarded by historians as the bridge between the Old World and American society."[32] Marc Lee Raphael, commenting on the Jewish community of Columbus, Ohio, observed that "American Jewish immigrants heartily accepted the public schools as vehicles for the assimilation of their children and as a means of upward economic and social mobility."[33]

However, several revisionist historians have questioned "the public school system as a path to economic and social opportunities."[34] Indeed, the public school was the subject of much ambivalence among some immigrant parents. Many immigrants regarded education as the door to success, while others perceived it as a means of erasing ethnic cultural values and practices.[35] While it was both, to a certain extent, it is more likely that Upcountry Jews—as businesspeople—tended to associate more strongly with middle-class values and viewed education as another means of fitting in and achieving economic success.

Comparatively, Jewish children attended school longer than other immigrant groups, whose parents anxiously awaited the time when their children could quit school and contribute to the family economy. The latter was typical among many urban immigrant groups, especially working-class Italians where children of immigrant parents sought employment at an early age exclusively for the purpose of contributing to the family income.[36] This pattern was repeated in the early twentieth century in manufacturing towns and cities across the nation. Similarities existed among working-class Jews in industrial cities where daughters frequently worked in garment factories.[37]

This pattern recurred in the early twentieth century in manufacturing towns and cities across the nation. Similarities existed among working-class Jews in industrial cities where daughters frequently worked in garment factories.[38] However, patterns were different in the Upcountry among Jewish businesspeople.

Traditional Jewish culture valued learning and parents believed their children could achieve upward mobility through education, as evidenced by the number of second-generation Jews who graduated from high school in the Upcountry. A random sampling of 150 children born to East European immigrants in the Upcountry reveals that one hundred percent of Jewish students attending school in the 1920s and 1930s, both females and males, graduated from high school. Anita Abrams graduated from Greenville High School and subsequently took a job as a stenographer at Saltzman's shirt factory; all five Bloom children, both male and female, graduated from Greenville High. The girls proceeded to work in their father's department store, while the boys went to college. Rebecca and Rose Campel graduated in 1930. Rebecca took a job as a stenographer in a Greenville office and Rose became a bookkeeper.[39]

Sadie August, who graduated from Spartanburg High School in 1920, worked as a stenographer in a local government office. In 1927, Judith Cohen and Bill Price graduated from Spartanburg High, and Bill joined Prices' Store for Men, the family business.[40] Herbert Shapiro and Alice Hecklin graduated in 1930. Shapiro went to work in his father's dry goods store and Hecklin worked in her father's shoe store.[41]

A year later, Lois Pollock and Abram Smith graduated from Spartanburg High, and Anne Price and Eugene Shapiro followed, graduating in 1933. Shapiro went to Wofford College, became a doctor, and opened a practice in nearby Asheville, North Carolina.[42] Helen Friendlander graduated in 1934, and left Spartanburg to attend college in New York City. Selmen Gelburd graduated in 1939 and joined his father operating their clothing store, the National Men's Wear Shop. Rosina and Joe Blumberg, of Dillon, also graduated in the early 1930s. Like so many others, Joe joined his father, Julius, a Russian immigrant, in the family business, the People's Dry Goods Company.[43] Every young Jewish person in Abbeville and Anderson completed their secondary education, graduating from local high schools.[44]

The children of middle-class business and professional families most resemble the high graduation rates of Jewish children. Because the Upcountry was the center of textile manufacturing the children of mill workers rarely made it to the eighth grade. Typically these children quit school at an early age to join their parents in the mills. In fact, it was not until 1918 that an act requiring mill schools receiving public funds make at least eight grades available to their pupils.[45]

Large numbers of Jewish high school graduates also entered institutions of higher education during the 1920s and 1930s. In doing so, they joined a nationwide increase of young people attending college, but Jewish youth were pursuing higher education in larger numbers than their non-Jewish peers. One study reveals that "nearly half of all college students in New York City were Jewish. Nationally, Jews made up less than four percent of the total population but more than nine percent of all college students" in the early 1920s.[46] Gerald Sorin reports that "although second-generation Jews reached the ivy-covered halls of academe well before other groups of the post-1890 immigration, it was not until the 1920s that Jews finished high school and entered college in substantial numbers. By the mid-1930s, fifty percent of the applicants to medical school and an equally disproportionate number of applicants to law school were Jewish."[47]

So many young Jewish people attended college that "most prestigious American colleges and universities," according to historian Leonard Dinnerstein, "had imposed quotas on Jews during the 1920s thereby severely restricting their educational and employment opportunities."[48] "New York University and Columbia University, for example, whose Jewish enrollments had reached forty percent, instituted quotas."[49]

Many Upcountry Jewish women and men attended southern colleges where Jewish student admissions were not restricted. Several students attended nearby colleges and lived at home, like Jack Bloom and his brother, Melvin, who both attended Furman University. Jack continued his education at Duke University law school, while Melvin pursued a PhD in organic chemistry at Duke.[50] Similarly, Simon Hecklin of Spartanburg lived at home while he attended Wofford College.

Other college-bound students ventured farther afield in the 1920s and 1930s, but most attended southern colleges such as the University of South Carolina, the University of Georgia, Clemson College, and the College of Charleston.[51] Several Jewish men with aspirations of a military career attended The Citadel in Charleston. Sam Lurey of Greenville enrolled in The Citadel and eventually retired from the US Army with the rank of lieutenant colonel.[52] Jewish males attending college and graduate school in the 1920s and 1930s frequently majored in business, law, and textile manufacturing.

Jewish women also pursued higher education at greater rates than women from native-born and other ethnic groups.[53] Numerically, there were far fewer Jewish women attending college in the Upcountry in the 1920s and 1930s than men, because most women secured jobs after high school or married. It is difficult to ascertain the number of Jewish women from the Upcountry who went to college in the 1920s and 1930s. Ceile Rosenberg attended Converse College, majored in sociology and became a social welfare worker in South Carolina.[54] Florette Visanska of Abbeville attended Goucher College in Baltimore and graduated in 1932.[55] Several other women attended the University of South Carolina and Converse College, which had a strong music program. These women typically majored in English, music, or childhood education, and many of them entered the field of teaching.

Annae Blotcky, the daughter of a Jewish immigrant, was one of two Jewish music teachers in Spartanburg, as well as the director of Wofford College Glee Club.[56] Dena Spigel, the daughter of Austrian-born David and Daisey Spigel remained in Spartanburg and taught piano until her marriage to Aaron Sachs, the president of Multiweld Manufacturing Company, and then relocated to Bessemer, Alabama.[57] Eunice Poliakoff of Anderson attended Peabody Conservatory of Music in Baltimore and took a job as a music counselor at a camp in that city.[58]

Rosa From of Union taught at the Fromwalt School in Atlanta after receiving her degree from Agnes Scott College in 1936. She gave up teaching when she married her husband, Myer Poliakoff. However, after his death, Rosa returned to work, succeeding her husband as owner and manager of D. Poliakoff Store in Abbeville. In 1997, at the age of eighty-two, she was presented with the Small Business of the Year Award.[59] These examples indicate the liberalizing effect of immigration on women and their daughters. Furthermore, it suggests a greater range of opportunities available to young women born into immigrant families who did not rely on their economic contributions for survival.

While Jewish traditions dictated that sons rather than daughters should be educated, that attitude was changing as Jewish immigrants adjusted to life in the United States. In small towns, like those of the Upcountry,

Formal education was an instrument of mobility, and as the historian Gerald Sorin points out, this concept developed fully in the 1920s.[60] One of the reasons for "the remarkable social mobility of the Jews is that they invested more, and earlier, in their own human capital than other groups, partly by staying in school longer."[61]

REINFORCING JEWISH BELIEFS AND VALUES

While Jews integrated into community life, there was, nonetheless, a fervent desire for Jews to retain a Jewish identity. Members of the Upcountry business community belonged to and supported religious congregations. In Spartanburg and Greenville, young people attended religious education classes, and prepared for their bar (and later) bat mitzvah. They learned Hebrew, became confirmed, and joined synagogue sponsored basketball clubs. Synagogue members organized local chapters of Aleph Zadik Aleph (AZA), which was a fraternal organization for Jewish teens and served as a central forum for the boys of the entire Jewish community. Local chapters organized softball teams and members played other AZA teams in Asheville, Columbia, Augusta, and Savannah.[62] In later years (the 1950s and beyond), Jewish youth attended Jewish camps located in the Blue Ridge Mountains of North Carolina.

Parents instilled a keen sense of Jewish pride in their children. While they played with non-Jews, attended schools and social events with non-Jews, they were raised to never forget they were Jews. Jewish merchants closed their stores for the High Holidays and parents kept their children out of school. Gloria From Goldberg of Union recalls that "it was drilled into Allan (her brother) and me that we were Jewish. When my dad closed his store for the High Holidays, he placed a sign on the door: "Closed for the Jewish Holiday."[63]

Rose Poliakoff of Union recalled "my [Orthodox] parents wanted us to know that we were Jewish, and they wanted us to maintain our identity. My mother wanted us to stay out of school for every holiday . . . not just Rosh Hashanah and Yom Kippur, but Sukkoth and other holidays."[64]

Jewish parents welcomed and even encouraged their children to interact with non-Jews, but when it came to marriage, they wanted their children to select Jewish partners. Allen From of Union, recalled, "on occasion, I would attend church with my non-Jewish friends and was always made to feel welcome. My parents had no problems with my ecumenical activities. My parents encouraged me to engage with my Christian friends but made sure I maintained my Jewish beliefs and values. I believe they thought—"this is fine now—but you are going to marry a Jewish woman."[65] As a high school student, Joan Meir of Greenville recalled that her parents allowed her to date whomever she wanted but when she went to college, she had to date Jewish boys.[66]

As southern Jewish communities grew, an intricate network of family and business alliances assembled for the purpose of bringing young people together. Various Jewish social and cultural societies provided a meeting place for young men and women, often leading to marriage. According to Jeanette Davidson Finkelstein, "Jewish young people got together on Sundays in Greenville where they attended dances and played cards. They came from all over the state so that young Jewish boys and girls could meet each other."[67] At one of these Sunday get-togethers, Jeanette met Jacob Finkelstein from Brooklyn whom she married a year later.[68]

Ida Lurey Bolonkin, who graduated from Greenville High School in 1939, did not believe in intermarriage and never dated a non-Jew. She met her future husband at an AZA meeting. "That's why AZA was so important," added her daughter, Joan Bolonkin Meir. It brought young Jewish people together, "it was their social life."[69] Very few intermarriages occurred before the 1950s and 1960s, attesting to the strength of Jewish identity.

FOODWAYS

Jews also maintained Jewish identity through foodways, a link with the Jewish past and a celebration of religious customs and traditions. Jews interwove food with the religious calendar and each holiday was marked by a special dish.[70] Eating matzah at Passover "reminded Jews of the haste with which the children of Israel left Egypt, and a morsel of bitter herbs to recall the anguish of their slavery."[71] *Latkes* (potato pancakes) for Hanukkah and hamantaschen (three cornered filled pastries) for Purim were typical delights, as were honey cakes for the Jewish New Year, and cheesecake and cheese blintzes that accompanied the spring holiday of Shavuot. The weekly Sabbath meals featured chicken soup, roasted meat, gefilte fish, cakes, and fruits.[72]

Southern Jews, however, "straddled two worlds," as Marcie Cohen Ferris describes in her examination of Jewish southern foodways. Ferris argues that southern Jewish cuisine "revealed both how they [Jews] merged with the cultures they encountered in the region and how they separated themselves from these cultures."[73]

Many southern regional dishes included pork, oysters, and shrimp, referred to as treif or trefa, a Yiddish word used for something that's non-kosher.[74] While most Orthodox and even Conservative Jews in the South kept kosher, some Reform Jews ate pork and forbidden seafoods.[75] In 1885 a conference of Reform rabbis in Pittsburgh had passed a Declaration of Principles that "all such . . . laws as regulate diet" are no longer necessary."[76]

This situation was not unique to the South. At a banquet held in Cincinnati in 1883, celebrating the initial graduating class of Hebrew Union College, founder Rabbi Isaac Meyer Wise invited major Jewish religious leaders from Orthodox to Reform to celebrate the event. Hoping to unite all American Jewish congregations, the evening ended in disaster when the food served included trefa, such as clams, soft-shelled crabs, and a shrimp salad, thus accentuating the ideological and religious rift between Reform and Orthodox practices even more so.[77]

Allen From of Union recalls that his grandmother kept a kosher home, ordering meat from Atlanta, and raising chickens in the backyard, slaughtered according to the laws of kashrut. His grandfather, Israel, however, "was not so Orthodox," and would eat forbidden foods. When he brought home treif, his wife "would send him to the backyard where he would sit on a tree stump and eat in the company of a horse that he kept from his peddling days."[78]

Most Jewish families, however, simply merged typical southern dishes with Jewish ones. Jack Bloom described the food his mother served as "kosher southern-country cooking, embellished with pot roast, fried chicken, chicken soup, chopped liver and sweet and sour meatballs. . . ." But he also ate grits, cornbread, and cobbler.[79]

Middle-class Jewish families in the South typically employed Black women to help with the cooking and cleaning, and frequently with the children. Black cooks introduced Jewish families to traditional southern cooking. At the same time, Black cooks learned how to prepare Jewish dishes. Ferris observes that while Jewish women ruled over the kitchen: "Black women asserted their authority through the dishes they prepared for Jewish families. Jewish and African American women created similar blended dishes such as lox and grits, sweet potato kugel, collard greens with gribbenes ('cracklins' made from rendered chicken fat or 'schmaltz'), sweet and sour shad, Sabbath fried chicken, Rosh Hashanah 'hoppin' john' (the black-eyed peas and rice dish traditionally served on New Year's Day), and barbeque brisket."[80]

Every Jewish family interviewed in the Upcountry employed Black cooks. In the Bloom household, Lucille prepared food alongside Mrs. Bloom, where they made traditional Jewish and southern meals.[81] Edward Gray fondly recalls Annie Cook who worked for his mother and grandmother.[82] Marian Feinstein's family grew up with a young Black woman named Minnie, who did all the cooking.[83] Susan Jacobs recalled that "most Jewish families in Spartanburg had Black women who worked for them and learned to cook

Jewish dishes." Susan eventually inherited the services of Marie, her mother-in-law's housekeeper, who instructed Susan "how to take care of the household and how to do things related to the children."[84] Linda Tanenbaum, who grew up in an Orthodox household reported that "the Black woman who raised us, learned the rules of kashrut, how to make all the kosher dishes and how to clean the house and china for Passover."[85]

The blending of traditional Jewish fare with Black southern cooking established connections between Jews and the local population that "strongly shaped regional expressions of Jewish life."[86] Being Jewish in the South meant consuming a fusion of Black and southern recipes with traditional Jewish dishes."[87]

CONCLUSION

Jews dominated the business landscape of the Upcountry and in this new world environment, a Jewish middle-class emerged that identified with middle-class American values: citizenship, homeownership, and education. While aspiring to such values, Jews nonetheless, maintained Yiddishkeit (identity as Jews) in a variety of ways. Marriage was one of the most important element of retaining identity as Jews because it guaranteed the persistence of the Jewish faith within a family from one generation to the next. By institutionalizing religion, observing High Holy days, and maintaining Jewish foodways, Jews in the Upcountry preserved and retained their identity as Jews. At the same time, they moved into middle-class neighborhoods dominated by non-Jews and educated their children, thus securing for the next generation the tools necessary to achieve social mobility.

CHAPTER 6

The Upcountry Goes to War

Beginning in the late 1930s, the people of Upcountry South Carolina watched with growing apprehension as Nazi aggression encircled Europe. On the home front, industries mobilized rapidly as the War Production Board worked with local industries to ensure maximum productivity for the war effort.

The outbreak of war in Europe, writes historian Courtney Tollison Hartness, "brought significant economic relief to the Upcountry." Beginning in the fall of 1939, "cotton prices climbed alongside rising demand generated by US government contracts with upcountry textile and apparel mills."[1] Approximately 500 mills with 3,176,638 spindles, 163,618 looms, and 9,361 knitting machines produced textile goods in the early 1940s, from parachutes to uniforms in response to military demands.[2]

By April 1942, Upcountry mills had converted fifty percent of their manufactured goods to army and navy twill, aerial delivery cloth, bomb parachute cloth, ski trooper tents, and mosquito netting for troops in Pacific locations.[3] Jewish manufacturing companies primarily manufactured clothing for soldiers' uniforms. While stationed in Europe, Lt. Colonel Harold Cohen was happily surprised when he opened a box of army shirts that had been manufactured at his family firm, the Dixie Shirt Company in Spartanburg. The company produced shirts and lightweight cotton uniforms for soldiers as did the Shirtmaster plants in Abbeville and Anderson, owned by the Kaplan family. Saltzman's Piedmont Shirt Company also did a brisk business resulting from government contracts.[4]

The Japanese bombing of Pearl Harbor on December 7, 1941, mobilized America's entry into World War II in a way that Hitler's atrocities against the Jews and his takeover of Europe could not. Approximately half a million American Jews answered the call to fight for their country. They served in every branch of the military and achieved senior rank as a commodore, generals, major generals, brigadier generals, vice admirals, and rear admirals.[5]

Nearly every young Jewish man in the Upcountry proudly served in the armed forces, mostly as enlisted men, but many as officers. American-born

Jews, like Italians, Poles, and Irish, serving in the military were the children and grandchildren of immigrants.

CAMP CROFT

On December 12, 1940, with urging from US Senator James F. Byrnes (who had resided in Spartanburg since 1934), work began on the new Infantry Replacement Training Center (IRTC) in Spartanburg, called Camp Croft. The 20,000-acre center was half the size of the city and was comprised of 600 buildings including mess halls, theaters, service clubs, fire stations, company offices, classrooms, a laundry, a bakery, a cold-storage plant, six chapels, nine barber shops, ten athletic fields, four boxing arenas, three swimming pools, two libraries, and a post office.[6]

According to Tollison Hartness, "after the United States became involved in the war militarily, Camp Croft trainees began to replace dead, injured, or missing infantrymen overseas."[7] After training in military customs, close-order drill, and rifle marksmanship, some recruits received specialty instruction in weaponry, including machine guns, antitank guns, and close support howitzers.[8]

On average, Camp Croft prepared between 65,000 and 75,000 recruits per year in their training programs. However, not all those stationed at Camp Croft were men training for warfare. Hundreds of women at the camp worked as nurses at the post hospital, and a Women's Army Corps (WAC) detachment was located there as well.[9]

Spartanburg residents soon adjusted to the bustling army camp with 200,000 soldiers who passed through the camp during its five years of existence. Both Jewish and non-Jewish retail business boomed as servicemen packed restaurants, theaters, bars, and grills. In the city itself, six United Service Organizations (USO) centers opened throughout the week for soldiers and civilians engaged in the war effort. Churches opened clubrooms for worship and entertainment, and community members opened their homes for the young soldiers stationed at the camp.[10] Camp Croft's 25,000 personnel, "including hundreds of local support jobs, injected the town with an invigorating mixture of patriotic military spirit and much-needed federal dollars."[11]

In March 1941, six army chaplains—three Protestants and three Roman Catholics—arrived at Camp Croft to lead services and minister to soldiers. A Jewish chaplain soon followed: David Eichhorn was stationed at Camp Croft for twenty-one months. Eichhorn recalled, "About a thousand new trainees came to the camp each week. During their first week, they were addressed by Protestant and Catholic chaplains of their battalions and myself since I was the only Jewish chaplain in the camp."[12]

Based on reported religious preferences of the soldiers, "the average number of Jews in training at any given time was about 1,500" according to Eichhorn. He noted that "about 10,000 Jewish soldiers received their basic infantry training at this post during my period of duty there. Among many others who were trained at Camp Croft and assisted me in conducting religious services were the sportscaster Melvin Israel (Mel Allen), comedian Sam (Zero) Mostel, and Vladimir Sokoloff, concert pianist."[13] Many of the Jews stationed at Camp Croft would become notable public figures years after the war ended. These included Ed Koch, the future mayor of New York City; Henry Kissinger, who served as secretary of state under President Richard Nixon; and the comedian, film, and stage star, Zero Mostel, who performed comic routines for civilians in downtown Spartanburg.[14]

Russian-born, Philip Plotkin of Brooklyn, immigrated to the United States in the 1930s and a decade later was fighting for America. Plotkin worked as a commercial artist and illustrator before he was drafted. While stationed at Camp Croft, he expressed his creativity as the editor of two battalion newsletters and by painting murals in several camp buildings during his off-duty hours.[15] He eventually fought in Normandy with Operation Overlord. An article about Plotkin and his artistic work at Camp Croft appeared in the *Spartanburg Herald Journal* in December 1941.[16]

Entertainment provided by and for the recruits made the Upcountry a lively place in the early 1940s. Jewish recruits who played musical instruments participated in the Camp Croft Band, which frequently played at downtown concerts and events in Spartanburg. The Jewish Welfare Board ran a USO, and Greenville's Beth Israel Synagogue offered dancing for Jewish soldiers on Townes Street every Wednesday night with a free dinner and recreation from three to eleven o'clock every Sunday.

In Spartanburg, six USOs, among them the Jewish Welfare Board, hosted soldiers stationed at Camp Croft. Jewish women working with the Jewish Welfare Board provided soldiers with books, meals, and board games.[17] As part of the Red Cross Garment Production Program, local women made clothing and shipped it to needy civilians in Europe. The Red Cross Surgical Dressing Core was organized in February 1941 and Spartanburg's Red Cross chapter provided yarn, wool, and other fabric for women to make into clothing and bandages.[18] Area churches and synagogues organized their members into teams for both the Garment Production Program and the Surgical Dressing Corps.[19] In these and other ways, Upcountry Jews, like Jews throughout the country and other religious groups, emphasized outreach, and welfare. One of the many forms of outreach included transporting Jewish soldiers to synagogue for services and fellowship. [20]

Several northern Jewish soldiers stationed at Camp Croft met local women and romances ensued. Like the soldiers posted at Spartanburg's Camp Wadsworth during World War I, Jewish soldiers at Camp Croft were the guests of townspeople for meals and companionship. Frequently matches ensued, and after the war, soldiers returned to Spartanburg to marry their wartime girlfriends.

Marian Fink met her future husband while he was in basic training at Camp Croft. She was a dancer entertaining the troops with the USO when she met Seymour Feinstein who played saxophone and clarinet with the Camp Croft Band. Feinstein became a regular at the Fink home and frequently brought his Italian friends there where they made Italian sauce for Sunday dinner. Marian and Seymour married in April 1944.[21] When the war ended, the couple settled in Spartanburg where they started several successful businesses, including a dance studio where "Miss Marian" provided dance lessons for thousands of budding dancers.[22]

Margaret Caul and Master Sergeant Joseph H. Wachter also met at Camp Croft. Wachter hailed from Buffalo, New York, the son of Russian Jewish parents. When the war broke out, Wachter volunteered for the army and was assigned to the Quarter Masters Corps at Camp Croft. Margaret, who was not Jewish, was a Wac (a member of the Women's Army Corps) stationed at Camp Croft when they met and fell in love. The couple married in 1945 and settled in Spartanburg, where Wachter eventually opened a jewelry store.[23]

THE GREATEST GENERATION

Jewish experiences in World War II solidified their status as American citizens while they earned the respect of the nation at large. Moreover, many Jewish men in the armed forces became conscious of themselves as Jews and took pride in their heritage. As the historian Deborah Dash Moore explains, "American Jews would discover not only how American but also how deeply Jewish they were."[24] This generation of American Jews demonstrated their patriotism, courage, and masculinity, fighting to defend the principles that attracted their immigrant parents and grandparents to America.

In the Upcountry, Jewish names linked to local businesses and industries appeared in hometown newspapers as husbands, sons, brothers, grandsons, and nephews marched off to war.[25] As difficult as it was for mothers and fathers to say goodbye to their sons, "most of them departed with their parents' blessings and prayers."[26] Some Jewish men were encouraged by their families to sign up, like Harold Cohen of Spartanburg, whose father, Max, said to him, "See what you can do for Uncle Sam."[27]

One of the first to enlist in the Army Air Forces after the Japanese attack on Pearl Harbor was 22-year-old Stanley D. Malinow. The son of a Russian immigrant, Malinow collaborated with his father in the scrap metal business in Spartanburg.[28] Harvey Saltzman of Brooklyn had relocated to Greenville to work for his uncle, Shepard Saltzman, at the Piedmont Shirt Manufacturing Company. With the outbreak of war, Harvey enlisted and served in the US Army where he held the rank of captain.[29] Sam Lurey of Greenville graduated from The Citadel in 1935, enlisted in the army in 1941, and was commissioned a Second Lieutenant in the Army Corps of Engineers in March 1943.[30] Lurey made a career in the army, serving in Korea and Germany, with the Army Corps of Engineers.[31]

All three sons of businessman Victor Davis, the only Sephardic Jew in the region, served during World War II. Jack was an army staff sergeant, Alex was in the US Air Force, and Louis was with the US Army Signal Corps. When the brothers returned to Greenville after the war, they worked at Davis Battery & Electric Company, the family business started by their father. The greatly enlarged business carried auto parts and accessories and remained in business for six more decades.[32]

Other Greenvillians who served in the armed forces were Jack Bloom, a graduate of Furman University and Duke University Law School, who served in the US Army at the rank of colonel. When he returned from the war, he opened a law practice and became the first practicing Jewish lawyer in Greenville.[33] Also, Harry, Louis, Marion, and Jack, sons of Rabbi Charles Zaglin, "served in some capacity during the war, although not all served overseas."[34]

In some small Upcountry towns, the young male Jewish population practically vanished during the war. In Anderson, nearly every Jewish son served in the armed forces. Louis Funkenstein, an executive officer served on the USS *Curtiss,* stationed in the South Pacific, and Alvin Fleishman also served in the navy. Abram Rosenblum, the son of Polish immigrants who operated a men's clothing store in Anderson, enlisted in the Army Air Corps in April

Davis Battery Electric Co., 1930, Greenville, courtesy of Bobbie Jean Rovner

1942.[35] A pilot for the US Army's "Mighty Eighth" Air Force, Rosenblum flew fifty-six missions before being shot down over Germany in April 1945. The decorated pilot returned home safely after three weeks in a POW camp in Austria, where he was released at the end of the war.[36]

Irving Abrams enlisted in the US Army upon graduation from Greenville High School and rose to the rank of lieutenant colonel. When he returned to South Carolina after the war he enrolled at Clemson College.[37] Ralph Tanenbaum of Spartanburg attended Wofford College for a year and was working at Carolina Loan and Luggage when he entered the US Army.[38] Max Massey, who settled in Spartanburg after the war and started a clothing business, served in the Army Air Corps 5th Division, from 1941–1945, in the Pacific theater. Massey received a Bronze Service Star for the liberation of the Philippines, two Bronze Stars for the Asiatic and Pacific campaign, and several World War II Victory Medals.[39] When Massey died at the age of ninety-seven in 2018, his obituary noted that he "exemplified the American experience and its ideals of loyalty and bravery."[40]

Solomon Abrams was the son of Lewis and Anna Abrams, Polish immigrants who settled in Orangeburg and operated a grocery store. Abrams became a celebrated lawyer in Greenville after the war where he served in the US Air Force and flew in combat as a bombardier. In early 1944, his plane was shot down over Pioeti, Rumania, where he was captured and taken as a prisoner of war. He escaped the camp after four months of imprisonment. When he returned home, Abrams finished his education at the University of South Carolina and attended Georgetown University Law School. He set up a practice in Greenville where he was known as a "tenacious trial lawyer," and served as an election commission chairman, where it was claimed, he was "one of the most capable, hardworking and dedicated people we've ever had involved in registration and elections in South Carolina."[41]

The five sons of David and Ella Poliakoff of Abbeville, Abraham Ellis, Marion, Myer, Arthur, and Samuel, all graduated from the University of South Carolina, and served in the armed forces. The eldest, A. Ellis, earned his medical degree from the Medical College of South Carolina and established a practice in Abbeville before the war. During the war he was a captain in the Army Medical Corps. Arthur served in the Army Pharmacy Corps for more than three years, and after the war, took a job as a pharmacist in Atlanta. Dr. Samuel Poliakoff, the youngest sibling, also served in the Army Medical Corps and was subsequently dispatched to Korea in late 1945.[42]

Captain A. Ellis Poliakoff kept a diary of his war-time experiences and some of his most poignant entries relate to Jewish religious observances. These entries demonstrate Moore's assertions that "under army auspices Jews achieved a group cohesiveness they never had as civilians" as they met other Jews and attended religious services.[43] The following are typical entries:

9 SEPTEMBER 1944:

I brought a Talith for the boy who was a passenger, conducting services. There were yarmulkes for those that needed them. We have a nice Kiddush cup. There were prayer books for all. All seats were taken, and I believe all members of the Jewish faith were present except a few. We were praying to the Almighty and I know everyone meant it . . . We also said the prayer for a safe voyage.[44]

17 SEPTEMBER 1944:

To-night is the eve before Rosh Hashana. I made arrangements for services . . . What a strange place to be holding services but we want to have services. The Lord has been kind to me, and I want to say my prayers especially at this time of the year.

27 SEPTEMBER 1944:

Fasted all day. We had [Yom Kippur] services this morning at 10 A.M., again at 2:30, and again at 7:30 pm. Boat drill interrupted the 2:30 service. Almost every Jewish person on board came to at least one service . . . I think we did right well, considering the circumstances and the fact that we didn't have a Chaplain.

Faith became important to soldiers faced with the daily threat of death, and as Moore notes, "Jewish soldiers often attended religious services to find fellowship."[45]

While Poliakoff was on a shore leave in Abbeville in December 1944, he wrote, "One thing I noticed which stood out to me after being around the sick and wounded, was the fact that no one seemed to be thinking of the war. It also seemed that everyone had somebody in the service somewhere. I suppose many had heavy hearts and were just masking their feelings. It was also at the time the Germans were pushing forward. Probably, it's best to be this way and not think too much of the war."[46]

While the people of Abbeville did not talk much about the war during that December of 1944, American soldiers on the Western Front geared up for some of the most grueling battles under the most treacherous conditions during that winter. Lieutenant Colonel Harold Cohen of Spartanburg was caught in some of the worst and most decisive battles on the Western Front during the harsh winter of 1944–45. His heroism earned him the highest honors conferred on a South Carolinian during World War II.

Cohen, the son of Russian immigrants who operated a garment factory in Spartanburg, was twenty-six years old when he enlisted in the US Army. He served his country with distinction as a remarkable military leader and a decorated war hero.

Lieutenant Colonel Cohen and Colonel Creighton Abrams, who would later be promoted to general and commander of operations in the Vietnam War from 1968 to 1972,[47] made up a spearheading team that put fear into the Germans when General George Patton's 4th Armored Division made its historic fifty-eight-hour, sixty-five-mile dash across the Rhine.[48]

Cohen moved up the ranks quickly, from a private to a lieutenant colonel and commander of the 10th Armored Infantry Battalion of the 4th Armored Division, a unit under the command of Patton's Third Army. Cohen and

Abrams helped the 4th Armored Division invent a new kind of American blitzkrieg and spearheaded the Third Army across France and through Germany during the brutal winter of December 1944. The "spearheading duo" devised new tactics involving speed, surprise, and the use of forward outposts to defeat the Germans in numerous campaigns. The Germans feared the 4th Armored Division, dropped leaflets, and posted signs for their troops warning them "Beware of Abrams and Cohen, Roosevelt's Highest Paid Butchers."[49]

The Abrams-Cohen team took part in numerous strategic campaigns in France, Belgium, and Germany. An important battle fought at Chaumont, Belgium, ultimately opened the way to Bastogne, a major campaign in the Battle of the Bulge. The 4th Armored Division reached Chaumont and occupied the town in December 1944, with Cohen commanding one of the division's battalions. The Americans encountered stiff resistance. German troops launched a counterattack and all the US forces, including Cohen's 10th Armored Infantry Battalion, retreated after heavy personnel and material losses. The next day the American forces prepared a new attack to capture Chaumont. On Christmas Day, 1944, American soldiers reattacked supported by the US Air Force. By the evening of December 25, they liberated Chaumont and Grandru, and on the following day made an opening to the encircled city of Bastogne.[50] The Battle for Chaumont is recognized by historians as one of the larger tank battles of the Battle of the Bulge.[51]

Abrams and Cohen led Patton's drive to the Rhine and directed the Moselle-Rhine-Saar campaign.[52] In military operations against German forces at Brecht in February 1945, Cohen displayed extraordinary heroism earning him a Distinguished Service Cross. The citation described Cohen's "devotion to duty which exemplify the highest traditions of the military forces of the United States . . . ."[53] Creighton Abrams called Cohen the "the best infantry commander in the army."

Near the end of the war Cohen had a short stay in an evacuation hospital because of hemorrhoids so severe that even General Patton was shocked upon making a personal inspection of his backside.[54] When Cohen was released from the hospital and on his way back to his unit, he was captured by the attacking German Sixth SS Mountain Division. Based on an interview with Cohen, writer and filmmaker Jim Sudmeier, wrote, "When caught in an American artillery bombardment, Cohen befriended the Germans by treating dozens of their wounds. In several days he escaped unharmed to the advancing US troops. Everyone had assumed he would be killed by the

Germans because he was Jewish. When [Creighton] Abrams walked into a room and saw Cohen sitting there, tears began rolling down his cheeks. They embraced each other and Abrams told him it was the happiest day of his life to know they were back in business together."[55]

Cohen and Abrams's feats during the war were recounted by newspapers across the US. In one front-page headline captioned "Nazis Stunned by Yank Speed," an Associated Press (AP) reporter interviewed Cohen on the drive to the northern gateway of the Nazi capital. Cohen laughingly said, "It would be a good story if you could say the 'master race' was being chased by two members of what Hitler calls the 'inferior race' but it ain't so. I'm the only Jewish member of the [duo]. Abe (Creighton Abrams) is a Presbyterian."[56]

A war hero, Cohen was awarded the Legion of Merit, four Silver Stars, three Bronze Stars, three Purple Hearts, the French Croix de Guerre, and decorated by the governments of England, Poland, Czechoslovakia, and Luxembourg.[57] Cohen also received the Distinguished Service Cross, the highest award for a combat soldier second only to the Congressional Medal of Honor. He accepted the honor in a manner that reflected his humility and simplicity: "My most prized possession is my American citizenship. My proudest claim is that I am an American patriot." These understated words are engraved on his tombstone.[58]

Sixty-five years later, Cohen was honored at Chaumont for his role in liberating the town and surrounding area from the Germans. On September 12, 2009, less than three years after Cohen's death, his children, grandchildren, and the residents of Chaumont honored Cohen and unveiled a plaque in his memory. The road leading through the town of Chaumont to Bastogne was named "Rue Du Colonel Harold Cohen," and Cohen was celebrated by the villagers as their "liberator."[59]

Harold Cohen was not the only Jewish hero from the Upcountry. Lieutenant Morton Sher of Greenville was an extraordinary fighter pilot, who, unfortunately, never made it back from the war. Morton Sher was the son of David and Celia, of Minsk. After emigrating from Russia the family settled in the small town of Gaffney in Spartanburg County, where they operated a junk yard and pawn shop. In the 1930s, the family moved to Greenville where Morton and his siblings attended Greenville schools and his parents became partners in a dry goods store.[60] As a young man, Morton participated in many high school organizations and was particularly active in the Aviation Club.[61]

Following high school graduation, Sher attended the University of Alabama for two years before enlisting in the US Army Air Corps in June 1941.[62]

At that time his father was operating the Piedmont Scrap Material Company and his mother was secretary-treasurer for the Greenville Paper Stock Company.[63] While his parents climbed the economic ladder to success through hard work and entrepreneurship, Sher's military career also advanced—a testimony to his aviation skills, leadership, and bravery.

Lieutenant Sher's heroics during World War II were captured in front-page news stories across the nation, among them the *Fort Worth Star-Telegram, The Atlanta Constitution,* and the *Pittsburgh Sun-Telegram.* A report published in the *San Francisco Examiner,* reported the "first-hand story of Lieutenant Morton Sher, the 21-year-old American fighter pilot from Greenville, SC, who made a forced landing in a remote region of China after participating in an attack on Jap-held Hong Kong." The story included a live interview with Lieutenant Sher, who reported,

> We took off from our base somewhere in China early one morning in October in a flight of six P-40s and contacted the bombers which we were to escort. Our target was Hong Kong. We reached it without trouble. The bombers circled and dropped their bombs. We headed for home. Suddenly, they were swarming after us. Major Tex Hill, on whose wing I was flying, sighted a formation of "Jap" Zeros climbing up at us on our right, aiming straight for the bombers. He gave me the attack signal, peeled off in a steep dive and went for the lead Zero. I followed him and picked the second one. My shots went into the canopy and through the pilot. The Zero fell off in a wild spin and crashed in the bay.

"With five Zeros (long-range, carrier-based fighter aircraft used by the Imperial Japanese Navy 1940–45) on his tail, Sher dove at them and opened fire. Three turned on him. He was forced down by engine trouble in a small field within Chinese lines while chased by two Japanese fighters. His only injury was a head bump, suffered when his plane nosed down.[64] He was hailed as a hero by 15,000 Chinese who called upon him to sing and make speeches."[65] Sher had many close calls. He was part of a group of airmen known as "The Walker's Club," consisting of eight US airmen in China who were forced down behind Japanese lines. After a period of eight weeks and many narrow escapes of contact with enemy patrols, the men of The Walker's Club reached their bases.[66]

In a ferocious aerial dog fight with Japanese Zeros and a tragic ending, Lieutenant Sher's bomber was shot down and he was killed in action and lost at sea on August 20, 1943.[67] A Gold Star casualty, Sher is memorialized at Tablets of the Missing at the Manila American Cemetery in the Philippines.[68]

The Greenville News reported that Lieutenant Sher flew in China under the famed General Claire Chennault, former commander of the Flying Tigers of the Chinese Army, and "had four Jap planes and several probables to his credit."[69] The story of Sher's China experience was recounted in full in *Fighting for America,* published by the Jewish Welfare Board.[70]

CONCLUSION

Nearly every young Jewish man who fought in the war was the son of a businessman or manufacturer. Distraught at the prospect of their sons shipping out for active duty, Jewish parents, nonetheless, supported the war effort and remained proud of their sons who served.

Jewish heroes like Cohen and Sher demonstrated courage and bravery. Anti-Semitic accusations that Jews were unfit for the rigors of army life, especially the infantry,[71] as Moore, in *GI Jews* points out, were proven wrong by the brave and heroic actions of soldiers like Cohen and Sher.

"World War II was the great watershed in the history of American Jewish identity," wrote historian Edward Shapiro, who asserts that "American Jewry emerged from the struggle convinced that they were no longer an exotic ethnic and religious minority but an integral part of American culture."[72] The experience of fighting side-by-side with other Americans, whether native-born or immigrant, solidified Jewish soldiers' sense of belonging.

Jewish soldiers showed their commitment, love, and patriotism for America by serving and fighting in World War II. As the sons and grandsons of immigrants, they made the ultimate sacrifice for their country. Local newspapers in the Upcountry reported on the heroics of Jewish men in service and proudly labeled them as their community's best and bravest. Their experiences in war gained Jews in the armed forces the respect of America, and for the first time, Jewish Americans felt fully assimilated into their local communities and America at large.

CHAPTER 7

Jewish Garment Manufacturing

Andrew Teszler and his father, Sandor, made textile history in South and North Carolina. Their story is even more significant as Holocaust survivors. Sandor Teszler and his sons, Andrew and Otto, survived the brutality of the Holocaust and the Communist takeover of Hungary, fled to England, and immigrated to the United States in 1948. Teszler, who was already established as a textile giant in Central Europe, transferred his skills and expertise to the United States, where he and his family found refuge and renewed purpose in the textile industry that so powerfully shaped Upcountry South Carolina.

The Teszlers are representative of the many Jewish textile and garment manufacturers who established companies in the Upcountry in the mid-twentieth century. European Jews as well as northern Jews launched new companies or transferred operations from the North to the Upcountry. The Upcountry received a major economic boost from World War II, a boost that accelerated in the postwar period transforming the region into an industrial powerhouse. Economic development and a population surge advanced during the years 1945–1954 and marked what the economic historian Marko Maunola calls "a golden decade of prosperity."[1] This chapter illustrates the key role of Jewish industrialists in the postwar surge of textiles and apparel manufacturing. These entrepreneurs poured millions of dollars into the local economy and provided employment for thousands of South Carolinians.

TEXTILE MANUFACTURING DURING THE POSTWAR PERIOD

In 1945, with the Upcountry's textile industry pulsating at full speed, the region's mills operated near maximum capacity in response to rapidly growing consumer markets.[2] The prosperity that World War II generated for the textile industry translated into better wages for workers and unprecedented profits for the industry.

The late 1940s and 1950s were years marked by incredible economic progress in the United States, yet the growth rate of South Carolina "surpassed . . . national averages by a wide margin . . . manufacturing nearly doubled the national growth rate."[3] No other region in the state matched the economic advancement of the Upcountry.[4]

Significant new mill construction took place in the Upcountry for the first time since the 1920s, but "mills were operating in a changed environment," according to historian David Carlton. No longer small-town industries, "some mills had been integrated into large corporations headquartered in New York."[5]

Giant textile corporations emerged through a process of consolidation, such as "J. P. Stevens and Company, which operated the four Victor-Monaghan mills, as well as the Dunean, Piedmont, and Slater Mills in Greenville. Eventually, J.P. Stevens owned eighteen mills in the Greenville area."[6] A wave of consolidations occurred in the Spartanburg region as well, with Reeves Brothers purchasing Saxon and Chesnee Mills in the 1950s.[7] Burlington Industries bought Southern Bleachery and Print Works in early 1965,[8] while multiple other consolidations occurred over the next several decades.

Important technological developments occurred from the 1950s to the 1970s that contributed to an improved work environment for the health and comfort of workers. New plants installed air-conditioning and mills became cleaner, no longer tainted by smokestacks and polluted air.[9] In addition to building entirely new plants, millowners upgraded their equipment and expanded their facilities.[10]

South Carolina had always been favorable to out-of-state companies wishing to relocate by providing substantial tax breaks, such as exemption from state property taxes and local taxes, and very low corporate taxes. In 1954, seven years after the passage of the Taft-Hartley Act,[11] which had favored unions and collective bargaining, the South Carolina assembly passed a right-to-work-law, affirming the right of every individual to work without being compelled to belong to a union or to pay dues to a labor union.[12] South Carolina was one of five southern states that offered massive tax exemptions to industries promising to relocate within their borders. According to historian James Cobb, "many economists bemoaned such practices, and both labor union leaders and politicians, such as Senator John F. Kennedy of Massachusetts, complained . . . that by dangling such enticements before northern employers, the southern states were essentially engaging in industrial piracy."[13] South Carolina's technical education system provided another motivation for companies to move south as it trained workers for the specific needs of individual companies.

South Carolina publicized the region's advantages to persuade investors to locate their industries in the state. By the end of World War II, historian James Cobb notes that "state development agencies sought out prospective investors likely to be interested in locating a new facility in the South," and relied on advertising, letters, phone calls, and personal visits by agency representatives to sell them on relocation.[14] Progressive businessmen such as Charles E. Daniel of Greenville, for example, spent $100,000 on advertising and promotion in 1954 alone."[15] Cobb notes that "many southern developers swore by the ads they placed in major national magazines. South Carolina promoters linked an aggressive advertising campaign that began in 1945 to the 600 new businesses that came into the state during the following two years."[16] These efforts contributed to a trend of manufacturers migrating from northern states to South Carolina that had commenced during the nineteenth century.

"The vision that inspired the Southern businessman was that of a South modeled upon the industrial northeast," wrote C. Vann Woodward.[17] Not surprisingly then, many of the textile giants attracted to the South Carolina Upcountry in the mid-twentieth century descended from northern textile magnates. In Spartanburg, for example, Frederick Dent, a Yale graduate, and the son of a textile man in Greenwich, Connecticut, relocated to Spartanburg in 1947. Dent assumed the position of president of Mayfair Mills, a textile manufacturing company with six plants, including five in South Carolina and one in Georgia. Dent "rapidly became one of the most visible economic, civic, and political leaders in the community."[18] President Richard M. Nixon appointed Dent, a highly respected expert in his field, secretary of commerce in 1973.[19] According to Rosabeth Moss Kanter, a Harvard business professor, "one significant action in 1954 set in motion a number of forces that eventually brought economic strength to the region as a major player in the global economy." The northern textile heir Roger Milliken moved his company's headquarters to Spartanburg, "a move that likely ranks as the single most important in the history of Spartanburg's textile industry."[20] Milliken served as president and CEO of his family's firm, Milliken and Company from 1947 to 2005. Considered the twentieth century's greatest leader in American textiles, Milliken was born in New York City and attended Yale University. When his father died, young Milliken succeeded him as president of the family textile enterprise. After Milliken moved the company's headquarters to Spartanburg, he built what became the world's largest and most dynamic textile and research facility.[21]

A Milliken presence had existed in Upcountry South Carolina since the 1880s, when Seth Milliken, Roger's grandfather, invested in a plant in Pacolet. During the next decade, the company boosted its presence in the South by buying interest in forty-two mills around the region. Milliken and Company grew to be the largest privately owned textile and chemical manufacturing company in the world, and the most innovative given its research, development, and technological capacities. The company eventually expanded to fifty manufacturing facilities in seven countries. In 1999, the trade magazine *Textile World* selected Roger Milliken as the textile industry's "Leader of the Century." From Spartanburg, he spearheaded forward-looking change in South Carolina, helping to create a thriving manufacturing and business environment throughout the state.[22]

According to economic historian Marko Maunula, "the changing nature of global textile markets, technological advances, and changing culture in the workplace were altering the local textile business." All aspects of the business were changing, "from the disappearance of the mill village to new types of factories and product lines."[23] Milliken's business practices led most of these changes.

JEWISH ROLE IN THE POSTWAR INDUSTRIAL SURGE

While a handful of Jewish garment manufacturers like Shepard Saltzman and Max Cohen, discussed in chapter 4, established apparel manufacturing companies in the Upcountry before World War II, their numbers multiplied after the war. According to Wofford College archivist Philip Stone, "garment manufacturers became interested in South Carolina. Speer's March 1945 industrial agent's report listed at least twenty textile and apparel prospects that hoped to come to the state. Among these were manufacturers of shirts, men's suits, women's apparel, undergarments, kids' clothing, a rayon yarn mill, and a textile finishing plant."[24]

Upcountry recruiting efforts moved beyond the textile industry and conscripted apparel manufacturers, thus attracting more Jewish-owned businesses to the region. Beginning in the 1940s. Proximity to textile mills, cheap labor, subsidies, and a union-free environment were inducements for northern garment companies to relocate to the Upcountry, a movement that was simultaneously occurring in other southern states such as North Carolina, Georgia, and Alabama. The arrival of Jewish apparel manufacturers and their upper-level management, including Holocaust survivors, contributed to the prosperity and economic progress that took place in the Upcountry in the post–World War II era.

The movement of Jewish manufacturers to the Upcountry has been over-looked in accounts of the relocations of capital from the North to the South. Most scholars examining the growth of manufacturing in the Upcountry in the post–World War II era leap from business titans like Roger Milliken to the era of massive international recruiting in the late twentieth century without reference to Jewish manufacturers.[25]

Garment manufacturing had long been dominated by Jewish immigrants centered in New York. In the 1940s, continuing a trend that started earlier with textiles, apparel manufacturers, seeking lower labor costs, moved to the South,[26] thus contributing to a new era of manufacturing growth in the Upcountry. Many of these companies were founded by the sons of northern clothing manufacturers like William Epstein, whose father manufactured clothing apparel in New York. After the younger Epstein arrived in the Upcountry in 1952 and established the Iva Manufacturing Company of women's apparel, he added five more plants located in Anderson and Abbeville Counties. These companies manufactured women's clothing including skirts, blouses, bathing suits and pedal pushers.[27]

Herbert Setlow also expanded his father's manufacturing business into South Carolina. His Russian-born father, Joseph, immigrated to New Haven, Connecticut, in 1913, and founded Setlows, a pants manufacturing company. Herbert entered the business with his father and established a subsidiary of the company in South Carolina's Newberry County in 1958.[28]

The Lewkowicz brothers of Rheims, France, relocated to Spartanburg in the 1960s. They opened Gaftan Sportswear Inc. in 1970, specializing in ladies' sportswear manufactured under their own label "L & K" (Love & Kisses). These French Jews also founded L & K Dyeing and Finishing Plant in Shelby, North Carolina, and another plant in Spartanburg. The brothers frequently visited France to observe the new European styles and introduce contemporary designs for the American market.[29]

At least thirty or more Jewish-owned garment factories launched in the Upcountry between 1940 and 1970.[30] These companies generated thousands of jobs and established factories in small towns with little or no industry as well as in larger cities where industries proliferated.

At the end of World War II, apparel manufacturers that had produced uniforms and parachutes during the war, converted to mass producing garments for Americans hungry for stylish clothing with the emergent fashion industry leading to a meteoric rise in consumerism after the austere years of World War II. Several Jewish manufacturers in the Upcountry appeared on the cutting edge of fashion design, stimulating consumer buying in the 1950s and 1960s. In the postwar years Jewish fashion designers and garment manufacturers put American style and fashion design on the map. In New York, Jewish Americans such as Anne Klein (Hannah Golofski) and Ralph Lauren (Ralph Lifshitz) blazed a trail in fashion design.[31] Simultaneously, Jewish garment manufacturers in the Upcountry created and produced new fabrics, such as double knits, and perfected new methods of dyeing, knitting, and apparel finishing. The goods they produced reflected the needs of working women and men as well as stay-at-home moms. The apparel factories established by Jews in the mid-twentieth century differed from the cotton mills that populated the Upcountry in the late nineteenth and early twentieth centuries. Women employed as machine operators made up the majority of those who worked in apparel factories. They did not reside in mill villages; rather, they lived in their own homes in the community where the apparel factory was located.

The clothing industry generated thousands of jobs for Upcountry women. These job opportunities came at a propitious time, with "the departure of low-wage agricultural workers, tenants, and small farmers,"[32] and together with numerous family-farm failures. Furthermore, as historian Melissa Walker argues, "white farm women's embrace of off-farm jobs . . . is indicative, not only of families' dire need for cash incomes, but also of many women's ambitions to participate more fully in the family economy by earning a paycheck."[33]

Additionally, as historian Julia Kirk Blackwelder points out, "postwar economic change . . . [created] a major transformation in the economic roles . . . of southern white women."[34] For Upcountry women, their changing economic roles resulted from employment opportunities in garment manufacturing. In fact, out of 19,330 females employed in Spartanburg County in 1950, 8,446 (nearly forty-four percent) worked as factory operatives in garment companies.[35] In the Upcountry, eighty-eight percent of all apparel workers were female by 1968.[36]

JEWISH INNOVATION IN FABRICS AND DESIGN SUBHEADING

One approach for examining select garment manufacturers in the Upcountry is to classify them by (1) innovations in clothing apparel and fabric design, and (2) manufacturers who grew their business into large corporations through a process of consolidation.

Growth through Innovation

Two Jewish-owned companies led the way in innovative contributions to the field of garment manufacturing with cutting-edge designs and state-of-the-art fabrics. Andrew Teszler and Jack Nachman created successful businesses because of their creativity, awareness of consumer desires, and marketing finesse.

Andrew Teszler and his father, Sandor, made textile history in South and North Carolina. Sandor (Alexander) Teszler was born in 1903 in Budapest and studied textile engineering at the prominent textile engineering program at Chemnitz University of Technology in Germany. Unable to study in Hungary because the Jewish quota for students had already been filled, he returned to Budapest to work in a knitting factory after completing his studies in Germany.[37]

Sandor and his brother, Joseph, who also worked in textiles, opened a hosiery and underwear factory, and merged with another prominent knitting factory in 1929. The two brothers operated the largest and most modern knitting plant in Central Europe, employing 1,800 workers and 120 clerical employees at its peak in 1944.[38]

Teszler and his wife, Lidia, had two sons, Otto, born in 1929, and Andrew in 1931. Following the German invasion of Poland and the outbreak of World War II, Germany invaded Yugoslavia on April 6, 1941. The district where Teszler's factory was located came under Hungarian control but continued to produce textile goods for the Hungarian government. According to the historian Mario Fenyo, the German high command assured Hungarians that their economic activities would continue unhindered.[39] For three years, the Teszler family remained unharmed and continued their textile operations.[40]

When the German army occupied Hungary in 1944, the situation for Hungary's Jews rapidly deteriorated.[41] The Teszlers were eventually rounded up and sent to a "yellow-star house" in Budapest, awaiting deportation. However, Sandor and Lidia were rescued by the vice-consul of the Swiss Embassy, Carl Lutz, who is credited with rescuing thousands of Hungarian Jews.[42]

On February 15, 1945, the Soviets liberated Budapest and the remaining Jews were left facing the horrible truth of what happened to friends and family members deported to the death camps. Sandor Teszler's father, brother, sister-in-law, nieces, and nephews, as well as his mother-in-law and father-in-law, had all perished in the Holocaust.[43]

Sandor tried to rebuild his business, but the Communist-controlled government seized his factory, claiming he collaborated with the Germans during the war. A Communist takeover ensued, and Sandor and Lidia fled to Great Britain to join their sons who they sent there earlier.[44]

In 1946, President Harry Truman proposed to Congress that Jews be admitted to the United States outside the quota system. Hasia Diner writes that the "bill authorized issuing 202,000 visas above the quota limit . . . for Jews and others who had been displaced by the war and could not return to their former homes, mostly ethnic Germans from countries that fell under Communist rule."[45] This slight relaxation in the number of Jews who could enter the United States after World War II made possible the Teszlers' immigration.

In January 1948, Sandor and Lidia settled in New York where another Teszler brother, Akos, a textile chemist who immigrated in 1927, had established a small textile factory on Long Island in the early 1940s.[46] When Sandor arrived, Akos made him a partner in the business and in 1952, after his death, Sandor took over the company. Andrew and Otto soon joined their parents in the United States, and both enrolled in the textile engineering program at North Carolina State University, a world leader in textile education and research. After graduation, Andrew obtained a job at a knitting plant in Delaware and Otto was recruited to work for the American Aviation Company in California.[47]

In 1959, David Schwartz, the president and chairman of the board of Jonathan Logan Inc. of New York City, the country's leading manufacturer of women's apparel, listened attentively to an idea from Andrew Teszler, a young, unknown graduate of North Carolina State University. Double-knit garments were already popular in Europe, and the younger Teszler had the idea to start the first double-knit garment operation in the United States. Schwartz liked Teszler's idea. After a feasibility study, the two men agreed on a unique plan for the new business, a vertically integrated manufacturing facility, producing a double-knit garment from raw fiber cut and sewn into high-quality, popular-priced garments.[48]

After purchasing textile machinery in Europe, Schwartz sent Andrew to Spartanburg to organize the Butte Knit Division for parent company Jonathan Logan.[49] When the mill opened in 1960, it was a small plant housed in a 20,000-square-foot facility. Eventually one of the most outstanding

Butte Knits distribution center, Spartanburg

operations in the entire textile garment industry, it produced double-knit dresses and ensembles for women.[50] Double-knit clothing flooded the markets in the 1960s when men and women began wearing more casual pants suits, tunics, and jackets. "Young women wore brightly colored stretch fabrics and men discarded the traditional suit for the "leisure suit."[51]

Andrew Teszler recruited specialists for his factory through familial and social networking, a common strategy employed by Jews. They also tapped into ethnic networks to fill the needs of executive and managerial staff. Many of the newly hired executives were New York City transplants while others were Jews who had been working in a variety of southern industries. Teszler hired Sam Witz of New York, a specialist in distribution, from parent company, Jonathan Logan. Marvin Siegel, hired as an accountant, later rose to vice president of finance. Barry Goldman, Siegel's brother-in-law, was recruited as a management trainee. Teszler hired Julius Blum of New York as a vice president in the early years of the company and appointed Richard Acanfora, comptroller. Jack Tobin, an expert pattern designer who had been collaborating with another southern firm joined Butte as did Lou Geller and David Adelman. Adelman had previously worked as an executive at Spartan Undies, another Jewish-run firm in Spartanburg.[52] Seymour Greenwald became a sales manager. Some of the transplanted northerners such as Acanfora, Siegel, Witz, and Tobin became presidents and board members of Spartanburg's Temple B'nai Israel.[53]

The connections between Andrew Teszler and the people he hired at Butte Knitting Mill ran deep. Many of them were Holocaust survivors like

Butte Knits employees, Spartanburg

himself. Joseph Rex, hired as director of public relations was born in Budapest, grew up in the former Yugoslavia, and joined the partisan movement resisting Nazis. The apartment in the Jewish house in Budapest where the Teszlers had taken shelter years earlier belonged to the grandparents of Joseph's wife, Sylvia Rex.[54]

Teszler hired Lajos Bruck, a Hungarian Jewish refugee as a salesman, a position he had previously held for a textile company in Hungary. Andrew Ehrenstein was another Hungarian Jew who had been a member of the Hungarian resistance movement. He and his wife, Magda, and son, Gabriel, were living in Israel when David Schwartz of Jonathan Logan hired Ehrenstein and brought the family to the United States so that Bruck could train in management at Butte.[55] These former resistance fighters and Jewish refugees found a patron in Andrew Teszler who provided them with a job and security in a growing company.

Teszler's commitment and compassion for other Holocaust survivors reveals a strong emotional tie to his Jewish countrymen with whom he shared so much. Coming together in a small city and a tightly knit religious community solidified the survivors and their families with enduring friendships and support from their temple community.

Teszler's hire of Jews from New York, other regions of the South, and across international borders from Europe and Israel to Spartanburg, reveals a movement of people and skills connected by Jewish ethnic networks. In the case of Butte Mill, the largest textile plant in Spartanburg with more than 3,000 employees, Teszler relied on Jewish ethnic networks to manage his firm. More importantly, however, the network that he relied on to build his enterprise in South Carolina reflects a complex linkage with other Holocaust survivors who had been educated in textile manufacturing in Europe and well equipped with skills and experiences to contribute to the building of industry in the local area.

In 1961, Sandor and Lidia sold their textile plant on Long Island and moved to Spartanburg to reunite with their sons. One year later, the senior Teszler launched Shannon Knit, a textile mill, at Kings Mountain, North Carolina.[56] Teszler's plant provided a major economic boost for the community of Kings Mountain and eventually provided employment for 200 workers. Sandor Teszler made the hour commute from Spartanburg to Kings Mountain until 1965 when he decided to sell the plant. As soon as Sandor sold Shannon Knit, Andrew asked his father to join him at Butte as vice president for overseas operations.[57]

The rise of Andrew's company, Butte Knitting Mill in Spartanburg, was phenomenal and meteoric. From 1960 to 1976, Butte expanded twenty-four times, building 2.2 million square feet of factory space in the Spartanburg area, and adding 2,400 employees.[58] The company also operated a division called Lana-Knit at Shannon Free Airport in Ireland. Sandor spent time in Great Britain improving operations of their facilities in London and Shannon. He returned to Spartanburg in 1967 and resumed working with Andrew at Butte in production and quality control.

Butte built or acquired twenty-six sewing factories from Pennsylvania to Florida and Arkansas. Sales of women's wear soared 17-fold between 1966 and 1971.[59] The double-knit clothing produced in Spartanburg with the Butte label rose as the cash cow of the Jonathan Logan line of clothing.[60] The mill produced many innovations that became staples of the fashion industry. They initiated new methods of dyeing, knitting, and finishing never utilized before and were first in the industry to use computers for design.[61]

In 1970, Andrew made a bold change. He broke from Johnathan Logan, Inc. and established his own vertically integrated knitting plant, Olympia Mills in Spartanburg and another plant in Tuscaloosa, Alabama. At Olympia

Mills, Sandor and Andrew produced polyester fabrics and employed 900 workers. Otto returned from Shannon, Ireland, in 1971, and joined his father and brother in the business.[62]

In May 1971, at the age of forty and at the peak of his career, Andrew Teszler died of a massive heart attack.[63] After Andrew's sudden death, Sandor became chairman of Olympia Mills. In 1974, Monsanto bought Olympia Mills just as the double-knit business was starting to go into a steep decline, turning it into the world's largest silicon wafer plant, maker of thousands of computer applications in 1979. In that same year Sandor Teszler stepped down as chairman and commenced his retirement.[64]

After Andrew Teszler's death many of his employees gave emotional testimonies of what Teszler meant to them. One worker remarked, "He was so sensitive to the lowest people in his plant, the most obscure, maybe not-too-well educated. He was always accessible to anybody . . . he was aware [of] illness or accident in everyone's family, and he never failed to inquire."[65]

Another worker commented: "He had a way of seeing potential in people that even they didn't realize they had."[66] One employee recalled: "One day he (Teszler) was wearing an expensive suede coat and a worker happened to compliment him on it, said he admired it. Teszler took his coat off, and gave it to the man, put it on him."[67]

In 1968, one of the veteran workers in the dress inspecting department, Viola Darby, was absent from work because her 5-year-old son, Jerry, was fatally ill with leukemia. Teszler organized a blood drive for the child and "when physicians decided his best chance lay in being transferred to St. Jude Hospital in Memphis, Teszler had the child and his parents flown there in his private plane."[68]

Mrs. A. Y. Woodward, a Black woman who identified herself as a friend and former employee, shared this about Teszler: "I know, personally, of a boy he put through college and of another man whose house was destroyed, and he gave him a check immediately for $1,000. The Black community will miss and mourn him—our little world right here is a better place because he was here . . ."[69]

The bonds of friendship and caring that Teszler fashioned with his employees resembles the paternalism practiced by many corporations in the early twentieth century. However, in this case, it was not an effort to keep unions out because Butte Mills was one of the few industries in the Upcountry that was organized, an issue discussed later in this chapter.

The Teszlers brought important skills from Hungary that were reinforced in the younger generations' educational attainment in the United States. Otto left Spartanburg after his brother's death and took a job in Jonesville, South Carolina, with Wellman Industries. Otto and his business partner, John Wellman, had a revolutionary idea for producing a new type of yarn made from waste in a small plant in Georgetown, South Carolina.[70] Otto did not remain there for long. After obtaining a master's degree in textile manufacturing, he taught textile research at North Carolina State College, before a final career move to California where he worked as an engineer at an atomic institute.[71]

Another Jewish garment company that led the way in design and creativity was Nachmans of Easley. A Russian immigrant who began producing ladies clothing in 1904, founded the L. (Louis) Nachman and Son Company of Philadelphia.

Louis' son, Jack Nachman, joined his father's business during the early 1930s after attending the Wharton School at the University of Pennsylvania. In the late 1940s, Jack sensed a need for a new fashion. "It was the beginning of the baby boom, and women needed something besides their daytime street clothes to wear around the house."[72] Nachman created the Swirl, "a wraparound house dress which became the at-home fashion of the era."[73]

In the 1950s, Jack Nachman became president of the company, and decided to relocate the Swirl operation. He wanted to be closer to where the cotton fabrics were produced to save transportation costs.[74] More importantly, he wanted a cheaper source of labor, something easily found in the nonunionized South.

Through business contacts in South Carolina, Nachman moved his company to the small town of Easley, about fifteen miles south of Greenville. According to his son, "We were the first people to come into Easley with major manufacturing. It was the start of all this employment."[75] The Nachman Company opened as the Easley Textile Company in October 1953, and Jack "renamed the family business Swirl, in honor of the company's most successful style." The completed plant was a state-of-the-art facility with all new machines.[76] Swirl, Inc., with corporate headquarters located in Easley, soon opened a second factory in nearby Ware Place that manufactured the popular Models Coat.[77]

Swirls were made in hundreds of different fabrics and decorated with embroidery, applique, lace, piping, and a variety of trims designed in a studio in Paris that collaborated exclusively with the company on fabric ideas. The basic shape of the dress included a bodice and sleeves cut in one piece and a full, gathered skirt, made with the "housewife" in mind.[78]

As styles continued to become shorter during the 1960s with the advent of the miniskirt, the company developed different lines for a more diverse consumer base. The first addition was the Park East label in 1964, which produced a shift dress, like the Lilly Pulitzer model of today. In 1965, they developed Swirl Girl, a younger, trendier line of casual dresses and lounge-wear.[79] Women made up the majority of workers employed at Swirl, and that combined with the absence of unions kept wages low. Most female employees worked as sewing machine operators, supervisors, fitting models, and graders. Other women worked as typists, secretaries, and personnel managers. Males filled jobs as industrial engineers and plant managers.

In 1970, Jack's sons, Lawrence and Jeffrey took over the family business and further refined the concept of at-home apparel by developing leisure-wear. The Concept 1970s label, born in 1971, featured long, flowing, and caftan-like garments. In 1975, the famous lingerie designer Bill Tice, the only designer to win a Coty Award for loungewear, was hired as the designer at Swirl where he had his own label. Tice was known for stylish robes and lounge-wear. His hallmark approach used rich colors and silks, giving at-home wear a less casual look.[80] Swirl also contracted with Geoffrey Beene for logoed polo shirts and Oscar de la Renta for nightgowns and robes.

The Nachman's two factories employed more than 1,000 people, continuing operations until the late twentieth century. For more than fifty years, they introduced new styles, fabrics, designs, and fashion concepts for the American consumer. By the late 1980s, however, Swirl was facing financial difficulties. The Nachman family sold the company in the fall of 1989, after being sued by four companies trying to collect thousands of dollars owed by the company.[81] The demand for fashionable leisurewear had run its course.

Growth through Consolidation

In addition to expansion through innovation, other Jewish manufacturers grew their businesses into large corporations through a process of consolidation, expanding by diversifying, building more factories, and acquiring others. This was a customary practice among non-Jewish manufacturers in the Upcountry, as discussed earlier in this chapter. Notable among Jewish garment industries that started out small and with a keen sense of business acumen expanded to other cities, states, and even to operations abroad, included the Piedmont Shirt Company, Max Shore, Kreiger, and Lowenstein.

The oldest and largest, Jewish garment manufacturing company in South Carolina was Shepard Saltzman's Piedmont Shirt Company. By the 1950s, Saltzman had created a growing textile empire from his original plant in Greenville. With three plants located in the Upcountry, including the East-will Sportswear Company that he purchased in Greenwood, Saltzman turned to Troy, Alabama, to purchase Pike Garments. With 1,700 employees in all its locations. The Piedmont Shirt Company was America's fourth largest manufacturer of shirts.[82] Saltzman's line of clothing expanded to meet consumer demands. In 1939 he added sportswear; in 1946, boys pajamas; and in 1952, an entire line of boys' wear.[83]

Saltzman hired many relatives and close Jewish friends from New York to work in his company. Harry Abrams joined Saltzman's firm in 1938. After gaining experience at the Piedmont Shirt Company, Abrams started his own garment company, as did the Austrian refugee, Max Heller. Heller said of Saltzman, "I would rather have worked at Piedmont than anywhere else."[84] Heller recalled the friendly relations between employer and employee at the shirt factory: "In Austria the boss was feared, and workers were treated as inferiors. Here, I realized a man was respected for what he does, not for what he's called."[85]

Saltzman is best remembered for his efforts to save European Jews by providing affidavits for them to leave the German Reich and assuring them employment at his company. In addition to sponsoring Max Heller, Heller's sister, and uncle, he eventually provided employment for Heller's future wife, Trude, and her father. Saltzman also spent many hours teaching Heller the English language.[86] Saltzman's adherence to Jewish morals and ethics motivated him to perform many mitzvahs during his lifetime.[87]

Saltzman demonstrated a deep interest in his employees. On the twenty-fifth anniversary of his company, he remarked, "It has taken me years to establish this relationship with the people in our plant and you can bet I am going to do all I can to maintain it." Saltzman believed that he established the closest relationship between the head of the firm and his factory workers of any other manufacturer.[88]

Nonetheless, the Piedmont Shirt Company experienced labor problems beginning in the late 1930s (see section on labor relations below). Following Saltzman's death, he was succeeded by his son-in-law, Martin Morrow, who kept the company operating until 1990, when it filed a Chapter 11 petition declaring $4.2 million in liabilities. Morrow stated that the company's troubles were caused by weakness in the clothing market, lower manufacturing costs overseas and high employee turnover.[89]

Another successful clothing manufacturer was Max Heller, mentioned above, who arrived in Greenville in late 1938 as a nineteen-year-old Austrian Jewish refugee. He spoke no English and the only person he knew was Mary Mills, a young woman he briefly met a year earlier in Vienna. The young woman, enjoying a grand tour of Europe, met Heller in a café. She was from Greenville, and he worked for a merchandising firm in Vienna. He gave her a picture of himself, and she gave him her address.[90]

The young Heller became desperate when Hitler's troops entered Austria in March 1938. Within hours, things changed dramatically. According to Heller, "Every policeman pulled out a swastika [and] put it on his arm." That evening as the family was eating their Sabbath meal, the Heller's wondered what they would do. "We've got to get out of here," Max said. He decided to write to the American girl he met in 1937 to see if she could help him get out of Europe.[91] Heller soon learned that to enter the United States he would need a guaranteed job. In broken English, he asked Mary Mills if there was someone who could "guarantee" for him. Increasingly, anti-Semitism grew more pervasive, especially among the young Austrians that Heller had grown up with and had known for years.[92]

In May 1938 Heller received a letter from the girl in South Carolina. "You probably thought I have forgotten you" Mills wrote. "But I have been trying to work something out for you." Mills had contacted Shepard Saltzman at the Piedmont Shirt Company and asked him to assist Heller in getting him out of Austria. Saltzman later said, "How can I not help? When she, a Christian, wants to help, [then] I, a Jew, must help."[93]

Heller and his sister, Paula, left Vienna on July 18, 1938. He carried his prayer book, a prayer shawl, and Star of David medallion given to him by his parents at his Bar Mitzvah. Paula and Max arrived in New York and boarded a train for Greenville, where they were greeted by Shepard Saltzman and Mary Mills.[94]

At 1:30 that afternoon, Heller started working at the Piedmont Shirt Company sweeping floors. Heller recalled the moment he entered the shirt company: "When I came into the factory everyone knew I was coming . . . I was probably the first refugee to come out of Europe, certainly after Hitler came to Austria. So, naturally, everyone was interested to meet me."[95]

Maxon Shirt Corporation, established by Max Heller in 1948, courtesy of the Coxe Collection, Greenville County Historical Society

Heller worked hard and rose in the company, initially as head of the shipping department. While he was happy with his job at Piedmont Shirts, his aspiration to own and operate his own company prompted him to leave Piedmont Shirts. Together with a business partner, Heller started the Williamston Shirt Company twenty-seven miles from Greenville. The business boomed. But in 1947 the partnership broke up and Heller sold his share.[96] In 1948, he achieved his dream: he established his own company, Maxon Shirts in Greenville, with forty employees in a 6,000-square-foot plant. In 1952, increasing volume made larger quarters necessary, and the company moved into a building on Court Street in Greenville. In its tenth year Maxon had 4,000 accounts and more than 600 people on the payroll. Twenty-six salesmen covered the country while Max kept a finger on the pulse of public likes and dislikes. His Carnegie-brand shirts had a reputation for quality and excellent value.[97]

By 1966, Heller's company, now a subsidiary of the Oxford Manufacturing Company, relocated to a larger plant and employed 700 workers, providing jobs to hundreds of women. Maxon Shirt Company had branch offices in New York, Chicago, San Francisco, Dallas, Baltimore, and Los Angeles. The company's products sold in all fifty states as well as Puerto Rico, Nigeria, Rhodesia, Bermuda, and Canada.[98] (Heller's relations with Black employees is addressed in chapter 8.)

After an extraordinarily successful and lucrative business career, Heller decided to sell his shirt company and pursue a new direction in life: public service. According to *The Greenville News,* "Many of Maxon's first employees were still with the company when he sold it in 1971." Close business associates attribute this to Heller's personal interest in his workers and to his understanding from "coming up the hard way." The local newspaper also reassured the community that nearly 500 jobs at Maxon Shirt would be saved because Land and Sea, one of the nation's best-known manufacturers of women's apparel, had acquired the facilities.[99]

David Krieger, a native of Kolno Poland, owned Emb-Tex, an embroidery firm with roots in New Jersey. In December 1924, when he was six years old, his mother died. A work opportunity brought his father, Morris Krieger, to the United States in 1935, with a plan to bring his four sons from Poland: David and Herman first and the two younger sons later. But Germany's invasion of Poland about a year after David and Herman had entered the United States ended the plan. David Krieger's two younger brothers and the extended family that had raised him could not leave and ultimately were murdered by the Nazis.[100]

Krieger served in the US Army, under General George Patton, where he decoded messages transmitted to his commander. Krieger returned to New Jersey after the war and worked for his father's company, Kaufman and Krieger, located on Broadway, in New York City. Two years later, he and his brother found an investor and started the embroidery company, Emb-Tex, New Jersey's largest embroidery firm. In 1961, their leading client, Eugene Stone of Stone Manufacturing in Greenville, persuaded the Kriegers to move the operation to Travelers Rest.[101] There, Krieger created the largest embroidery company in the world, that by 1988, employed 750 people.[102] It doubled in size with added plants from Canton, Ohio, to Hong Kong, growing to 2,000 employees.[103] Krieger purchased the world's largest embroidery machines from Switzerland for his plant in Travelers Rest and then purchased the American Trim Products subsidiary, which doubled the size of Emb-Tex.[104]

Krieger then founded Krieger Corporation, which did the same thing as Emb-Tex but was built with newer technology. Eight years later he started another company known as the Kemco Company. This shop opened with eight embroidery machines that embellished pillowcases, sheets, curtains, and American flags. To highlight their work, Krieger and his wife, Page, opened a retail store in Greenville that Page operated.

While other textile businesses had taken their plants outside the United States during the 1970s, Krieger claimed he had no plans to leave Travelers Rest. "I love this country too much to ever leave it, and many people here in this plant are like family to me. Some of them have worked for me for 40 years."[105]

In 1979, Krieger sold Emb-Tex to the Hillman Company of Pittsburgh soon before the company ran into financial difficulties. In the 1990s Emb-Tex and American Trim, which shared common ownership with Emb-Tex of Travelers Rest filed for protection from its creditors under federal bankruptcy laws. Emb-Tex defaulted on nearly $12 million in loans and held $7 million less in inventory than it reported to Security Pacific, whose loans to the company were secured by inventories, equipment, and other assets as security. The company went into receivership in April 1990,[106] and reopened under a new owner. During the years that the Kriegers operated the company, it was widely recognized as the leading embroidery company in the world.

The Carolina Blouse Company, organized by the Russian immigrant, Max Shore (in Philadelphia in 1933, opened its first South Carolina plant in the 1940s. After serving in World War II, Shore moved his operations to Greenville, where his company opened with seventy-five machines and fewer than one hundred employees. The company expanded by building additional manufacturing plants in Greenville and Woodruff. By 1960, 1,700 employees worked in three plants, making it one of the largest women's blouse manufacturing companies in South Carolina.[107] Shore had two sons, Reuben and Sidney, who entered the business with their father and maintained offices and showrooms in the heart of the fashion district in New York City. The company designed blouses that sold nationally and advertised in *Mademoiselle* and *Harper's Bazaar*.[108]

Shore strongly felt that "he couldn't have achieved the tremendous success of his company that he achieved here in any northern industrial city." He "induced other northern manufacturers to move to this area since he found the local workers so capable and loyal."[109] Macshore Classics, Inc. eventually grew out of the Carolina Blouse Company, which remained a family-owned business producing high-quality products for homes and the hospitality industry, including draperies, shams, bed skirts, duvet covers, decorative pillows and bolsters. Macshore found its top international trading partners in Antwerp, Shanghai, and Genoa, Italy. Three generations of the Shore family kept the business operating for more than eighty years.

Shore remained popular with his employees for the benefits he provided, such as paid vacations and hospitalization insurance.[110] He was also known for assisting his workers. Shore helped Jack Weinman, a salesman for Macshore Classics go into business when he could no longer travel as a salesman after contracting polio. Weinman wanted to open a bowling alley and, "determined to aid in his rehabilitation," Shore gave him encouragement and "a loan needed to translate the dream into a reality."[111]

No longer able to compete with cheap imports, the company reduced its workforce from its high of 1,800 workers in the 1960s to ninety in 2004.[112] Three generations of Shore family members operated the business until its closure in 2004. The factory outlet store remained in business until 2016.[113]

If anyone rivaled the likes of Roger Milliken and his textile empire it was Leon Lowenstein. Considered one of the top cotton manufacturing giants "in the world," the Lowenstein family owned and operated fourteen plants by 1985 in South Carolina alone.[114]

M. Lowenstein and Sons began with Morris, who emigrated from Germany to New York City during the 1860s. In 1889, he established a cotton goods firm with his son, Abraham. At the start, the business jobbed yarn goods, towels, sheets, pillowcases, and imported linen damasks and toweling that Morris purchased from a brother-in-law in Germany.[115] In addition to the familial business networks that Lowenstein and other Jews created in the United States, they also tapped into family enterprises operating internationally.

In 1909, the company passed the million-dollar sales mark, and each year thereafter the sales volume exceeded the prior year.[116] After two years at City College, Leon, Lowenstein's youngest son, attended officer training school and entered the army in 1918. That year, Morris passed away at about the same time the company incorporated with a net worth of $2.75 million.[117] Abram succeeded his father as president of the company, and Leon became secretary-treasurer. Together, they decided to start finishing goods in a company-owned plant. Leon hired a textile expert to join the converting organization and the brothers established a bleachery, dyeing, and finishing plant in Rock Hill, South Carolina, with plans to employ 500 people, with eventual expansion plans that might require 800 employees.[118] During the building of the Rock Hill Printing & Finishing Company, Leon commuted almost every week by train between New York and Rock Hill. Unlike other northern Jewish manufacturers, Lowenstein never established a home in South Carolina. Instead, he operated the company's southern plants from his New York office and hired local executives who managed the local companies.

After Abram's death in 1936, Leon became president of the company, and purchased multiple plants in the South. Within a couple of decades, M. Lowenstein and Sons textile dynasty rose. The company became a public corporation in 1946, with a listing on the New York Stock Exchange the same year the company attained sales of $101 million.[119]

After World War II, the company expanded into the manufacturing of greige cloth (unfinished, undyed woven or knitted fabric) by purchasing several well-established textile mills in the Southeast: Merrimack Manufacturing Mills in Huntsville, Alabama, in the 1940s, and in 1946, the Orr Mills in Anderson, South Carolina.[120] After purchasing Orr Mills, a company established in 1899, Leon Lowenstein sold the Orr Mill village homes to his employees as part of his policy of providing homeownership at a modest cost to those who worked in his mills.[121] This provided hundreds of workers the opportunity to become homeowners, giving them independence, equity, and providing them with a stake in the community. Homeowners were proud that they were living in their own homes and not a "company house." The opportunity to purchase a mill home was particularly important for women who could not have purchased a home on their own. This practice was not unique; however, textile mills throughout the Upcountry cut costs by dissolving mill villages and selling village housing to their employees. This process started in some mills before World War II, accelerated afterward, and was largely complete by the 1950s.[122]

Some of the employees of Orr Mill who purchased homes included Zora Louise Day, who worked at the mill her entire adult life. She never married and only had a seventh-grade education. Nonetheless, in 1949, she purchased the mill house she had rented from the company and remained there until her death in 1991.[123] Ruth Cleveland Attaway was born in 1892, married, and worked at Orr Mills. Widowed in 1920, with a daughter to support, she continued working at the mill. In 1949, she purchased her company house on Lyons Street in the mill village where she provided a home for her daughter, a son, her mother, and a twenty-year-old cousin.[124] Another example is Evie Reynolds, who moved from Georgia for a job as a textile worker in Anderson. There is no evidence that she ever married, but she had a son living with her in the mill village. In 1949, Reynolds purchased the home she rented from Lowenstein.[125]

In the 1950s, Lowenstein acquired Spofford Mills in Wilmington, North Carolina, and Covington Mills in Covington, Georgia,[126] as well as Entwistle Manufacturing Company in Rockingham, North Carolina and Chiquola Mills in Honea Path, South Carolina. He renamed Entwistle, "Aleo Manufacturing," (in honor of the founder's two sons—Abram and Leon). Aleo then added four merchandising subsidiaries: Classic Mills, Plisse Corporation of America, Lenworth Corporation, and Wearever Fabrics Corporation.

The Chiquola Manufacturing Company, established in 1902 in the Upcountry town of Honea Path, produced coarse sheeting and print cloth. It gained fame for the bloody strike—the Uprising of 1934—when seven workers were killed and thirty wounded.[127] Under Lowenstein's leadership, Chiquola's workforce stabilized and grew to 800, producing blended sheeting, tobacco cloth, gauze, and print cloth.[128]

The M. Lowenstein and Sons company acquired textile products other than fabric with the purchase of Wamsutta Mills in New Bedford, Massachusetts, and moved the operations to Lyman, a small town in Spartanburg County. The acquisition brought with it, in addition to garment and industrial fabrics, the famed Wamsutta sheets, towels and pillowcases.[129] Wamsutta No. 1 and No. 2 mills were constructed in Anderson, and each plant ran nearly half a million spindles and nearly 1,000 looms.[130]

By the 1950s, the Rock Hill Printing & Finishing Company became the largest textile finishing plant in the world, employing 1,300 workers. This proved to be a decade of massive expansion as Lowenstein purchased several additional mills that produced print cloth in Gaffney, in Spartanburg County, Limestone Manufacturing Company No. 1, and Limestone No. 2, with about 700 workers.[131] In 1956, the Independent Board of Judges in the Financial World Annual Report Survey judged the annual report of M. Lowenstein & Sons as the best of the textile industry.[132] Two years later, Lowenstein added a synthetic division to his empire, known as the Lyons Division in Anderson.[133]

In a major buyout, Lowenstein acquired the complete cotton operation of Pacific Mills, one of the great names in textiles, initially founded in 1852 in Lawrence, Massachusetts. It manufactured prints and fancy cottons as well as worsted goods in its woolen mill operations. With the purchase of Pacific Mills, Lowenstein added five mill properties and a finishing plant including the Columbia, South Carolina, division known as Granby and

Olympia Mills, which employed 1,300 by 1992[134] This made the company one of the largest producers of domestic fabrics in the country.[135]

A pioneer in creating new fabrics and finishes, Lowenstein realized the importance of textile research and development. For that reason, he built a modern research product development laboratory in Anderson in 1959.[136] M. Lowenstein and Sons design studios became the largest in the world with locations in New York and Paris, where colorists and stylists created a constant flow of patterns. A sales force of nearly 200 men in New York and twenty field offices throughout the United States and Canada sold to customers in more than sixty-five countries. The company grew into one of the largest exporters of cotton and blended fabrics in the world.[137]

Lowenstein knew people, their needs, and tastes, and cashed in on the desire of consumers to be well-dressed and fashionable. His company catered to small garment-manufacturing companies by selling fabrics to them direct, "giving them credit on modest terms, and helping them see the advantages of selling fashion merchandise at prices that would attract mass consumption."[138]

In total, Lowenstein operated fourteen mills in the Carolinas that included piece goods under the brand names Lowenstein, Pacific, and Wamsutta, and new products such as draperies, and industrial and decorative fiberglass fabrics from the company's Clark-Schwebel Fiberglass subsidiary.[139] Additionally, his subsidiary, the Lowenstein Cotton and Storage Corporation in Anderson, handled the company's cotton purchase operations that, in the 1950s, housed 700,000 bales of cotton.[140]

In little more than seven decades, M. Lowenstein & Sons grew from a modest business in a small store to a textile empire. The corporation prospered during the 1960s and 1970s, but retrenched during the 1980s by closing some mills, selling off certain product lines and its children's wear fabrics. In 1986, Springs Industries purchased M. Lowenstein and merged its operations with its own.[141]

Wendall Fabric Corporation is the only known Jewish textile company still operating in the Upcountry in 2023. Established in 1946 by Alan Silverman of Brooklyn, the grandson of Russian immigrants, Wendall Fabrics Corporation is one of the leading specialty textile fabrics weaving companies in the United States.

Silverman attended Georgia Tech with intentions of becoming an electrical engineer but dissuaded from doing so because he was a Jew. This was an era of quotas keeping Jewish students within numerical boundaries set by the university. According to his daughter, Cathy Lewson, university personnel encouraged him to major in textile engineering, a field that hired Jews.[142] Thus, Silverman graduated from Georgia Tech with a degree in textile engineering, returned to New York, and started working in a chemistry lab. Eventually, he entered business with his uncle, Frank Silverman, who sold seat-cover materials for automobiles. Because of continuous labor strikes in New Jersey where he purchased the material, he started looking for companies in the South to manufacture seat covers and found one in Blacksburg, South Carolina, thirty-five miles from Spartanburg.[143]

With financial support from his father and uncle he secured the Blacksburg firm. Isadore Wendlowsky bought into the business and the mill was renamed Wendall Fabrics Corporation. The company eventually moved into other lines: air filtration products, acoustical material used for speakers, upholstery material, shade cloth used in farming, and geotextiles. At its peak during the early 1970s, it employed 300 people[144] and shipped its products to Africa, Japan, England, Germany, Australia, and Canada.[145]

Beginning in the 1970s, Wendall Fabric Corporation cooperated with Gardner-Webb College, a private, Christian university located in Boiling Springs, North Carolina, by providing students with internship opportunities For a small town with a population of under 2,000 in Cherokee County the internship opportunities available at Wendall are an important part of this community's support for young people.

One of the reasons this Upcountry company continues to thrive is because of their ability to adapt to new product designs. From manufacturing seat covers, the family modernized its technology and its products, creating goods for a modern market such as air filtration, acoustical material, and geotextiles.

LABOR RELATIONS

There is no uniform model for labor-management relations between Jewish manufacturers and their employees in the Upcountry. Some Jewish employers provided benefits and a living wage to their employees, while others, particularly small companies, had no formal labor policy, relying on a flexible system of negotiations for improved wages and benefits. Employees at several Jewish manufacturing plants joined unions, while other workers refused to be organized. Various Jewish manufacturers battled against labor unions, but others did not resist them. Simply put, Jewish manufacturers demonstrated no monolithic response to labor unions or in their treatment of workers. Comparing Jewish manufacturers to others, there is one small variation. More Jewish manufacturers in the Upcountry were open to labor unions than non-Jewish manufacturers. Non-Jewish millowners, as well as smaller manufacturers, adamantly opposed labor unions.

The South Carolina Upcountry had an anti-union reputation. Since the days of large-scale industrialization in the late nineteenth century, paternalistic millowners rigidly controlled mill workers. Anti-union efforts by community boosters, textile magnates, and community elites kept unions out of the Upcountry for the most part, "despite the violent labor unrest of the 1930s, culminating in the 1934 massacre at Honea Path, where a confrontation between striking textile workers and the police-backed millowners led to the deaths of seven strikers."[146]

As Marko Maunula and other scholars have observed, the 20th century's success in recruiting northern textile manufacturers to the South was in large part based on its scarcity of unions."[147] That does not mean, however, that Upcountry textile and garment workers were passive and unwilling to fight for better wages, benefits, and working conditions. Moreover, several companies established in the Upcountry as subsidiaries of northern corporations, like Butte Knitting Mills, imported its contract with the International Ladies' Garment Workers' Union (ILGWU) to the South. Thus, as the historian David Carlton maintains, "Spartanburg had successfully kept unions out, but union toeholds appeared in newly arriving" manufacturing companies.[148]

Several Jewish-owned companies were at odds with New Deal policies of the 1930s. On May 30, 1935, *The Greenville News* charged Saltzman's Piedmont Shirt Company with returning to pre–New Deal code wages and hours, as wages were reduced and hours increased.[149] On the heels of that report, the Employees Association of the company released a statement affirming that "a settlement of wage scales and hours was reached which met with unanimous approval of all employees of the company."[150] The committee maintained that "no strike was held or intended at this plant . . . the confusion . . . was motivated by a few excitable employees." Furthermore, the association indicted newspaper reporters who were only creating a "scoop for the papers." The Employees Association pledged to the management "undivided loyalty in cooperating with problems which may yet arise due to code adjustments."[151]

Two days later, on June 2, 1935, the shirt company took out a half-page advertisement imploring the public to "Judge Us Fairly," and proceeded to defend their labor practices by noting that "at no time did sweat shop conditions exist as it did in other factories in the industry." They continued their defense stating, "Our piece rate scales were higher than they should have been to work as a detriment to us rather than a benefit." Furthermore they noted the fact that there had never been a strike at the plant.[152]

In fact, the shirt company had reduced wages by 25% and increased working hours from thirty-six to forty and forty-four hours a week. Some of the employees refused to go to work in view of the cut. To this charge Saltzman retorted that "his company's wages had been 25 percent above the code and that wage readjustments were necessary because of chaotic conditions certain to come in anticipation of reduced prices."[153]

The Employees Association had decidedly taken a position to portray Saltzman's management in the best light possible, and management followed up by reassuring the public that there had never been a strike at their plant, an activity loathed by most southerners. While the responses of the Employees Association as well as the company's management assuaged the public's fear, the Piedmont Shirt Company continued to have labor-relation problems. The very fact that an Employees Association existed at all was problematic.

Employee associations, according to historian Nicki Mandell, composed of "employer and employee representatives [who] met to debate and then jointly resolve disputes, adjust wages and hours, and monitor working conditions." However democratic this sounds, Mandell maintains that corporate executives retained absolute veto power over these decisions.[154]

Two Upcountry Jewish firms had company-sponsored employees' unions, the Piedmont Shirt Company and M. Lowenstein & Sons, but in the late 1930s, they were ordered to halt the organization by the National Labor Relations Board according to Section 7(a) of the 1935 Wagner Act, which stipulated those employees should have "the right to organize and bargain collectively through representatives of their own choosing, free from interference, restraint, or coercion of the part of employers." Consequently in 1939, the National Labor Relations Board ordered the Piedmont Shirt Company to halt the employees' unions.[155] The shirt company had two unions, "one for white employees and the other for negroes." In a case brought against the company by the Amalgamated Clothing Workers of America, the company would be required to reimburse employees for all dues paid since July 5, 1935, if such recommendations were adopted by the labor board.[156]

Similarly, M. Lowenstein & Sons "was accused of fostering a company union for its office employees in violation of the Wagner Act, in charges filed with the professional workers." The union petitioned the labor board for an election which would establish its right to represent Lowenstein office employees.[157]

The Dixie Shirt Company in Spartanburg found itself in trouble with the Fair Labor Standards Act in 1942, when a decree was filed against the company and its president, Jack Cohen. In criminal contempt proceedings, a fine of $6,100 was assessed against the firm, "but would be suspended if the company paid its employees or former employees back wages owed them under the Fair Labor Standards Act of 1938." The company pled guilty but contended that it was not a willful violation.[158]

A major unionization movement emerged after World War II when the Textile Workers Union of America (TWUA) were determined to organize southern mills. The movement formed an important part of the Congress of Industrial Organizations (CIO)-led Operation Dixie that sought success in the South to secure their future nationally.[159] Some successes occurred among Jewish firms, but also, failures. For example, "when the International Ladies Garment Workers Union (ILGWU) worked to get bargaining rights for JaLog Industries in Spartanburg, (a subsidiary of Jonathan Logan), it had trouble getting workers' signatures for their union cards, despite the company's positive attitude and cooperation with the union drive. Some workers went to management expressing their desire to remain neutral from unionization."[160] A frustrated regional director of the American Federation of Labor and Congress of Industrial Organizations (AFL-CIO) complained "even though a union is given to them on a silver platter, they are still reluctant to accept it."[161] Similar to unionization efforts elsewhere in the Upcountry, attempts to unionize JaLog failed. A host of reasons contributed to the failure of unions to organize at JaLog and other industries. Nonunion workers received higher wages, owned homes, and automobiles, and, thus, were resistant to outside forces that unions represented.

Spartan Undies and sister plant, Gaffney Maid, two other Jewish-run operations in the Upcountry, forcefully encouraged their employees to join the union. In 1964, employees were told that they must join the ILGWU or the plant would be closed. Both companies were subsidiaries of Jonathan Logan of New York, which also operated Butte Knits. David Schwartz, chair of the board of Jonathan Logan, told the *Spartanburg Herald* that he hoped Spartan Undies and Gaffney Maid employees would "get me off the hook," by joining the union. The company was in favor of employees unionizing in accord with an agreement between Jonathan Logan and the ILGWU. Yet again, employees resisted. Art Irwin, a lawyer representing several employees of Spartan Undies, said a petition opposing unionization was being circulated at the plant.[162] Finally, however, a union contract was signed in September 1964.

Even though Jewish manufacturers admitted one of the reasons they relocated to the South was to avoid unions, it was common for Jewish-run textile and garment manufacturers to support unionization efforts at their plants when faced with the prospect. While the older, New England-owned cotton mills fiercely opposed unions, Jewish-owned and operated plants in South Carolina had New York City origins, where unionization was common, making them more open to and supportive of labor unions. Furthermore, as subsidiaries of New York companies, they often had no choice but to honor union contracts forged in the North.

Throughout the South, several mills established or purchased by Leon Lowenstein experienced strikes and union activity beginning in the late 1940s. In November 1949, the TWUA began organizing Orr Mill in Anderson. By January 1950, the first membership cards were distributed, "individual workers were called to the company office" (administered by local managers) and dissuaded from engaging in union activity.[163] Fierce opposition to unions occurred in Anderson County known for its long history of violent labor troubles dating back to strikes in 1919 and 1920. In 1937, CIO organizers were beaten and driven out of town at gunpoint. In 1950, the Anderson Citizens Committee organized to fight "subversive influences," and published a letter to the TWUA telling it to get out and stay out.[164]

In 1949, three of Lowenstein's mills achieved eighteen-month contracts with the TWUA, affecting three thousand employees. Workers won a company-paid insurance program including hospitalization, life insurance, and surgical benefits. Seniority and leave-of-absence clauses were improved, eligibility period for vacations was reduced to six months, and a rule stricken that denied vacation time to workers absent more than twenty-six days a year.[165] By 1956, the TWUA had organized five of Lowenstein's mills and was negotiating for two others.[166]

That same year, the Dixie Shirt Company was ordered to halt anti-union acts at their company in Spartanburg. A court ruling enforcing a decision by the National Labor Relations Board (NLRB) reported that "the shirt manufacturing concern had waged a vigorous campaign in defeat of the union by threats and intimidations of employees on the part of Dixie's supervisory officials." Furthermore, the opinion declared, an employee, "Dorothy Gaston, whose work had been previously satisfactory, was discharged for what the NLRB said was apparently union activity." The opinion stated that "Dixie must stop the unfair labor practices contained in the NLRB findings, and Miss Gaston must be offered her former position." The board believed that she had lost her job because she led the drive to obtain a union in the factory, which employees wanted because the company announced new piecework rates that would result in wage cuts.[167] In the Upcountry, it was often women, such as Dorothy Gaston, who organized and led unionization movements.

During the 1960s, the ILGWU organized Butte Knitting Mills, which had a long-standing relationship with Butte's New York-based parent company, Jonathan Logan.[168] Rosalie Tucker had experience with unions in the North where she had lived and worked before coming to Spartanburg. Surprised to find that the ILGWU was organizing Spartanburg, she quickly joined. Furthermore, she distributed union cards to other workers in the sewing room and began signing them up. Tucker recalled that the ILGWU got into Butte mainly because of the piecework rates. According to Tucker, "They paid so much money for each dozen you done. If they set it at one hundred pieces for eight hours, you had to make over one hundred to make any money. If you done more than that they'd up the rate. . . ."[169]

During the 1960s, Butte employees walked off their jobs several times. In April 1969, workers engaged in several wildcat strikes. A labor dispute of approximately 800 members of the ILGWU walked on Tuesday, April 10, after alleged production schedule alterations resulted in a cutback settlement. Negotiations took place with Butte management and most workers were back on the job Wednesday morning.[170] Notwithstanding the occasional strike, most employees declared that "labor relations with Andrew Teszler were generally good"[171] at a time when modernization in the textile and garment industries was affecting many Spartanburg workers.[172]

Teszler, however, provided benefits for employees that were not negotiated by the union. He exhibited concern for his employees' well-being by providing on-site medical care and a variety of educational, recreational, and social activities. One of the most noteworthy programs he offered workers was the opportunity to acquire a high school equivalency diploma. He engaged four teachers to come to the mills each Tuesday and Thursday afternoons from 4:45 to 7:15 to conduct classes in English, history, math, and science. Peggy Williams, who "always regretted leaving high school," passed her equivalency exam after taking classes at the mill. A third-shift knitter with two children, Teszler saluted her, noting, "I consider your achievement as the first proof of success of this worthwhile program."[173]

As part of his medical support for employees, Teszler introduced an industrial foot health program in 1966. Since many employees had to stand on the job all day, they frequently suffered foot problems. A Spartanburg podiatrist was retained to conduct a program of reducing the foot and leg problems among Butte's employees. He offered his services every Wednesday (in the emergency room at the plant on Interstate 85) during breaks and lunch periods and before and after working hours. A treatment room opened and launched a program of basic research pertaining to foot and leg discomfort as it pertained to Butte employees As a result, new floor matting installed throughout the plant softened the floors.[174]

Teszler promoted an atmosphere of socialization among employees through a series of company-sponsored events, including dinners and a kiddie party for employees' children at Christmas. Employees received Halloween packages in October, and summer picnics provided food, entertainment, sports, and music.[175]

By the mid-1960s, the Piedmont Shirt Company, under the leadership of Saltzman's son-in-law, Martin Morrow, had changed its management style and benefits to reflect the growing trends occurring in modern manufacturing plants. The company offered vacation pay, free life insurance and free hospital and surgical insurance. Employees were provided with paid holidays, free medical services were provided weekly, and registered nurses were on duty all day.[176] With the exception of a few small victories for organized labor, the overall defeat of unions in the South Carolina Upcountry ended in disappointment for the unions, cementing the reputation and character of the South Carolina Piedmont as decidedly anti-union.[177]

Jewish Philanthropy and Civic Involvement

The prominence of Jews in civic philanthropy reflected their growing affluence in society.[178] Jews had always given generously to Jewish charities and Jewish institutions, but with the success of Jewish businessmen and manufacturers in the mid-twentieth century they were often giving outside of the Jewish community. Eric Goldstein and Deborah Weiner maintain that "philanthropy became a vehicle for Jews to assert their place in local civic affairs and highlight their role as responsible citizens."[179]

Many non-Jewish industrialists in the Upcountry gave liberally to local charities and building projects.[180] In Spartanburg the Teszlers were the most generous Jewish philanthropists in the Upcountry in the mid-twentieth century.

Sandor and Andrew Teszler were deeply involved in Spartanburg events and were extraordinary philanthropists. Father and son contributed to Spartanburg and were the most recognized Jews in the community. Andrew was a devoted civic leader and his generosity brought benefits to the entire Spartanburg community that endure to the present day. He purchased the first intensive-care heart unit and the first heart scanner for Spartanburg General Hospital. He also spearheaded a campaign to raise $950,000 to open the Charles Lea Center for the education of disabled children.[181] In 1969, Andrew became a member of the board of trustees at Wofford College and donated money for the building of a new campus library that honored his father.[182] The new $1.5 million Wofford College Library was dedicated on March 28, 1971.[183] Teszler served on Governor John C. West's Commission on Human Relations. He and his family were active members and supporters of Temple B'nai Israel, and his generous donations made possible the construction of an education building at the temple.

Sandor Teszler remained engaged with the Spartanburg community as a member of downtown Rotary, the Spartanburg Chamber of Commerce, and as a trustee of the Charles Lea Center. In 1997, Wofford College awarded him an honorary doctor of humanities and at the age of ninety-three, the faculty voted to make him a professor of the humanities.

After his death at the age of 97 in 2000, Wofford College created the Sandor Teszler Award for Moral Courage and Service to Humankind, a fitting memorial to a Holocaust survivor whose intelligence, perseverance, righteousness, and kindness made him who he was: a prosperous textile entrepreneur, a devoted family man, and a pillar of the southern community that became his home. Teszler's obituary noted that "his constant example of integrity, industry and deep concern for human values made him an outstanding and well-loved leader in all endeavors and spurred all those associated with him to strive for excellence in their professional and private lives."[184]

Very few Jewish businessmen were as engaged in the community or as generous as the Teszlers. However, many Jews gave liberally to their synagogues and Jewish causes. For example, the Abrams family were Reform Jews. Harry Abrams, president of Raycord, desperately wanted to worship in a vigorous religious community. During the 1930s, the Temple of Israel in Greenville was inactive due to financial problems caused by the Great Depression, so Harry set about revitalizing the congregation. His son, Irving, was also active in the Temple as well, and in the 1960s he was elected president of the statewide B'nai B'rith.[185] The younger Abrams was deeply involved in community activities, belonging to the Elks Club, the Walden Masonic Lodge, and the Hejaz Temple of the Shriners.[186]

Max Shore, of Macshore, Inc. and his family belonged to Congregation Beth Israel in Greenville, where he was chair of the building committee for a new structure. When it was completed in 1958, the first-floor assembly room was named the Shore Youth Center in his honor.[187] Shore was also active in the United Jewish Appeal, serving on the conference sponsoring committee of the Emergency Carolina Regional Conference. These members felt "keenly the responsibility of American Jews to come to the aid of their fellow Jews overseas."[188]

Throughout his life, Lowenstein was a major philanthropist, contributing generously to colleges and organizations, particularly in the New York area. However, Lowenstein did not give back to the southern communities where much of his fortune was made. As a resident of New York, and later, Miami, Lowenstein contributed to colleges and foundations in those two cities. Buildings bear his name at Fordham University, New York's St. Vincent's Hospital, the nurses residence at Mount Sinai Hospital in Miami Beach, Temple Emanu-El in Miami Beach, and auditoriums at the Jewish Guild for the Blind.[189]

In 1960, Lowenstein was appointed to the board of lay trustees at Fordham University and served as honorary chairman of the board of Hillside Hospital in Long Island. He was a board member of St. Vincent's hospital in New York City and director of Mt. Sinai Hospital in Miami Beach. In South Carolina, Lowenstein established the Lowenstein Scholarship, an award presented annually to an outstanding graduating son or daughter of an employee pursuing a career in textiles.[190]

His support of Jewish organizations was a lifelong commitment. He served as honorary vice-chairman of the United Jewish Appeal, president of the Federation of Jewish Philanthropists of New York, and honorary vice-chairman of the Anti-Defamation League of B'nai B'rith. Lowenstein received the Human Rights Award, presented by the Joint Defense Appeal (JDA) for his philanthropic activities for Catholic and Protestant causes as well as the JDA.[191]

Regardless of the stature and success of Jewish entrepreneurs in Upcountry South Carolina, restrictions enacted years earlier prohibited Jews from membership in private dining clubs in both Spartanburg and Greenville. It was the 1970s, and times were changing. During an era of expanding civil rights, the leadership of southern communities recognized that it was time to end exclusionary policies against Jews. Frederick (Rick) Dent, who succeeded his father as president and CEO of Mayfair Mills, suggested the time had come to all allow Jewish membership in the Piedmont Club. The board of directors voted unanimously to allow Jews in the former all-white, Protestant, male, and old-South private club.[192] Similarly, Greenville's Poinsett Club followed suit. When Spartanburg businessman and community leader, George Dean Johnson, developed the Carolina Country Club and residential community, he warned that restrictions against Jews would not be tolerated.

Decline of Textile and Garment Manufacturing

From the 1970s onward, South Carolina textile manufacturers competed unsuccessfully with developing countries. Many firms went under and after 1977 the decline accelerated.[193]

By 1985, the impact of technology and foreign competition meant serious problems for textiles and garment manufacturing. Betsy Wakefield Teter noted that "increasing automation brought computers to every machine on the floor . . . and with automation came job loss. Between 1972 and 1985, automation was the primary factor in the loss of 700,000 textile jobs."[194]

It was impossible for American manufacturers to compete with cheap imports. In 1985, the typical upcountry textile worker was making $6.50 an hour, while a Chinese worker was making $0.20 an hour. Imports of textile and apparel imports tripled from 1980 to 1990, reaching sixty percent by 1990, resulting in a loss of "six out of every seven apparel jobs in Spartanburg County between 1971 and 2002."[195]

Several upcountry manufacturers who supported global textile manufacturing also supported a controversial new government program that allowed them to ship cloth to the Caribbean to be sewn in low-wage factories and then sent back to the United States as "American made" goods and apparel.[196] Textile manufacturing survived for several more decades, though drastically reduced in size and scale. Garment manufacturing, however, took a major hit as apparel companies, unable to compete with cheap, imported goods closed their doors. Upcountry South Carolina was in transition in the mid-to-late 20th century and major economic transformations took place.

CONCLUSION

This chapter demonstrates the significant role of Jewish manufacturers in the postwar surge of textiles and apparel manufacturing in Upcountry South Carolina after World War II. The era reflected prosperity for the Upcountry and Jews contributed to that end. The postwar period witnessed large numbers of Jewish entrepreneurs who brought their technological expertise and recruited a class of savvy managers to fill executive and managerial positions at their plants. Many Jewish manufacturers transferred skills and training received in Europe and applied it to their new American environment. Furthermore, ethnic networks comprised of family members and compatriots from the old country provided employment links stretching from Europe and Israel to New York and South Carolina.

Jewish textile and garment manufacturing plants provided employment for more than twenty-five thousand people in the Upcountry from the 1940s to the 1980s, when textile manufacturing began to decline because of competition with foreign-made goods. The impact of the manufacturing companies, however, reached far beyond the Upcountry. Many Jewish-owned companies were on the cutting edge of fashion and in-vogue fabrics. Their marketing skills reached across the United States and into European and Asian countries.

Upcountry businesspeople and town boosters were receptive to and welcomed these enterprising Jews, not because they were Jews, but because they were innovators who contributed to the progress and prosperity of Upcountry South Carolina.

CHAPTER 8

Jewish–Black Relations

Evidence of Jewish–Black collaboration appear in South Carolina during the early years of the twentieth century when the philanthropist, Julius Rosenwald, committed himself to improving the lives of Black individuals in the South. Rosenwald helped advance Black lives through education and building schools in partnership with Black citizens. In South Carolina alone, his funding helped build more than five thousand schools.

In 1919, the *Spartanburg Herald,* writing on the progress of Black schools in the county noted that "Mr. Julius Rosenwald, the head of the Sears, Roebuck Company of Chicago has established a fund to aid in building better schoolhouses in the rural districts of the south for colored people. Already more than 300 in the South have been aided from this fund. In this county two schools have been completed, one is in the course of erection and several communities have plans on foot to establish Rosenwald schools."[1]

Rosenwald, born in 1862, the son of German-Jewish immigrants made his fortune as the head of Sears, Roebuck and Company. A substantial philanthropist, Rosenwald, "probably the greatest white patron to join the crusade for Black education," according to Hasia Diner, enthusiastically supported the NAACP and its struggle for civil rights.[2]

A wealthy individual, driven by a sense of purpose to do good, Rosenwald pledged his support to create better educational facilities for Black children in the South. As historian John Hope Franklin maintains, "Nothing was more persistent in the first half of the twentieth century than the disparity between the money spent for the education of white children and that spent for the education of black children."[3] Rosenwald became committed to improving Black schools and narrowing those discrepancies.

Rosenwald's schools resulted from his friendship with Booker T. Washington. Following Rosenwald's donation of $25,000 to Tuskegee Institute, Washington prompted him to construct small rural schools in the South.[4] Rosenwald's foray into school construction for Blacks began with his provision of funds to help construct one hundred schools in three Alabama counties. Rosenwald articulated a visionary plan that included funding from state governments and private donations by local Blacks and whites. In fact, these sources were to provide money equal to or larger than the amount donated by Rosenwald.[5] While Rosenwald contributed the bulk of the financing, the Black community, in addition to providing funding, had to provide labor and materials. Diner notes that "where communities could not raise the cash, the men and women would literally build the buildings, offering their labor as their share of the cost." Additionally, Rosenwald solicited contributions from Jewish and non-Jewish white donors.[6]

Initially, Rosenwald's efforts focused on elementary education, but his vision expanded to support for Black high schools and teacher training institutes.[7] Believing that Black students should have access to higher education, Rosenwald helped prepare young Black students to attend Black colleges like Howard, Fiske, and others, which Rosenwald also supported.[8] By 1932, the year of his death, more than 5,000 Rosenwald schools existed in the South, including 450 in South Carolina. Nearly one hundred Rosenwald schools were erected in the Upcountry, including twenty-four in Spartanburg County and twenty-nine in Greenville County.[9]

Two Upcountry residents, Lugene Gist, and Mattie Sims Savage attended Rosenwald schools. Lugene, born in 1915 in Union County, recalled in an interview conducted several years ago that members of the Black community helped build the school. She noted that Joe Walker, a carpenter, and her father, who could read blueprints, contributed heavily to the construction of Poplar Grove School in Sanduk. The Black community raised money for the school by selling box suppers and hosting barbeques while white landowners contributed building materials.[10] Black citizens' participation building and raising funds for Rosenwald schools brought the Black community together with a spirit of optimism for the future of their children.

Mattie Sims Savage, who attended Beatty Bridge Elementary in Union described her Rosenwald school as a one-room schoolhouse where the teacher provided lessons in English, geography, spelling, and arithmetic. Often, children were late for the 9:00 morning start of classes as they often worked in cotton fields before walking to school. One of Mattie's most memorable events occurred when her teacher took students on a trip to visit Allen University, an all-Black college in Columbia.[11] By exposing young Black students to institutions of higher education in South Carolina, the teacher affirmed Rosenwald's vision that Black youth should be prepared for higher levels of accomplishment.[12]

Thousands of Black children who attended Rosenwald schools proceeded to college and became teachers, nurses, social workers, and ministers. A study conducted by two economists in Chicago estimated "that thirty percent of the educational gains achieved by African Americans in the 1910s and 1920s could be attributed directly to the Rosenwald schools."[13]

At Rosenwald's death, tributes poured in from across the country in his honor. W. E. B. Du Bois praised him: "The death of Julius Rosenberg brings to an end a career remarkable especially for its significance to American Negroes." Rosenwald's philanthropic endeavors in support of Black people reflects an effort to alter the racial divide in America by providing greater opportunity to Black individuals. In addition to his belief that Jews had an obligation to assist other Jews and support Jewish causes, Diner notes that "his upbringing in Reform Judaism had trained him to believe that as a Jew he had to right the wrongs of the world."[14]

Rosenwald was the first Jew to become involved in efforts to improve the lives of Blacks citizens in the South Carolina Upcountry but not the last. Community-building endeavors bridging the Black and white divide were tackled by twentieth-century Upcountry Jewish mayors and these efforts continue to the present day.

As discussed in earlier chapters, Jewish relationships with Black people have a long history in southern states. Jewish peddlers provided Black families with access to goods in the rural south. Later, Jewish merchants, whether in small villages, towns, or cities, established relations with Black clientele who frequented their stores.

Several historians examine the relationship among Jewish merchants and their Black customers. In his study of Jewish merchants in the South, Clive Webb writes that Black people "were always the last to be served and seldom allowed to try on clothes" in most white-owned business establishments.[15] However, "Jewish tradesmen," he asserts, "treated African Americans with care and consideration [and] they accorded them a stronger sense of personal respect than other storeowners."[16] Steven Hertzberg, in his study of the Jewish community of Atlanta agrees, stating that Jewish businessmen "treated their customers with a civility that the latter rarely received from white southerners."[17] Clive Webb also notes that "Jewish merchants earned a reputation among African Americans for being more willing than other white businessmen to offer both credit and basic courtesy to Black customers."[18]

Relationships between Jewish merchants and their Black clientele in the Upcountry reveal instances where merchants treated their Black patrons with courtesy and respect. Black people shopped in Jewish-owned stores in Spartanburg as no clothing stores existed in the Black southside neighborhoods that otherwise bustled with grocery stores, restaurants, and hotels.[19] Frank Nichols Jr., a resident of the southside recalls that he and other young Black men shopped at [Jewish] stores like Prices' and Greenewalds. "Those stores," he recalled, "had real nice and some expensive clothing. We didn't have a lot of money, but we worked odd jobs just to buy one or two pieces so we could dress nice and neat."[20]

Jewish businesses allowed Black patrons to try on clothes and use the same dressing rooms as whites. Black customers tried on clothing at Jeanette Finkelstein's Chesnee dress shop.[21] Allen From noted that his grandfather's store in Union allowed Black customers to try on shoes. An elderly Black man told From that in other stores Blacks patrons had to "measure the length of their foot with a string, go to the store and ask for a shoe of that length."[22] In the 1950s, From's father hired Black workers to assist Black customers.[23]

Jewish retailers extended credit to Black customers at a time when few white businesspeople did. Edward Gray of Kosch and Gray Jewelers in Spartanburg reported that Black patrons composed about fifty percent of his clientele. Beginning in the 1940s, his parents offered in-store credit to Black clients, "who lined up on Saturday mornings to make payments on their jewelry purchases."[24]

In a 2009 interview with Dorothy Cohen, who at ninety-three continued to operate Jack's Economy Store in Spartanburg, she noted that many of her clientele were Black individuals. She, too, offered in-store credit to her Black customers, and added, "I treat them like I want to be treated. I won't sell them stuff I don't think is right."[25] In interviews with Bobbie Jean Rovner and with Susan Zaglin and Larry Zaglin of Greenville, they noted that Black customers "were our bread and butter. You have to treat your customers with respect."[26]

Jewish businesspeople may have quietly tested southern racial mores in their daily business interactions with Black customers, but that does not mean that they were challenging the status quo. As historian David Goldfield declared, "To know one's place and to act accordingly was important for getting along in the South, especially before the civil rights era."[27] Edward Gray of Spartanburg also believes that southern Jews upheld racial mores, "but on their own terms. In their own stores they treated Blacks like any other whites."[28]

Marian Feinstein of Spartanburg corroborates, noting that "they went along with the racial mores of the South but inside their own stores they treated African Americans like very special people."[29] Feinstein's statement raises important questions about Jews' status in southern towns. While Jews in the Upcountry were well assimilated and experienced little anti-Semitism, there was, nonetheless, a feeling that southern cultural traditions regarding race must be upheld.

CIVIL RIGHTS ERA IN THE UPCOUNTRY

In the mid-twentieth century the Upcountry fit the quintessentially southern paradigm, dominated by economic exclusion and segregation. Black individuals lived in run-down, shabby sections of town, and Black children attended inferior schools. The economist Marko Maunula asserts that "the Upcountry was archetypical of the South Carolina Piedmont, with its blue-collar racism, condescending middle-class illusions of benevolence, and widespread white conviction that local African Americans were content with the racial system that prevailed in the region."[30]

During the first half of the twentieth century, racial violence deeply tarnished Greenville's reputation as a progressive city when five lynchings took place between 1905 and 1933. The Willie Earle hanging in 1947 garnered national attention when a white mob hanged Earle, a Black man suspected of murdering a white cabdriver. Thirty-one men confessed to lynching Earle. A few months later, a jury of twelve white males acquitted the defendants on all counts.[31]

As civil rights issues heated up during the 1950s in Greenville and other areas of South Carolina, the NAACP became a major vehicle for securing civil rights for Black people. Black high school students worked closely with the NAACP, and local Black ministers provided needed leadership for the movement. The civil rights activist James Felder dates the beginning of the Greenville movement to December 1959, when native son Jesse Jackson came home for the Christmas holidays from the University of Illinois.[32]

Born in 1941, and raised in Greenville, the nationally known civil rights leader Jesse Jackson grew up in the city's segregated neighborhoods, a mix of poor and middle-class Black individuals,[33] and attended the all-Black Sterling High School. A good student, class leader, and superb quarterback,[34] Jackson longed to attend Furman University, but it was segregated, like all other southern institutions, so he left Greenville for the University of Illinois. Ironically, when Jackson went to Illinois, "he did so as the recipient of surprising solicitudes on the part of the white order of Greenville."[35] Bob King, Furman University's football coach and an Illinois alumnus, watched Jackson play several high school football games. Impressed with Jackson's performances, he encouraged the University of Illinois to offer Jackson a scholarship.[36]

While Jackson attended classes at the University of Illinois, the Greenville NAACP invited baseball great Jackie Robinson to speak at its meeting on October 25, 1959. When NAACP leaders took Robinson back to the airport after his talk, Robinson and the rest of the group took seats in the main lounge. Airport officials soon arrived and asked the group to move to the colored lounge. Robinson reported that "we purposely bypassed a small, segregated corner of the terminal labeled Colored Lounge, for we knew that a ruling four years ago ended segregation of interstate travelers in public waiting rooms."[37] This incident incited a protest march by Greenville's Black community that originated at the Springfield Baptist Church, headquarters for the civil rights movement, on New Year's Day, 1960, and continued to the airport. Marching with the peaceful protestors calling for an end to segregation, Jesse Jackson joined with hundreds of other Black Greenvillians.[38] This event launched Jackson's role as a civil rights activist.

In an interview conducted with Jackson in August 2016, he revealed the torment he suffered because of the discrimination directed against him as a Black man. His activism did not start, however, until the Jackie Robinson incident and another event that touched him personally. In Greenville during a Christmas break while a student at Illinois, Jackson could not obtain books he needed from the "Colored Branch Library." He tried desperately to procure them from the white "public" library but was prohibited from doing so. He swore to himself on the way back to Urbana "that someday he was going to use the public library."[39]

The following summer, Jackson, along with seven other Black Greenvillians, staged a forty-minute sit-in at the public library. Arrested and charged with disorderly conduct, the "Greenville Eight" as they became known, ended up in jail.[40] This marked the beginning of Black direct action in Greenville. After several more student sit-ins, the threat of federal action forced the desegregation of the library.[41] In Greenville, demonstrations against a segregated library system ended peacefully after Attorney Donald Sampson, the city's first Black lawyer, sued in federal court for the desegregation of the public library. On September 2, 1960, under the direction of the mayor and city council, all Greenville library branches closed to prevent court ordered desegregation. Distraught at the libraries' closings, public pressure motivated the mayor to reopen all the libraries, and the city dropped its charges against the demonstrating youths.[42]

At about the same time, protesters commenced targeting downtown lunch counters. On July 21, 1960, a fight broke out following a sit-in at Kress's lunch counter. The incident, involving more than thirty white and Black teenagers resulted in a week of clashes between Blacks and whites "exchanging gunfire, rocks, and bottles."[43] Demonstrations continued into 1961 targeting whites-only skating rinks and other lunch counters.

Southern historian Steve O'Neill maintains that "the threat of economic sanctions by the executive branch of the federal government pushed Greenville's business elite to weigh profits against the continuation of segregation."[44] On July 1, 1961, with threat of suspension of contracts by the federal government for South Carolina textile plants practicing segregation, Charles Daniel, a leading Greenville businessperson, former US senator, and a powerful economic voice in the state, gave a talk at a watermelon festival in Hampton, South Carolina. Known as the "watermelon speech," it reflected Daniel's concerns about the future of the state's economic progress in a segregated society. He asserted that for the economy to improve and attract outside investors, white South Carolinians must "forsake some of our ways." He urged economic and political leaders to "handle [the desegregation issue] ourselves . . . or it will be forced upon us in the harshest way. Either we act on our own terms, or we forfeit the right to act."[45] In the words of one Greenville textile man, Daniel's speech "gave the blessing of the establishment to desegregation."[46]

Student sit-ins continued in Greenville and Spartanburg throughout 1961 and 1962."[47] George Foster, a junior at the all-Black Carver High School in Spartanburg and a member of the youth chapter of the NAACP, participated in marches and sit-ins in Columbia and his hometown of Spartanburg. He led one of the first local sit-ins at Woolworths in Spartanburg in 1960. Young Black individuals approached the lunch counter and took a seat and white spectators attacked the demonstrators. After a confrontation with "two big white men coming through the door toward us like they were going to kill us . . . someone called the police," he recalled. Arrested and incarcerated, the two white men spent only a few hours in jail before their release.[48]

According to one newspaper account, "Olin Emory, 20, walked to the counter and struck one of the Negroes, then grabbed him by the shoulders. The other white man slugged the second Negro behind the ear . . ."

Detectives, who had been forewarned about the demonstration, arrested the white men and the two Black demonstrators.[49] While white onlookers often threw punches, African American demonstrators remained peaceful, never striking back.

Carole Moore Richard took part in a demonstration at Woolworths in Spartanburg on July 27, 1960, along with thirty other Black students. She recalled that "once there, we sat down. We were ordered to leave. There were white people standing around jeering at us . . . they literally roped us into the seats. As we were leaving, the white people, mostly men, spat on us and continued to jeer."[50] The *Spartanburg Herald* of July 28, 1960, confirmed this account and added that a mob did, in fact, chase some of the Black youth to South Liberty Street and some fighting ensued. In 1963, one year before the Civil Rights Act of 1964 outlawed segregation in public places, negotiations between Black and white local leaders quietly integrated lunch counters in Spartanburg.[51] Local Black leaders, such as the Reverend Booker Sears and the Rev. J. Leon Pridgeon, worked behind the scenes with white civic leaders to avoid violent clashes in the civil rights struggle, according to Black residents Beatrice Hill and Brenda Lee.[52] Upcountry whites implemented partial accommodation and practiced moderation in their relations with Blacks, which kept race relations from turning violent. Economic historian Marko Maunula maintains that South Carolinians who thought of themselves as refined southerners, "hated to be lumped together with extremist, violence-prone states such as Alabama and Mississippi, preferring instead a polite, subdued handling of racial issues."[53]

According to Jack Bass, a Jewish South Carolinian, civil rights activist, author, journalist, and coauthor of *The Orangeburg Massacre,* South Carolinians practiced moderation during the civil rights era because "historically, an aristocratic racism had dominated the white South Carolina social and political structure—a racism in which Negroes were looked upon as children rather than as a lower class of being and in which lower-class whites were also looked down upon. It contrasted with the democratic racism that prevailed in the Deep South in which all whites shared a sense of equality because they were white."[54] According to Bass, the system of aristocratic racism put a premium on an orderly society, which prevailed in South Carolina. Early on, "low-country planters and wealthy men of commerce in Charleston had attempted to develop an aristocratic society. In race relations, it developed as paternalism."[55] From this so-called aristocratic racism "a white social structure emerged which seemed to value stability almost as much as segregation."[56]

Upcountry whites denounced the Ku Klux Klan and other forms of racial extremism. Local white leaders took gradual steps beginning in the 1950s to include Black people in public positions. The hiring of two Black police officers in 1950 and 1953 in Spartanburg together with improved funding for the town's Black schools and periodic urban renovation projects in Black and white communities helped to instill some sense of progress. "In elections, Spartanburg white voters joined most of the [Upcountry] in supporting business-minded, moderate segregationists over the more dedicated, fire-breathing brand of white supremacists."[57]

When Ernest "Fritz" Hollings became governor in 1959, "he adopted a defiant approach to the validity of *Brown vs. Board of Education* in his inaugural address." Originally opposed to school desegregation and a defender of white privilege, Hollings maintained a vociferous stand against violence and was more concerned with public safety than demonstrations for civil rights.[58] However, Hollings broke from traditional southern racial customs when the state's economic future was at risk because of segregation. According to historian David Ballantyne in his discussion of the governor's plan for South Carolina's industrial development,[59] "By the end of his term, Hollings was counseling peaceful compliance with the federal court order to admit [African American student] Harvey Gantt to Clemson."[60]

Meeting together in 1961, Greenville business and community leaders decided segregation had to go. Charles Daniel, a leading businessman in Greenville, explicitly stated that "South Carolina should treat its Black citizens fairly and provide them with decent education and employment opportunities."[61] The South Carolina historian, Walter Edgar, notes that Daniel's remarks "were the first public indication that men in positions of power were willing to abandon segregation. The following year, the Greenville Chamber of Commerce formed a biracial committee to end segregation."[62]

Courtney Tollison Hartness maintains that desegregation of South Carolina's public and private universities demonstrate the state's desire to integrate peacefully.[63] She asserts that desegregation at South Carolina institutions of higher education did not take place amid violence. However, in most cases, it did not come voluntarily. Desegregation ensued at the two largest public institutions in the state—Clemson University and the University of South Carolina—because of lawsuits filed by Black students.

The belief that desegregation in South Carolina "was conducted with grace and style," as is often asserted, is challenged by O'Neill, who believes that this interpretation is a product of white memory, not Black memory.

Based on interviews and personal conversations with Black individuals, public forums, and unpublished memoirs of local residents, O'Neill argues that "white Greenville was not moved by a desire for justice or a spirit of equality."[64] Black residents recall the arrests, the resistance of the white establishment, the court victories, and the indignities they faced in fighting for rights guaranteed by the Constitution.[65]

After much resistance, in 1963, South Carolina began to dismantle Jim Crow segregation. In Greenville and Spartanburg, Blacks and whites reached accommodation rather quickly. One of the reasons these two cities may have moved speedily on resolving the racial issue rested with the international companies they were courting. Community leaders, fearing that European companies would not relocate to a region rife with racial conflict, did not want the civil rights movement to derail industrial development.

With the handwriting on the wall, in 1963, outgoing Governor Fritz Hollings told the legislature: "If and when every legal remedy (to desegregation) has been exhausted, this General Assembly must make clear South Carolina's choice . . . As determined as we are, we of today must realize the lesson of one hundred years ago and move on for the good of South Carolina and our United States. This should be done with dignity. It must be done with law and order."[66]

This statement contributed to the assumption of Hollings as a "moderate" governor in terms of civil rights. However, he became committed to the cause only after his election to the United States Senate.

While the Upcountry made much progress in the transition from the old order to the new without a single death attributed to civil rights protests, violence and retribution did occur elsewhere in the state. On September 15, 1967, at the dawn of desegregation, the all-Black Sterling High School in Greenville mysteriously went up in flames, as did Springfield Baptist Church in 1972.[67]

Moreover, civil rights protests resulted in the deaths of Black students in February 1968, when violence erupted in Orangeburg in the lower part of the state. Students at the all-Black South Carolina State College and Claflin College protested racial segregation at a local bowling alley and other privately owned local businesses. Cleveland Sellers Jr., a South Carolina native and a civil rights activist, joined the protestors. An organizer for the Student Nonviolent Coordinating Committee, Sellers encouraged student groups to demand courses in Black history and culture at the University of South Carolina.[68]

Hundreds of students gathered at South Carolina State where they built a bonfire and supposedly taunted law enforcement. Claiming they heard gunshots, highway patrolmen opened fire in the dark on about 200 unarmed Black students. The confrontation ended with three Black students dead and twenty-eight people wounded. Sellars, tried and sentenced to prison, served one year behind bars while the white policemen were acquitted.[69]

Apart from the Orangeburg massacre, the civil rights movement in South Carolina was met by little violence compared to other Deep South states. In the Upcountry the movement seemed uneven. The Greenville movement developed with more organization and leadership and protests occurred more frequently than in Spartanburg where little direct action took place. For the most part, white leadership in Spartanburg conducted racial negotiations "in private meetings rather than the streets."[70] Racial accommodations may have quelled issues for the time being but, PhD candidate Andrew Gutkowski observes, they "failed to radically reroute political power."[71] In Greenville, incremental steps toward Black integration occurred in 1969 when Dr. E. L. McPherson became the first Black person elected to the city council.[72] James Talley became the first Black person to serve on city council in 1981 and was elected as Spartanburg's first Black mayor in 1993.

JEWS AND CIVIL RIGHTS IN THE UPCOUNTRY

While many Jews supported the goals of the civil rights movement, "public support for Black equality threatened to undo generations of peaceful coexistence between southern Jews and their white neighbors."[73] Many historians agree that many Jews remained on the sidelines during the civil rights movement and rarely spoke out.[74]

Jewish silence could have signaled fear, or it may have reflected ambivalence or even opposition toward desegregation. In Charleston, for example, "a handful of members of the Reform congregation, Kahal Kadosh Beth Elohim, were rabid segregationists," according to Rabbi Burton Padoll, who led the synagogue from 1961–1967.[75]

The sons and daughters of Jewish business owners in the Upcountry maintain that friendly relationships existed between Jewish businesspeople and their Black clientele. There is certainly evidence to support that assertion, but that does not necessarily mean that Upcountry Jews supported the civil rights movement and desegregation.

Allen From of Union maintains that his parents "brought up their children with no malice toward anyone or any group of people, even though they played no part in the civil rights movement."[76] From added that Jews showed respect toward Black people but, in retrospect, he "wishes we had done more."[77]

Spartanburg attorney, Gary Poliakoff, noted that his parents, both very liberal, supported the movement. He also reasoned that Jews in Spartanburg "philosophically came around to civil rights,"[78]suggesting that some Spartanburg Jews may have been hesitant about supporting civil rights in the early years of the movement but gradually embraced the cause.

In fact, throughout the entire South, there existed a great deal of ambivalence among Jews regarding civil rights, contrary to "conventional opinion . . . that Jews are one of the groups that consistently support civil rights causes and promote the welfare of minorities in the United States."[79] Northern Jews and northern Jewish rabbis could more easily adopt a strident position in favor of racial equality but southern Jews "did not want to be perceived as different by other southerners."[80]

According to Leonard Dinnerstein, author of *Anti-Semitism in America,* "despite the participation of many Jews in the civil rights movement, the level of commitment has differed in various parts of the country."[81] Recognizing that most southern Jews were businesspeople who depended on the patronage of their white neighbors, "they thought it wise to fit in with the accepted customs of the community. In smaller towns, they avoided public airing of controversial views, and claimed as their own the community's standards of thought."[82] Dinnerstein's paradigm has been echoed by historians who agree that while many Jews privately advocated for Black equality, most adopted the racial mores of their communities.[83]

No records exist to suggest that Upcountry rabbis publicly addressed race issues during the civil rights era, but examples from Charleston and other regions in the South provide insight into Jewish attitudes. In studies conducted throughout the South, scholars found that rabbinical leadership in matters of civil rights varied from place to place based on the size of the city, the degree of cosmopolitanism and liberalism of local communities, the background of the rabbis, direct association with racism, prior participation in other reform activities and the position of the clergy in the South. Individual rabbi's positions on civil rights often depended on the makeup of the congregation as well. Furthermore, vocal and active desegregationists tended to be more prevalent among newcomers to the region than Jewish segregationists who hailed from long-time established southern families.[84] Dinnerstein wrote that "in the South, it is rare for a Jew to support publicly controversial issues . . . while many privately believe the Negro should have equal rights, few came out and said so."[85]

Two Charleston rabbis, who happened to be Northern transplants, spoke out on civil rights issues: Gerald Wolpe and Burton Padoll.[86] Rabbi Gerald Wolpe received ordination at the Jewish Theological Seminary. The Conservative Charleston synagogue Emanu-El recruited him for their rabbi in the mid-1950s. The first rabbi in Charleston (and possibly in all of South Carolina) to speak out against segregation, Wolpe found himself being criticized by some people in his congregation for taking a public stand on civil rights.[87]

In a 1999 interview he revealed that several people in his congregation might be labeled "absolute segregationists, while others might be called emotionally segregationist."[88] Wolpe witnessed the daily conflicts between Blacks and whites in Charleston, including Black boycotts of white businesses. While he denounced segregation, Wolpe thought very carefully about trigger words in his sermon, noting that "the Jewish community was very vulnerable at that time,"[89] and Black customers might boycott their stores."[90]

Frequently interviewed by the local newspaper, radio stations, and out-of-state media groups, Wolpe found himself in an awkward position when asked, "What do you Jews believe about segregation?" Typically, he answered: "I can't tell you what Jews believe about segregation because I haven't interviewed every Jew. But I'll tell you what Judaism thinks about segregation."[91] As a professing Jew, Wolpe could not accept it. Wolpe believed that civil rights demonstrations in Charleston remained relatively quiet compared to other places in the South. When asked why, he responded, "Charleston always had the feeling it was the center of civilization in the middle of [a] raucous society. The veneer of civilization was enough to keep things quiet."[92]

Rabbi Burton Padoll, an Ohio native who attended Hebrew Union College, a Reform Seminary, served a Massachusetts congregation before he was hired at Charleston's Reform synagogue, Kahal Kadosh Beth Elohim. Leading the congregation from 1961 to 1967, Padoll described himself as "messianic regarding integration."[93] His public support for civil rights and his fiery sermons met with trepidation by his synagogue's membership. "The congregation as a whole wasn't ready," he recalled. "There were a handful of people . . . who were really wanting someone to come and guide them and help them in terms of this whole issue of civil rights . . . there were all these people in the middle who really didn't know what to do. They were scared."[94] Padoll, himself an activist, noted that Jewish merchants on King Street "were concerned that if they treated Blacks the way Blacks wanted to be treated, their white customers would abandon them."[95] Moreover, he asserted, "Even in a city where Jews had not experienced anti-Semitism, they worried that they would suffer the consequences if the rabbi started stirring things up. Jewish businesspeople feared they would become targets of the segregationists in the community." Cynically, he added, "As long as Blacks were getting it, that's alright, but they didn't want Jews to be getting it too."[96]

In a sermon delivered on April 14, 1961, Padoll moralized: "Don't any of you ever make the mistake of telling me to stick to the Bible and the prayer book and leave social reform and politics alone—because these are precisely the issues that the Bible and liturgy are about."[97] Padoll recalled that some "would get up and leave in the middle of a sermon on civil rights."[98] Rabbi Padoll eventually curbed his opinionated sermons when it came to preaching civil rights in his congregation. He stopped preaching about civil rights and instead, held discussions after services where members of the congregation could discuss issues with him, "and it started to work."[99]

Padoll remained publicly involved in the movement and joined Black sit-ins at lunch counters in Charleston.[100] In South Carolina, Rabbi Padoll seemed an anomaly. Throughout the state, most rabbis remained silent. As the South Carolina historian of Jewish history Dale Rosengarten, commented, "I think it's safe to say southern Jews kept a low profile during the height of the movement."[101] This should not be surprising considering the difficulties southern rabbis faced. Many rabbis tried to balance a private commitment to racial equality on the one hand, with security concerns for their members on the other.[102]

By the 1990s, South Carolina rabbis, no longer afraid to speak out about race relations, and well-integrated into southern life, became activists in the Upcountry, advocating for a more equitable society. Times had changed and by the 1990s, speaking out on behalf of the problems that continued to plague the Black community became acceptable. Rabbis joined other white community leaders leading efforts to address issues of poverty and Black inequities.

Rabbi Sam Cohon, elected rabbi at Temple B'nai Israel, arrived in Spartanburg in 1994. He promoted interfaith activities and ushered in a period of rabbinical leaders committed to social justice. Following the tragic drive-by murder in Spartanburg of Ernest Rice in 1994, a Black community leader who coached teenage boys in evening basketball games, Rabbi Cohon joined a movement called "Stop the Violence Collaboration." In the aftermath of Rice's death, a broad range of civic, religious, and business leaders organized and discussed what could be done to stem the tide of violence and gang activity in the city.[103] Cohon, an active member of the group, also participated in Spartanburg's Human Relations Committee, an organization that acted as a constructive force in race relations. Jane Turner, a member of that organization noted that Rabbi Cohon "was a catalytic influence on the committee." No rabbi had ever been involved in Spartanburg in that way before.[104]

Cohon led local efforts to support a small, historically Black Baptist church in Williston destroyed by fire in 1995 during a rash of church burnings in South Carolina. The congregation of Temple Beth Israel raised more than $10,000 to rebuild the Black church during a "Sabbath of Support" weekend in 1996.

Cohon's activism on behalf of Spartanburg's Black community marked the beginning of local rabbis speaking out and advocating for social justice, both in Spartanburg and Greenville. While the issues confronting Black people have changed since the civil rights era, the pressing matters of racial inequalities and economic disparities between Blacks and whites continue. Upcountry rabbis have become leaders in outreach efforts to the Black community.

In 2003, Temple B'nai Israel hired Rabbi Yossi Liebowitz to succeed Sam Cohon, who left Spartanburg for a large synagogue in Arizona. Liebowitz, a Reform rabbi, attended Hebrew Union College in Cincinnati. Once in Spartanburg, Liebowitz carried on the tradition of closer relations with the community and expanded on them. Describing himself as "an ambassador of the Jews to the community," he is known for his wit and sharp sense of humor.

Liebowitz forged strong ties with local ministers, both Black and white, who share a commitment to promoting ecumenical relationships and community outreach. He is a frequent speaker at community events including Martin Luther King Unity Celebrations in Spartanburg. In May 2018, Liebowitz organized and led a successful interfaith event called "The Pilgrimage of People" to Washington, DC. The group, made up of white and Black members of local religious organizations, included Jews, Catholics, Methodists, Presbyterians, and Baptists. They discussed the common concerns of people having suffered from oppression and discrimination and the common narratives shared by Jews, Black people, and Native Americans and visited the Holocaust Museum, the Native American Museum, the African American Museum and African American monuments.[105]

Sam Rose, the current rabbi at Greenville's Reform Temple of Israel, reflects the desire of the temple community for their rabbi "to be out and about," according to Melinda Menzer, a synagogue member. A frequent speaker at local churches addressing issues of anti-Semitism, Rose is committed to racial equality and serves on the Diversity, Equity, and Inclusion Stakeholder Team for the Greenville County public schools. Rose helped establish the Greenville County Interfaith Justice Network, which is affiliated with the Direct Action and Research Training Center (DART). Rose attends DART seminars in Selma, Alabama, sponsored by the Union for Reform Judaism (URJ) focusing on integrating issues of racial justice in High Holiday sermons, issues that he also raises with children in his classroom.[106]

While Upcountry Jews and their rabbis kept a low profile during the civil rights era, Jewish manufacturers in the region took actions that created equal opportunities for Blacks in their establishments. The following examples illustrate progressive policies implemented by Jewish firms toward their Black employees, often before civil rights laws passed.

Textile mills in the Upcountry operated under provisions of a 1915 law passed by the South Carolina General Assembly making it "unlawful for any person, firm, or corporation engaged in the business of cotton manufacturing to allow or permit operatives of different races to labor and work together in the same room."[107] Consequently, textile manufacturing became "white work," and Black individuals who found employment at the mills worked "outside" in arduous jobs as loaders and handlers of heavy cotton bales, cleaners, and sweepers.[108]

During the 1940s and 1950s, pressure mounted to provide equal employment opportunity for Black workers. In 1961, President John F. Kennedy signed an executive order calling for equal opportunity employment for companies filling defense contracts. Judith Bainbridge, a Greenville local historian, writes that "it didn't take long for major mills in Greenville who produced for the military to notice." She reports that in a June 1961 meeting of 400 textile executives from the Carolinas, they agreed that "given the executive order, Negro employment on a new basis was coming."[109]

Not content waiting for federal mandates, Black individuals took matters into their own hands. In 1961, a small group of Black residents in Spartanburg demanded that textile mills be integrated. As Betsy Wakefield Teeter noted: "Buoyed by a new federal law that prevented discrimination by US defense contractors," about two dozen Black residents began visiting the personnel departments in Spartanburg County mills in early summer 1961." . . . Assisted by the NAACP, they filed the nation's first discrimination complaints against southern textiles and brought federal scrutiny to most of the major mills in Spartanburg County."[110]

According to historian Timothy Minchin, "Black activism in the area of employment was generated largely by the Civil Rights Act of 1964, which accelerated the racial integration of the textile industry and produced a new confidence among African American workers."[111] The Civil Rights Act of 1964 outlawed discrimination based on race, color, religion, sex, or national origin, and established a permanent Equal Employment Opportunity Commission (EEOC). Consequently, hiring and retention of Black employees increased dramatically. "Between June 1965 and June 1966, South Carolina mills hired five thousand Black workers and, between 1966 and 1967, Greenville mills doubled the numbers of Black men employed and added substantial numbers of Black women."[112] In South Carolina, "less than 5 percent of mill employees were Black in 1964; by 1976, nearly one in three textile workers in the state was Black."[113]

As also seen with labor relations, there is likewise no uniform model for Jewish–Black relationships in textile and apparel manufacturing in the Upcountry. Some Jewish manufacturers faithfully followed South Carolina segregation laws while others disregarded them. However, evidence shows that Jews frequently hired Black people to work "inside" mills and factories and did so before nondiscriminatory civil rights acts were enacted.

Jewish manufacturers had been among the first to integrate their workforce. Irving Abrams of Raycord stated that his garment manufacturing company was the only plant in Spartanburg that hired Black workers in the 1940s and 1950s.[114] When racial integration took place in the 1960s, Abrams reported that it went well, and he promptly promoted a Black woman to head one of the departments. This was highly unusual since Black workers rarely moved into supervisory positions before the Civil Rights Act of 1964. When the company hired Black women in the sewing department, a white sewer told Abrams she would not work next to a Black woman. He replied, "well, you'll just have to go home." Eventually, the white woman adjusted. In the 1960s, Abrams claimed that about twenty percent of his workforce consisted of Black workers.[115]

Shepard Saltzman hired Black workers at the Piedmont Shirt Company in Greenville before the Civil Rights Act of 1964 became law. Departments, however, were segregated according to jobs assigned by race. Black women generally worked as pressers and white women as sewers. Saltzman's new hiring practice met with resistance from certain elements in the community. This included frequent written threats sent to Saltzman by the KKK.[116]

After establishing Maxon Shirts in Greenville, Max Heller declared, "I integrated our work force. We had a sewing factory and I had white people working next to Black people. Never did I have a complaint. Not once. Never." However, a surprise inspection by a state official reminded him he was breaking the law by having whites and Blacks working together. To placate the state inspector, Heller agreed to separate the workers by race and set up temporary work bins between the sewing tables.[117]

By 1966, Heller's company, now a subsidiary of the Oxford Manufacturing Company, relocated to a larger plant and employed 700 workers. Custom dictated that even Christmas parties be segregated. Heller publicly upheld local mores and in December 1960, a local newspaper article pictured Heller presenting awards to several Black female employees. The caption noted that a company party was held "Tuesday night for its Negro employees. . . . A similar party will be held for White employees Friday at the plant."[118] Outwardly, Heller observed the racial mores practiced by South Carolinians. However, in the privacy of his own plant, Heller made some courageous moves regarding integration long before civil rights laws passed. One day he removed the signs that designated white and Black drinking fountains and white and Black bathrooms. White and Black workers, forced to use the same facilities, "did not say a word about it," according to Heller.[119]

The racial segregation that dictated life in the South deeply troubled the Hungarian Jewish refugee and textile manufacturer, Sandor Teszler of Spartanburg. As a Jew who experienced the humiliation of segregation in Europe, forced to wear a yellow star, Teszler could not abide by these racist practices. Recalling Teszler's abhorrence of Jim Crow laws, his friend Oakley Coburn, recalled that Sandor and his wife, Lidia, sat in the "colored" section of the segregated train station in Spartanburg every time they took a train.[120]

Shortly before Teszler opened his plant at Kings Mountain, the mayor of the small town visited Teszler and said, "Hopefully you will have only white people working for you." A few days later, a local Black minister also stopped to see him and said, "I hope you will hire Black people." Teszler responded, "Look Reverend, I belong to the minority in Europe, and you can't tell me about being a minority . . . when the time comes, I will call you and you will recommend to me high school graduates, boys, and girls, from honest families."[121]

Jewish refugees' persecution in Nazi-occupied Europe shaped their response to American racism. Teszler hired both Black and white workers at Shannon Knit. No segregated bathrooms, water fountains, or dining areas existed in his factory. Several years before the Civil Rights Act of 1964, Teszler boasted: "My plant was fully integrated, with thirty percent of my workers being Black. I was probably the first man in the history of North Carolina who had integrated a plant."[122] According to Teszler, "In 1963, people were coming from all over Gastonia and Charlotte to look at the first integrated plant in a real Southern town."[123]

Like his father Sandor, Andrew Teszler was also a refugee who fled Nazi-occupied Europe. The younger Teszler, also sensitive to issues of racial discrimination, operated his textile company as an integrated plant. Stella Coln Lee, a Black employee, "was so happy to get a job and a good salary at Butte Knit," according to her daughter, Brenda Lee Pryce. Pryce recalled that her mom had been working in a tearoom at Converse College when she talked to a textile man who encouraged her to apply for a job at Butte. Hired as a presser, years later she became involved in union activities. She was elected shop steward, a surprising position for a Black woman working in a plant with a predominantly white population. She successfully negotiated with management for better wages. According to Pryce, "Black workers got the wages they wanted at Butte."[124] Even though she represented the union, Pryce claimed that her mother always said positive things about the Teszlers."[125]

Brenda Lee Pryce also worked at Butte Mills in the 1960s and 1970s and noted that Teszler hired Black workers long before the Civil Rights Act of 1964. In a recent interview she observed that "very few Black women worked in manufacturing until Butte opened in Spartanburg. The Teszlers made a positive impact on the community, and they were very community oriented."[126] Pryce does not recall any negative feelings on the part of Black employees toward Andrew Teszler or any of the mill executives, almost all of whom were Jewish. Butte created a welcoming atmosphere for Black employees, and never segregated restrooms or water fountains according to race. Pryce also observed that "for the first time, African American women and men who found employment with Teszler were paid wages that allowed them to purchase homes."[127] Perhaps one of the most important opportunities Teszler provided his Black employees—voter registration drives located in front of the plant—encouraged workers to exercise their right to vote.[128]

Brenda Lee Pryce, who started out in the sewing department at Butte Mills, moved up rapidly, a most unusual occurrence since in most mills Black workers' "main grievance was that they were restricted to lower-paying jobs" once they entered the mills. Minchin reports that "companies hired blacks in increasing numbers but placed them in poorly paid positions and refused to promote them to skilled or management jobs."[129] With a degree from a local business school, Pryce advanced to a position as a keypunch operator. Eventually, she won promotion to department supervisor where she managed both white and Black workers. Her immediate supervisor financially supported her work with the NAACP as well as her civil rights activism.[130]

Pryce became deeply involved in politics and civil rights. After she attended college, Congressman James Clyburn appointed her campaign manager for his congressional run. In 1995, she became the first Black woman from Spartanburg elected to the South Carolina Legislature. She served House District 31 for ten years and returned to Spartanburg, where she remains a political and civil rights activist to this day.

The integration of South Carolina's textile industry was momentous because it employed the largest number of workers and dominated the economy of the Upcountry. Barriers were slowly removed to African American employment in textiles. In 1960, Blacks accounted for only three percent of the workforce.[131] By 1970, Black employees in South Carolina's textile mills, knitting mills, textile dyeing and finishing mills, and yarn and fabric mills totaled 50,428, while white employees totaled 279,994. Black workers thus constituted about fourteen percent of the total workforce in textiles and garment making by 1970.[132]

Those numbers continued to grow over the next decade. The influx of Black workers into textile manufacturing and garment making provided Black people with an unprecedented opportunity to move out of the lowest rungs of the economy and compete more equitably with white workers.

Upcountry Black people made slow, but substantial progress in the 1960s and 1970s. The economic advancements they made because of being hired in textile mills improved opportunities for both Black men and women but did not provide them with political power. In Greenville, it would take a Jewish mayor committed to civil rights to make decisive steps toward giving Black residents a voice in their community.

JEWISH POLITICIANS AND RACE

Looking back on his decision to enter politics in the early 1970s, Heller remarked, "When I ran for public office, I was quite clear what I believed in.

I believed that we needed to be integrated."[133] His political career took place during a critical period in southern history when a new image of the South worked toward improved race relations during the civil rights struggles of the 1970s.[134]

Having achieved great wealth in the garment industry, the Austrian Jewish refugee entered public service because "Greenville has been good to me."[135] He was elected to the Greenville City Council and served from 1969 to 1971, implementing policies that focused on keeping youthful offenders from becoming hardened criminals and addressing the lack of decent housing for the poor. As president of the Greenville Housing Foundation, Heller worked to provide improved housing for families of low and moderate incomes throughout the county. Both issues had a major impact on the Black community.[136]

Heller won many friends among the voters during his first and only term as councilman. Greenville residents appreciated his businesslike approach to city affairs, and his efforts to improve housing and race relations won the support of both white and Black constituents. His work on the city council gained the attention of many community leaders who persuaded him to run for mayor. Running as a Democrat, Heller was elected mayor of Greenville in 1971 with a seventy-percent majority.[137] His election was not an anomaly for the South. According to the 2017 Goldring/Woldenberg Institute of Southern Jewish Life, more than 200 Jewish mayors have served in the South since the late nineteenth century.[138]

Greenvillians' overwhelming support for a Jewish mayor suggests that the community saw Heller's political philosophy in line with its own. The fact that he was Jewish apparently had no significant bearing on his ability to get elected. His political success, as Baker notes, "in a conservative, mid-sized southern city demonstrates that a Jewish politician could serve as a symbol of progress in the Sunbelt South while his status as a Jew could also elicit relatively little attention from voters more concerned with governmental efficiency, growth, and policy than ethnicity [or religion]."[139]

Heller had an opportunity to make a strong statement about civil rights. His first hire as mayor of Greenville was the appointment of a Black secretary, the first at city hall.[140] Heller desegregated all departments and commissions in city government and, working with the police chief, made sure that new hires were based on the qualifications of the candidates and not the color of their skin.[141] Under Heller's leadership, the first full-time Black city employee at the administrative level was hired to head a new department in city government. Herman Greene became the city's first community relations coordinator in 1972.[142]

As mayor, Heller devised strategies to bridge the divide between the Black community and city government. Thomas Faulkner, who worked in the Community Development Office, recalled that Heller convened city council meetings in Black neighborhoods so residents could express their concerns to council members. In 1973, Black residents aired "complaints about substandard housing, sanitation problems and poor street conditions."[143] Responding to these matters, Heller's administration used federal funds to aid low-income neighborhoods and constructed community and recreational centers.[144] Faulkner pointed out that Heller took major steps to bring the community together and led the forces to create and do something about the problems.

Black residents also had the opportunity to lodge complaints by phone with a service known as the "hungry ear." The complaint or suggestion was then passed on to an appropriate department, and volunteers at City Hall followed up with a call to inquire if the problem had been successfully resolved.[145]

While race relations improved in Greenville during Heller's two terms as mayor, critics from the Black community charged that there needed to be "a greater degree of Black participation in the social, political and professional areas."[146] Dr. W. F. Gibson, chairman of the Black Council for Progress and the mayor's Human Relations Committee, said he would "like to see expansion of the appointments of Blacks to the boards and commissions of the city and county, especially those that have been totally closed to Blacks and poor people."[147] He also urged increased employment of Black people in city and county government.

On a visit to Greenville in 1973, Reverend Jesse Jackson, by now a nationally recognized civil rights activist, met with Heller. Impressed with Greenville's overall improvements, he nonetheless pointed out the ways that racism continued to plague the city: "Greenville with its industrial base is uniquely situated in the state and the nation with a comprehensive economic plan. I am personally impressed with its potential. I am equally disturbed by the missed opportunities. Since I left home much has changed in Greenville. I am proud of that, but it is my observation today that while the social relationship between Blacks and whites has changed, the economic relationship has not."[148] Jackson also pointed out the absence of blacks on city or county council. He lamented, "We have no Blacks from Greenville to represent us in Columbia or in Washington."[149] In 1981, Lillian Brock Fleming, one of the first Black women to graduate from Furman University, became the first Black person elected to serve on the Greenville City Council.[150]

Despite criticisms, "Heller maintained the support of many Black Greenvillians, co-chairing a task force on improving race relations in Greenville after his retirement from politics."[151] Several Black community members who admired the efforts Heller had been making in the field of civil rights expressed their appreciation, as one woman did in a June 1988 letter: "I want you to know that I sincerely appreciate everything that you have done for Black people in Greenville city/county and in the state of South Carolina. You are such an inspiration to so many people, especially me. I like the way you think . . . and your devotion to your religion. Above all, your love for people regardless of race . . ., I love you! Mazel Tov!!"[152]

Lottie Gibson, a Black Greenvillian and a civil rights activist, summed up Heller's impact on the community: "Please know that freedom, justice, and equality in Greenville County has come very slowly. Max Heller was a force for trying to bring about some level of equality in Greenville County, being of the Jewish race himself and having felt so many ills and been so disrespected. But because he was a man of justice and stood for freedom and equality, he was able to get a lot done for the city of Greenville."[153] Gibson served on the Greenville County Council and represented District 25 for twenty-five years before her death in 2016.

During Heller's years as mayor he created opportunities for whites and Blacks to convene and discuss problems faced by the Black community. His efforts to improve the lives of Black people reveal a strong commitment to diversity and civil rights. As a Jew who suffered persecution because of race, Heller knew what it felt like to be a victim of segregation and refused to be a part of a system that oppressed others. Greenville had a long way to go in creating a more equitable society, but Heller started the process.

James Talley, the first Black mayor of Spartanburg, served the city nearly a decade and a half before William (Bill) Barnet, the first Jewish mayor, took office in 2002. The Black community took immense pride in having a Black mayor with whom they had grown up. A highly respected teacher and coach who had been raised in the segregated neighborhoods of Spartanburg, Talley understood the problems his neighbors faced. Black residents believed they had power with a Black mayor, and he probably would have won reelection if he had run for a second term.

Bill Barnet became mayor following a grassroots movement and write-in campaign that resulted in a runoff, which he won. He had broad name recognition in Spartanburg because of his work in the community, his generous contributions to civic improvements, and his reputation as a business leader.[154] Nonetheless, several people phoned his campaign organizers stating that they would never vote for a Jew.[155] In a community that historically welcomed Jewish businesspeople, latent anti-Semitism reared its ugly head at the prospect of a Jewish mayor holding the top position in local politics.

Barnet also had to deal with Black peoples' misgivings. Mary Thomas, for example, noted that "Black people were comfortable with Talley. When Bill Barnet won, the Black community did not celebrate. Blacks saw him as another white elite in the community."[156] Mayor Barnet faced issues of serious racial inequalities in Spartanburg and decided to tackle them head-on. One of Barnet's greatest challenges centered around the issue of environmental injustice. Tensions ran high among Black residents of Arkwright, the site of two abandoned textile mills just outside the city. Arkwright, home to two superfund sites (contaminated locations due to hazardous waste), included the former city landfill and an abandoned fertilizer plant, along with a thirty-five-acre chemical plant, and six brownfield sites (contaminated abandoned industrial facilities).[157]

Since the 1970s, Arkwright residents had noted high rates of cancer, birth defects, and mysterious illnesses in their community.[158] Black residents lacked the political power to make their concerns heard until Harold Mitchell, a state legislator, and a Black resident of Arkwright founded Re-Genesis, an environmental justice organization headquartered in Spartanburg.[159] After much frustration and unrelenting pressure from Re-Genesis, the movement to cap the landfill ultimately succeeded, In 1999, as Andrew Gutkowski writes, "the city council—in response to mounting federal and grassroots pressure—officially accepted responsibility for both siting and failing to properly secure the Arkwright landfill and offered to set aside funds to redevelop the area."[160] According to Barnet, "the city spent a lot of time and effort dealing with it and ultimately, after spending eight million dollars, fixed the problem by capping the landfill and cleaning up the surrounding area."[161]

The Arkwright issue notwithstanding, Barnet still had to earn the trust of Black residents. According to Ed Memmott, Barnet's city manager, the mayor slowly established credibility with Black people in Arkwright by delivering what he promised. Barnet attended every meeting held by Black residents and built trust by having frank discussions of their problems.[162] Kathy

Dunleavy who worked as a community liaison for the mayor boasted that, "Barnet was everywhere." He attended services in every Black church and became a familiar face to the congregants. Once a week the mayor's team visited each store owner to understand the issues Black businesspeople faced.[163] He made condolence visits each time a Black family lost a member.[164] Russell Booker, a leading Black educator who considers Barnet his mentor, explains: "Bill believed he was the mayor of all the people in Spartanburg. When he took office, he started talking to people and recognizing what was truly going on in the [Black] community." Booker added that, at first, Barnet faced skepticism but he "gives his time, and his treasures, and the people trust him."[165] Mary Thomas added that "Bill still has some trust issues with several Blacks in the community, but he is consistent and stays the course."[166]

In his early years as mayor, Barnet began drawing up a plan for the city's improvements on the Southside, one of several African American residential areas. In 2010, the C. C. Woodson Community Center, a 27,000-square-foot facility reopened after a $7 million renovation project.[167] The center represents one of the earliest projects Barnet initiated to revitalize Black neighborhoods that had fallen victim to urban renewal in the 1970s.[168]

One of Barnet's many strengths included fundraising. He was a former businessman, board member (Bank of America, the Duke Endowment, and Fleet Boston Financial Group), chair of the Palmetto Business Forum, and past president of the South Carolina Textile Manufacturers.[169] Barnet's connections with major businesses and philanthropic organizations, as well as his personal influence, enabled him to raise millions of dollars for local initiatives.

Furthermore, Barnet contributes his own funds to create programs that benefit the Black community. Believing that education is the single most crucial factor in success, Barnet paid for local Black children to attend the Dartmouth Bound summer program, designed to give participants an in-person experience of daily college life at Dartmouth. The program, open to rising high school seniors, encourages students from underrepresented backgrounds, including students of color, of low income, and who are the first in their families to attend college, to complete college applications. The program also provides students with mock admission interviews and discussions with professors about classes and research possibilities.[170]

Following his mayoral service, Spartanburg city leaders, including the newly elected mayor, Junie White, approached Barnet and asked him to lead the revitalization of the Northside. Barnet launched the most ambitious redevelopment effort ever attempted in the city—the Northside Initiative. The initiative, renamed Northside Development Group (NDG), focuses on a part of town at the site of a former major textile factory, Spartan Mills, home to a large Black population. Barnet led a team of area residents and stakeholders who re-envisioned how a low-income neighborhood with poor infrastructure, high crime, and scant opportunity could achieve upward mobility.[171] Barnet raised millions of dollars for the project, including monies from Jerry Richardson, the founding owner of the NFL Carolina Panthers, and the Duke Endowment.[172]

Mitch Kennedy, assistant city manager and a member of the Black community working with Bill Barnet, created the Northside Voyagers, a group of Black residents responsible for approving proposals introduced by the Northside Development Group. As chair of the development group, Barnet insisted that the undertaking be a community project and not a city project. He was adamant that the people living in the Northside community define and drive the outcomes. Believing that trust is fundamental to the project, Barnet continues to work hand in hand with Northside residents.

Barnet entered a partnership with Purpose-Built Communities, a nonprofit initiative launched in Atlanta to help local leaders across the country create healthy and sustainable urban neighborhoods with the goal of enabling low-income families to break the cycle of poverty. Purpose-Built Communities bring together leaders and community members working to improve equity and opportunity in neighborhoods across the country. Knowledge sharing and collaboration tackle the complex challenge of intergenerational poverty to achieve racial equity, improved health outcomes and upward mobility for residents.

The Northside Development Group and the Northside Voyagers, led by President Tony Thomas, partners with major nonprofits in the city as well as local colleges.[173] The Northside encompasses more than 400 acres and approximately 1,850 people, more than eighty percent of whom are poor and Black people. The NDG purchased abandoned and dilapidated buildings to spur housing and commercial real estate development. Since 2013, more than 450 new or renovated affordable family housing units have been constructed, along with the T. K Gregg Community Center.[174]

The infrastructure of the Northside improvements includes state-of-the-art lighting and streetscapes. Educational facilities like The Cleveland Academy of Leadership (formerly Cleveland Elementary School) is at the heart of the Northside community. In 2019, The Franklin School was established. The school is a $10 million facility, and a model child development center operated by Spartanburg County First Steps in partnership with Wofford College, the University of South Carolina Upstate (USC Upstate), and School District Seven.[175]

Russell Booker, a former superintendent of Spartanburg County School District Seven, and executive director of Spartanburg Academic Movement (SAM), served as the first Black principal in the county after integration in 1970. Having grown up in Spartanburg, he possesses keen insight into the state of race relations in the city. In a recent interview with Booker, he shared some insights into Black perceptions of Bill Barnet. He revealed that "Blacks in the community, especially the Northside residents, trust him, because what he says, he does. There is always skepticism among races but he [Barnet] has always been true to his word. They've seen the successes, and it energized them."[176]

Mary Thomas, however, has a different take on Barnet's leadership: "Bill has done more to raise awareness in his own community of white privilege, and helps whites understand why they should care as well. Having come from a place of comfort and privilege, he advocates for people who never dreamed of access to better living. He is in a position of power to get his friends and colleagues to invest in the Northside, and to understand and change the paradigm." Thomas added that the Northside project is all about advancing racial equity and Bill's work is all about providing a way for individuals to gain a pathway to success.[177]

Unlike Heller, who cites his Jewish identity as the source of his moral and ethical foundation, Barnet is less sanguine about the impact of Judaism on his life. He credits his parents for setting an example of thoughtfulness and respect for others and teaching him to be a contributor to his community.[178]

Following Barnet's service to Spartanburg, Junie White, a Baptist who converted to Judaism, became mayor in 2009 and was reelected in 2013 and 2017. White, born in Gaffney in Spartanburg County to a sharecropping family, served in the US Navy from 1957 to 1961. He married Irene Segal, a Jewish Canadian woman in 1961 and returned to live in Spartanburg. He eventually purchased a gas station and, not knowing anything about cars, hired the best mechanics he could find. In the late 1970s, he converted to Judaism so that he and his four children could be united in worship with their mother. He assumed a leading role in the life of the temple and served many years as president of the congregation. According to Rabbi Yossi Liebowitz,

White makes major financial contributions to the temple and serves as advisor-at-large to rabbis and congregants alike.[179]

White received overwhelming support from the Black community "who loves him," according to Booker. For decades, White has quietly supported the Black community in a myriad of ways. From hiring Black people to work at his gas station beginning in the early 1960s, to supporting Black businesses, White is an exceptional friend of the Black community. Stories of his compassion, caring, and generosity abound in Spartanburg. Always ready to support Black children by purchasing their Little League uniforms and buying bicycles for those whose parents cannot afford them, he even repairs cars free of charge for needy Black community members.[180] White took young men under his wing and taught them the ways of life and how to be successful men.[181] In a newsletter published by Temple B'nai Israel on October 1, 2018, Rabbi Liebowitz once declared Mayor Junie White as mensch of the month.[182]

White may have been considered a mensch by the Jewish community, but not by a sibling, who lamented at their mother's funeral that she died of a broken heart because her son had turned away from Jesus and the Christian faith and now stood with the Jews.[183] The largely Christian community of Spartanburg, however, did not share that feeling and instead lauded White for being one of the community's most generous, caring, and philanthropic members.[184]

Unlike Mayor Barnet, a New York Jew who had no experience with Jim Crow segregation, Mayor White grew up in Spartanburg and attended segregated schools. His understanding of the Black community's problems and his assistance to needy Black people won him their support. White's desire to help lift Black people out of poverty launched the Northside Initiative which he entrusted to Bill Barnet when Barnet left office. White thoroughly supported the former mayor's work and provided city monies to fund the project. His focus on inclusiveness empowered not only Black community members but the LGBTQ community when he defended and marched in a Gay Pride celebration, stating, "We have laws that protect against racial discrimination, and it is time to protect those of different sexual orientation."[185]

CONCLUSION

Black-Jewish relations in the Upcountry benefitted from several factors: Black people comprised a minority population, unlike the Lowcountry, with historical Black population majorities. Jewish merchants established good relations with their Black clientele, offering them credit and allowing them to use changing rooms to try on clothing. Black people had more employment opportunities as Jewish manufacturers hired Black workers long before integration was an established fact. Finally, Jewish political leadership in Upcountry cities instilled values of racial equity in city hiring and promoted dialogue between whites and Blacks in their communities.

Jewish mayors in the Upcountry took a public stand against segregation and the economic obstacles faced by Black residents by creating programs that helped lift Black people out of poverty. Bill Barnet launched Northside Development Group, a multifaceted program creating middle-class housing, recreation centers, schools, and most importantly, leadership from the Black community to decide their future. These efforts are ongoing, but the legacy of Jewish leaders in Spartanburg and Greenville shifted the predominant white power structure narrative to include the voice of Black residents.

CHAPTER 9

The Jewish Role in a New Economy

Jewish retail business influence reached a peak in the 1950s and 1960s and then severely declined in the following decades. Jews had dominated retail business throughout the Upcountry, providing their clientele with everything from men's and women's clothing to fur coats and army surplus goods. While Jewish family-owned businesses dwindled, a younger generation of Jewish entrepreneurs created innovative means of retail marketing, anticipating today's one-price chain stores.

At about the same time, however, Jewish involvement in politics, culminating in the election of Jewish mayors in both Greenville and Spartanburg, led to a revitalization of both cities and recruiting efforts that resulted in the relocation of international companies to the Upcountry at a time when textile and clothing manufacturing was in decline.

THE DECLINE OF JEWISH RETAIL BUSINESS

The advent of shopping malls built on the outskirts of America's cities beginning in the 1960s resulted in deteriorating main streets once home to bustling business districts. City centers had been at the heart of Jewish merchant life, and along with the passing and retirement of first- and second-generation Jewish businesspeople, and the proclivity of their descendants to enter professions, Jewish-owned retail stores became rare.

Jewish retail businesses prospered in the Upcountry until the late 1960s, while only a small number persisted into the late twentieth century. At the mid-century peak, Jews owned and operated nearly sixty percent of Spartanburg's downtown businesses.[1] Only a handful of these businesses like Kosch & Gray Jewelers, Jack's Economy Store, and Prices' Store for Men in Spartanburg persisted into the twenty-first century.

Jewish businesses continued to be ubiquitous in small towns throughout the Upcountry where Main Street retailers made up the heart of the shopping district. Jewish merchants in small towns tended to prosper for a longer period of time because they were often the only retail stores with no competing

Price's Clothing Store, Main St. Celebrating 103 years.

shopping malls existing nearby. In Easley, Sarlins Department Store and Fedders Fashions provided merchandise to the small community. Fedders had ten employees, some of whom worked there for forty-four years until the store closed in 1984.[2] In Chesnee, Jeanette Finkelstein continued to operate the women's store, opened by her father in the 1920s, into the 2000s. Froms Department Store in Union, founded in 1904, continued a brisk business from one generation to the next until 1974; and in 1952, another family member opened Harry From's Ladies Shop that remained in business until 2004.[3] The Rosenberg Mercantile Company, an Abbeville business firm recognized as one of the oldest men's clothing stores in the Carolinas, acted as the main purveyor of goods in Abbeville celebrating its 100th anniversary in October 1972.[4] Herby Rosenberg, a descendent of the Rosenberg family, owned and operated retail liquor stores in Abbeville and Greenwood for forty years. In the early 2000s he sold the Abbeville business to a new owner who continues operating the liquor store under the Rosenberg name.[5]

The 1960s and 1970s marked the last hurrah for most Jewish-owned retail businesses in Spartanburg and Greenville. While they continued to do well, their days were numbered. In Greenville, like Spartanburg, only a few Jewish-owned retail businesses survived into the late twentieth and early twenty-first centuries. Among those were Carl Proser's Cancellation Shoe Mart that closed in 1996, and Sedran's Fur Shop that prospered for more than sixty years until 2015, when Stan and his wife, May, retired. Today, Zaglin's army and navy store in Greenville operated by Jeffrey Zaglin, continues the business his father started when he returned home to Greenville after serving in World War II.

As with most American cities, downtown businesses began shifting to the outskirts of town with the construction of shopping malls stripping city centers of once-vibrant retail districts. By 1960, 4,500 malls had been built in the United States and by 1975, 30,000 malls had been built,[6] Only a few Jewish businesses successfully relocated to shopping centers and malls. With an automobile in almost every driveway, shoppers were no longer restricted to downtown stores and could easily reach newly built malls located on the outskirts of town. While most Jewish merchants went out of business, an occasional large department store expanded to nearby towns. Meyers-Arnold, the Jewish owned department store located on Main Street in Greenville since the 1910s, continued operating successfully with eight stores throughout the Carolinas and Georgia. In the 1970s they added a location at Westgate Mall in Spartanburg and later sold out to Upton's Department Store in the late 1980s.[7]

Several Jewish businesses moved away from the area, unable to compete with department stores operating in newly constructed shopping malls. Susan and Larry Abelkop of Spartanburg moved the family business, Fox's, several times to make room for urban development. Larry's father had purchased the shop on North Church Street in the 1930s, but the store was forced to move in 1966 along with ten other businesses to make room for a city-built parking lot.

Not all Jewish-owned businesses specialized in retail. Several businesspeople dealt with scrap metals including the Yoffe and Tanenbaum families. In 1950, the two families opened Arrow Steel Products in Spartanburg. What started as a scrap yard eventually became a steel company as the family began handling "new" steel, a spin-off from scrap and salvage. According to Rick Tanenbaum who eventually managed the company, Arrow Steel was a family affair. His uncle started the business, and his father joined it in 1954. His aunt, Thelma Yoffe, did the bookkeeping, and a cousin, Michael Yoffe, joined the family business when he returned from serving in the US Air Force from 1968 to 1975. Rick's brother, Saul, joined the company for a short while and worked in the family business sporadically until he went to college. Saul rejoined Arrow Steel about the time it was purchasing more new steel and entering the field of fabrication. Rick Tanenbaum became the sole owner following the deaths of elderly family members. He operated the company until his retirement in 2020, selling it to a steel company from North Carolina.[8]

Marion Finke Feinstein's dance studio operating since 1946,[9] achieved tremendous expansion in the 1960s.[10] As her studio attracted ever increasing numbers of students, she moved to a larger facility and established Miss Marion's School of Dance on Reidville Road in Spartanburg's west end. Over the years she taught thousands of students, including actors Celia Weston and Andie McDowell.[11]

Feinstein hired a staff of teachers who taught tap, modern jazz, ballet, pointe, clogging, and gymnastics. Her three daughters and four granddaughters followed in her footsteps and also became dancers. The dance studio, one of the largest and most successful in the Upcountry, prospers today, under the management of Marion's daughter, Lori Feinstein Axelrod.[12]

Jack Steinberg, a retired lieutenant colonel in the US Air Force Reserve, and a University of Kentucky graduate, managed the Better Beer Company before establishing Steinberg and Associates Insurance Company in 1969. Jack's son, Hank Steinberg, is now the president of Steinberg and Associates, an insurance brokerage that offers employee health insurance, estate planning and private client services to midsize businesses and individuals. Likewise, at a time when no Jewish insurance companies operated in Greenville, William Rosenfeld, of Asheville, North Carolina, relocated there and opened the William Rosenfeld Insurance Company in the 1930s. After merging with other family members, the firm continues operating today under the name Rosenfield-Einstein Associates.[13]

Jewish business enterprises in the mid-to-late twentieth century continued to be family operated. Similar to the familial networks that functioned in the late nineteenth and early twentieth centuries, these linkages remained strong among Jews and defined the growth and persistence of business practices.

INNOVATIONS IN RETAIL MARKETING

While Jewish-owned businesses were slowly declining in the Upcountry, one individual, Henry Jacobs of Spartanburg, redefined innovation in marketing

and retail business in the early 1960s. One of the most successful Jewish businesspeople in the Upcountry in the late twentieth century, Henry Jacobs had
been raised in Spartanburg. His grandfather, Abe Morris, came to the city
in 1914 becoming part owner of the Standard Cloak Company, a store that
specialized in lingerie and women's clothing. Henry's mother, Sylvia, acted
as a buyer for the company and made frequent trips to New York City with
her father.[14] Jacobs graduated from Spartanburg High School, and earned
a degree in business administration from Babson College in Massachusetts.
After serving in the US Navy during the Korean War, he married Susan
Cohen of Fall River, Massachusetts. The couple eventually returned to Spartanburg where Henry joined the family business.[15] Eventually, Jacobs took
over the management of the Standard and expanded its home base in Spartanburg to a chain of twelve stores throughout the Upcountry and Georgia.

In August 1984, Jacobs established One Price Clothing, a retail business
specializing in women's and children's clothing and accessories. The business
was part of a growing number of off-price retailers selling deeply discounted
clothing bought from manufacturers faced with overproduction, canceled
orders, or liquidated items. One Price Clothing was one of the earliest businesses of its kind. "There's no sticker shock," explained Jacobs, "because
everything is priced the same . . . $6.00." With continued expansion, by 1996
the company had grown to 645 stores in twenty-seven states, and twenty-
nine in Puerto Rico.[16] Jacobs' innovation in retailing was commented on in
the business section of a Paris newspaper: "One Price is revolutionizing the
US retail market, and other retailers have paid tribute to the chain's success
by opening their own version of limited price stores."[17]

Three years after the store opened, One Price Clothing's common stock
was introduced in the NASDAQ National Market System.[18] The company
received praise year after year for its business success. In 1987, *The Charlotte
Observer* announced that One Price Clothing Chain performed highest among
new Carolina offerings.[19] *Business Week* listed the company as one of the
top five small new corporations in the country and it ranked eighth in *Forbes
Magazine's* list of the "200 Best Small Companies in America" in 1989. The
list ranked companies with sales between $5 million and $350 million by their
five-year average return on equity, a measure of profitability.[20]

Reflecting Jewish values of philanthropy, Henry and Susan Jacobs contributed immeasurably to the community of Spartanburg, the University of
South Carolina Upstate, and Temple B'nai Israel, where they were active
members. In 1993, USC Upstate recognized the Jacobs with Founders Day

Service awards for their commitment to improving education and health care and funding scholarships for minority students.[21]

JEWISH BUSINESS AND POLITICAL LEADERSHIP

Jewish business leaders frequently became politically involved in their communities. As successful businesspeople, they were highly visible and respected by community members. Throughout the South and well beyond, Jews engaged in political activities as legislators, senators, and public officials.

Jewish political involvement in South Carolina has a long history dating back to Francis Salvador, elected to the First Provisional Congress of South Carolina in 1774.[22] After World War II Jewish political engagement increased, and Jews from every region of the state, male and female, were elected to the state legislature.[23]

Locally, Matthew Poliakoff of Spartanburg was elected to the South Carolina House of Representatives in 1944 and served seven terms as a Democrat. Known as a champion of the working class, he cosponsored a minimum wage and maximum hour bill and another bill creating a Labor Relations Board.[24] Poliakoff focused on improving the lives of mill workers and mill villages. He authored legislation to reduce hazardous waste into the streams, and legislation that required mills to provide water and sewage in the mill villages and sanitary facilities in the factories.[25] Sylvia Dreyfus, a New York native, was the second Jewish Democrat from the Upcountry to serve in the South Carolina House of Representatives from 1976 to 1978. A progressive and a feminist, Dreyfus supported a number of bills considered unpopular by the majority of voters in her district. In 1977 she opposed a prayer bill arguing that "prayers belong in the home rather than in public schools."[26] In the heat of debate over the bill, Dreyfus suffered verbal attacks by some of the advocates of the bill who asked if she believed in God.[27]

An ardent feminist, Dreyfus not only supported the Equal Rights Amendment, but held discussions in her home focused on sexism in the Bible.[28] In 1978 Dreyfus issued an amendment aimed at encouraging The Citadel to admit women into its Corps of Cadets. It failed, but she succeeded in bringing the issue to a public forum.[29] Viewed as too liberal by many of her constituents, Dreyfus served only one term in the South Carolina legislature.

Jews served as mayors in South Carolina as early as 1833, when Mordecai DeLeon became mayor of Columbia. Three other Jews also served as mayors of the capital city. Jews became mayors in Georgetown, Kingstree, Eutawville, Latta, Florence, Lake City, Darlington, Manning, Sumter,

Greenville, and Spartanburg.[30] With a total of nineteen Jewish mayors, South Carolina trailed behind other southern states who elected Jews to manage their towns and cities. Texas leads with fifty-two Jewish mayors, followed by Florida, Mississippi, and North Carolina, all with twenty or more Jewish mayors since the nineteenth century.[31]

With the South having had surprisingly high numbers of Jewish mayors, it is worth pondering how Jews were elected in a relatively conservative region with large numbers of southern Baptists also elected. Most Jews in the South from the late nineteenth to the mid-twentieth century were business-people who owned shops on "main street." Thus, they were well-known in the community. Further, many Jewish businesspeople engaged in civic life and joined fraternal and secular organizations that brought them into con-tact with other businesspeople and professionals. Jacob Morrow-Spitzer, a PhD candidate, notes that Jews "generally had the support of community elites," because "their mercantile interests allied them with the southern mid-dle class."[32] The business and entrepreneurial success of Jews was admired by the community in an era when business savvy often translated into lead-ership and success.

Jewish businesspeople had the distinction of leading the largest cities in the Upcountry: in Greenville Max Heller, and in Spartanburg, Bill Barnett and Junie White. Heller and Barnet were visionaries who saw beyond the immediate problems plaguing Greenville and Spartanburg. Working with their local chambers of commerce, city leaders, and members of the Black community, Heller and Barnet enlisted the best and brightest to help solve the problems that plagued their cities through federal grants, donations, and public-private partnerships. Junie White, grew up in Spartanburg and under-stood the problems of race and inequality in the city. Individually, he men-tored Black men and supported the Black community with his own personal resources.

Max Heller

Max Heller understood the many challenges that Greenville faced in the 1970s. After serving on City Council from 1969–1971, Heller was elected the Democratic mayor of Greenville in 1971 with a seventy-percent majority.[33] As did other Jewish businessmen elected mayors in the 1970s including Mutt Evans serving Durham, North Carolina from 1951 to 1963, and Sam Massell, mayor of Atlanta from 1970 to 1974, Heller faced challenges of economic decline, civil rights, crime, and deteriorating downtowns.[34]

Heller's leadership focused initially on the decline of downtown Greenville. Serving at an especially critical time in the city's history, Main Street had seriously deteriorated since the late 1950s as shopping malls on the outskirts of the city rendered downtown obsolete. Main Street stores closed and boarded up, and streets became deserted. Vagrants sought refuge in the abandoned Poinsett Hotel, once a downtown landmark.[35]

Under the direction of Heller and the leadership of local businesspeople, a "Total Development Plan" was initiated by the chamber of commerce in 1976. The cornerstone of Main Street's renewal included plans for a $30 million downtown hotel, office buildings, a convention center and city commons project, financed jointly by the city and private business. Heller promoted public-private partnerships for downtown's benefit.[36]

In late 1978, Greenville secured a federal Urban Development Action Grant for $7.4 million, one of the first in the nation.[37] With these funds, the city acquired land on North Main Street, and with the active involvement of leading businesspeople, the new hotel and convention center started to take shape. The Hyatt Hotel Corporation initially refused to build a hotel on Main Street, citing the size of Greenville as a reason not to invest. Not content with that answer, Heller did a little research and discovered that the mother of Hyatt's CEO came from the same Polish town as his mother. Heller paid a visit to Jay Pritzker at Hyatt corporate headquarters in Chicago to inform him of their important old-world connection. Their shared Jewish background with mothers from the same European shtetl sealed the deal. Hyatt agreed to build the 330-room Regency Hotel, and the city approved a convention center atrium and a five-story office building.[38]

Working closely with the Greenville Chamber of Commerce, Heller shaped "Vision 2005," which called for ambitious goals including a new performing arts center, a year-round school for the arts, a research park, and a coliseum. With a $10 million pledge from the Peace family, owners of *The Greenville News,* community support was kindled for building a cultural center at the heart of the city. Another $42 million was raised and the Peace Center for the Performing Arts was built, a stunning architectural structure.

During his tenure as mayor, Heller made major improvements to the physical features of Main Street and it began to take the shape of a European village with green spaces, flower planters, and areas for outdoor dining, similar to what Heller experienced growing up in Austria.[39]

Heller's major challenge, however, was the economy. In the 1970s, Upcountry centers of the textile industry faced new challenges and environmental controls, worldwide inflation, and foreign imports. Spartanburg and Green-ville leaders refused to remain passive while the economic engine driving the Upcountry's well-being for more than one hundred years worsened. In an era of growing global markets, Heller embraced the idea of courting inter-national firms to establish their companies in Greenville.

Business leaders in both cities tackled the economic downturn in the textile industry by enticing major businesses and industries to relocate to the Upcountry.[40] Heller created the South Carolina Research Authority and worked closely with Governor Richard Riley to bring new business and industry to the Greenville area.

Continuing a pro-business tradition that evolved after World War II, the Southern historian Lacy Ford maintains that South Carolina ramped up its efforts to attract business and manufacturing to the state. He notes that "state policy makers and gubernatorial administrations passed bipartisan legislative support to bring impressive levels of outside investment to the state."[41] Moreover, South Carolina had passed a right-to-work law in 1954, had a favorable tax and regulatory climate, and a system of state financial incentives including relatively cheap industrial sites developed largely at state expense.[42] South Carolina experienced remarkable growth as new manufac-turing jobs came from outside the original cotton-textile field in related industries such as chemicals and synthetic fibers.[43]

The most significant business deal that Heller achieved as mayor occurred in 1975, when the French tire giant Michelin, selected Greenville for its first American plant. Heller worked tirelessly to convince Michelin to invest in Greenville. Both he and the governor made several trips to France where they lauded the excellent training that Greenville Technical College would pro-vide the local workforce. Furthermore, the state agreed to cover the cost of sending future upper management to France to learn the business and train at headquarters.[44]

Michelin ultimately built plants in Greenville, Anderson, Lexington, and Spartanburg. It also built a test facility for research and development in Laurens. To consolidate operations and manufacturing, Michelin made the decision to relocate its North American headquarters from New York to Greenville.[45] This was a remarkable achievement for Heller and Greenville, as Michelin became the cornerstone of manufacturing and business devel-opment along the I-85 corridor extending from Charlotte to Atlanta.

Heller and the business leadership of Greenville joined Spartanburg busi-ness leaders and the Spartanburg Chamber of Commerce, chaired by Richard

Tukey, to entice international companies to the Upcountry. Spartanburg had already created economic ties with Germany, Switzerland, and Italy; and when the 1992 announcement that BMW would locate its first-ever manufacturing facility outside of Germany in Spartanburg County, it was lauded as "South Carolina's biggest economic victory."[46] Following years of massive lobbying by governors, senators, public officials, business elites, and German manufacturers operating in Spartanburg, BMW's choice of location became a powerful symbol of faith in the new Spartanburg, the rapid internationalization of the community, the global perspective of its leadership, and the quality and quantity of its workers.[47]

According to Harvard economics professor Rosabeth Moss Kanter, "By systematically upgrading their ability to meet the needs of manufacturers," Greenville (and neighboring Spartanburg)[48] were becoming a vital component of a global economy.[49] James Cobb, agrees, noting that by the end of the 1970s South Carolina was the acknowledged pioneer in international recruiting. The state drew some forty percent of its annual increase in investment capital from outside the country. For the first time, annual industrial recruitment reached the one-billion-dollar mark.[50]

While Heller was courting international firms for Greenville, Bill Barnet, another Jewish business leader and future mayor of Spartanburg, was managing his family's business relocation to the Upcountry. William Barnet & Sons, an Upstate New York Jewish-owned business known for its innovations in textiles, soon became a player in the global market.

William (Bill) Barnet

Long before recycling products were seen as both ecofriendly and potentially profitable, the Barnet family made a business out of it. William Barnet & Son stood out as one of the more forward-looking corporations to relocate to the Upcountry in the 1960s. The history of the company began in the mid-nineteenth century when Meyer Barnet, a German Jew, escaped the political revolutions taking place in the German states and immigrated to the United States. Barnet and his family made their new home in central New York, where he earned a living as a peddler. From peddling to founding a shoddy business in 1898,[51] the family purchased scraps from various mills, recycled, reclaimed them, and then sorted, dyed, and processed them for resale.[52]

With the advent of synthetics at the end of World War II, William Barnet & Son began moving in new directions as the firm transacted business with southern textile mills. With the growth of synthetics in textiles, the company developed contacts with various producers and customers in southern states.

In the early 1960s, according to third-generation William "Bill" Barnet, the company expanded to the South because "the textile business goes where labor is abundant and competitive, where there are fewer environmental restrictions, and wherever logistics, like transportation, make it easier to make textiles."[53] Another third-generation family member, Tom Barnet, associated with the business for a short time, elaborated on the family's reasons for moving south, remarking that "the South was energy efficient, had an untapped labor supply, a more receptive business climate than the northern states, and greater supplies of raw materials."[54]

The South offered cheap labor and abundant energy, and the major synthetic chemical companies producing nylon, polyester, and rayon resided in the South. Tom Barnet also noted that, in addition to access to raw materials, cheaper transportation costs attracted relocation to South Carolina.[55]

The company's first move to the South occurred in 1960 when it purchased a hosiery mill in Tryon, North Carolina, just over the South Carolina state line, transforming it into a recycling plant which processed natural and synthetic fibers.[56] A trailblazer in breaking down gender and race barriers in the workplace, Bill Barnet noted that the company hired women for jobs that typically only men performed, such as running machinery, operating forklifts, and other better paying jobs. It also hired Black workers to do the same jobs as white workers. The latter policy proved controversial since the locals lived in and supported a segregated society.[57] Nonetheless, the northern-based company persisted in providing a nondiscriminatory work environment.

In 1971, Bill Barnet moved to Spartanburg and became president of Barnet Southern to distinguish it from William Barnet & Son in the North. Barnet, who earned bachelor's and master's degrees from Dartmouth, led the expansion of the company from its flagship plant in Arcadia in Spartanburg County, to plants in Kinston, Cartersville, and Milledgeville, Georgia.[58] In 1986 Barnet acquired the family business and became the sole owner.

The company entered the worldwide market in 1990 with the purchase of Cherotan, an operation headquartered in Aachen, Germany, and a secondary facility located across the Belgian border. With this purchase, "Barnet Europe" was born with additional plants in Germany and Italy. The company then turned to Asia and started doing business in China, India, and Hong Kong, and expanded into Central America, South America, Australia, and Africa. The flagship company, still located in Spartanburg, continued employing hundreds of local residents. By the 1990s, nearly 1,400 local people worked for the company.[59]

Barnet operated the corporation until 2001 when he sold it to a management team, divesting himself of the business. The company, although no longer operated by the Barnet family, still operates under the name William Barnet & Son, and serves a world market of fibers, polymers, and yarns to more than seventy countries worldwide. In March 2023, the company will be 125 years old and exemplifies the rise of a Jewish immigrant who started life in America as a peddler and rose to the head of a company, that under the leadership of his descendants, became a worldwide player in the global economy.

Back in Greenville, Heller's contributions to the diversification of industry and recruitment of foreign companies to the Upcountry during his years as mayor resulted in more than 65,000 new jobs created in Greenville County. Subsequent to his terms as mayor, Heller's appointment to chair the State Development Board occurred following a lost bid for Congress in 1986. Perhaps it was serendipitous for South Carolina that Heller did not make it to congress, for the economic development that ensued, in large part, was a result of Heller's initiatives working as chair of the State Development Board, an appointment made by the governor after Heller's congressional loss.

In his bid for Congress, Heller had been well ahead of the Republican candidate, Carroll Campbell, fifty-one percent to twenty-nine percent.[60] But Campbell's campaign manager, Lee Atwater, future chair of the Republican National Committee, found the way to victory was to remind the electorate that Heller was an immigrant and a Jew.[61] Furthermore, Don Sprouse, an independent candidate who petitioned his way onto the ballot, stated that "everyone who goes to Congress should be a Christian."[62] He asked the voters, "can you vote for a foreign-born Jew who does not accept Jesus Christ as his personal savior?"[63] Heller's numbers started dropping. He lost the election, but graciously stated, "I don't think Campbell was anti-Semitic, but he used whatever was available." Heller received numerous letters from local residents, sickened by the religious bigotry displayed in the campaign.[64]

Heller's run for congress reveals a race laden with anti-Semitism, but it was not the only episode of anti-Semitism he faced while mayor. In 1975, in an attempt to bring people together and foster a more cohesive city, Heller created the mayor's prayer breakfast, open to all denominations and all races. With the announcement of an interfaith dialogue, demonstrators from the conservative evangelistic Bob Jones University marched with placards stating, "How can you follow a man who doesn't believe in Christ," and referred to Heller as "The devil in sheep's clothing." Undaunted, Heller continued his mayor's prayer breakfasts year after year.[65] Heller experienced other silent forms of anti-Semitism in Greenville. In the 1960s, the private Poinsett Club's membership policies prohibited Jews from joining. A similar exclusion that existed in Spartanburg kept Jews out of the Piedmont Club. In 1968, Heller declined the invitation to a dinner honoring South Carolina Governor Robert McNair at the Poinsett Club, stating "people of my faith are not welcome as members and because of this I have declined invitations to any affairs taking place there."[66] While Heller had the support and backing of a majority of Greenvillians, these anti-Semitic episodes reveal an unease among many members of the community uncomfortable with a Jewish mayor. Similarly, when Bill Barnet was nominated for mayor in Spartanburg, episodes of anti-Semitism surfaced there as well.

Recognized as a major business leader who successfully led domestic and international companies, Barnet became a major player in Spartanburg politics when, in 2001, he was elected mayor following a write-in campaign engineered by a grassroots movement. Barnet was widely recognized in the community for his generous contributions to civic improvements, and his reputation as a business leader.[67] Nonetheless, several community members made anti-Semitic comments to campaign organizers stating that they would never vote for a Jew.[68]

As mayor, Barnet committed himself to several vital initiatives. A large part of his focus involved encouraging investment and the retention of business, both domestic and international. As did Heller, he worked closely with the chamber of commerce and local investors to establish, among others, the corporate headquarters of Extended Stay Hotels; QS/1, a health care and governmental software technology company; and the Edward Via College of Osteopathic Medicine (VCOM). He also led a capital campaign to establish the George Dean Johnson Jr. College of Business and Economics downtown as an expression of USC Upstate's metropolitan mission.

In addition to closing the Arkwright site (discussed in chapter 8), an environmental hazard that affected hundreds of Northside residents, Barnet worked on building the South Church Street retail center. While Spartanburg's Main Street was not as grim as Greenville's when Heller took office, Barnet redesigned Morgan Square at the center of downtown as part of a new vision for the central business district adding parking garages to provide desperately needed downtown parking.

Committed to improving educational opportunities through excellent schools, Barnet was the driving force behind the Franklin School, a $10 million early childhood education learning center in the heart of the impoverished and racially segregated Northside. Since his retirement from politics, Barnet continues his work with a team of "resident navigators" to redesign the poor neighborhoods of the Northside into a Purpose-Built Community, also discussed in chapter 8.

Heller and Barnet provide two distinct, yet similar models of leadership in the Upcountry. Heller became mayor in 1971, a time when the textile industry was seriously declining in the Upcountry. As a result, he pursued industrial diversification and actively recruited companies from all over the world to South Carolina. He chaired the State Development Board for five years, from 1979 to 1984, and according to Richard Riley, "It was the most important appointment I made as governor."[69]

Heller's vision for Main Street took shape with his leadership and the public-private partnerships he nurtured. With the help of prominent city fathers like Charlie Daniel, Alester Furman, Roger Peace, Tommy Wyche, the Hipps and Timmons families, and others, Heller revitalized Greenville's downtown. His pathbreaking improvements continue with his successor, Mayor Knox White.

Bill Barnet, who became mayor in 2001, did not face the same severely declining textile industry as did Heller. As noted earlier, his company was already leading the turnaround with its global expansion. Neither did he inherit a rapidly deteriorating downtown as did Heller. Nonetheless he faced equally difficult challenges. Spartanburg had been racially divided as a result of residential segregation and the environmental hazards in the predominantly Black neighborhood of Arkwright (discussed in chapter 8). Barnet met the challenge head-on and worked with the leadership of Re-Genesis to end the environmental crisis in the Black community.

Following his two terms as mayor, Barnet pursued public-private partnerships launching a massive revitalization of Spartanburg's Northside, a largely Black neighborhood characterized by poverty, crime, and inadequate housing. Today, the Northside is a growing community of newly built affordable and market-rate homes, providing economic, social, recreational, and educational opportunities for its residents.

Both Heller and Barnet were visionaries who committed themselves to urban revitalization benefitting all citizens, Black and white. Both mayors were recognized for their business as well as civic accomplishments. A few of

Main St. Greenville's bronze sculpture of Mayor Max Heller, dedicated by a grateful community. Photo by Ben Stockwell.

Heller's most notable awards and recognitions include his appointment as a trustee at Furman University where he was also honored with an honorary doctor of laws in 1975; the Bell Tower Award for service and leadership in 1998, and the Heller Service Corps named in honor of him and his wife, Trude, who also received an honorary degree from Furman in 1999. Heller received honorary degrees from Clemson and Winthrop Universities as well. The Jewish Historical Society of South Carolina honored Max and Trude with the Order of the Jewish Palmetto in April 2007.

The recipient of multiple awards for his community leadership and public service, Barnet received the Drummond Award for Statesmanship in April 2007.[70] In 2010, the Kiwanis Club honored Barnet as Citizen of the Year for his exceptional contributions to Spartanburg through civic engagement and leadership in government, commerce, and philanthropy.[71] Barnet's reputation as a leader and visionary is reflected in his appointment as a Converse College trustee, an honorary doctorate awardee of the University of South

Carolina, a member of the board of Duke Energy and the Palmetto Institute, a nonprofit think tank aimed at bolstering per capita income in South Carolina.

Barnet's accomplishments are recognized beyond the local community, as he serves as a trustee for the Duke Endowment and a member of the board of directors of Fleet Boston Financial Group and the Bank of America. Barnet sums up his commitment to civic service and philanthropy stating, "It is good for those of us who have been given much to give back."[72] Consequently, Barnet and his wife, Valerie Manatis Barnet, have given generously from their personal resources to the community of Spartanburg.

Barnet practices the values of Judaism passed along to him by his German-Jewish parents including sharing his substantial resources as well as his time and talents with those in need around him. Heller, a European Jewish immigrant, was raised in an Orthodox home, and retained a strong identity as a Jew, even conversing in Yiddish with his wife, Trude. As a member of Beth Israel, he served as president of the congregation, led a Zionist organization and was active in the National Conference of Christians and Jews.[73] According to Rabbi Julie Anne Kozlow of Congregation Beth Israel, "Heller was a pillar of the synagogue. That Heller chose to live in the shadow of his temple speaks volumes about the man and the family he raised."[74] It was said that Heller "lived his religion in everyday life."[75]

Max Heller's service to the community and his desire to make Greenville a better place was recognized officially when he turned ninety years old in May 2009. A bronze sculpture and storyboards were unveiled in his honor on Main Street. Known as the Max Heller Legacy Plaza, his life is memorialized with photographs and interpretive panels, from his escape from Nazism to America, to his business life and public service.

CONCLUSION

After riding the crest of textile production for nearly a century, the Upcountry was threatened with the demise of their cash cow. Local chambers of commerce worked with city and county leaders and adopted a policy of international recruitment, resulting in the establishment of hundreds of foreign companies. Jewish mayors were instrumental in bringing global companies to the Upcountry and worked hand in hand with community leaders to achieve that goal.

South Carolina was not the only state to change the direction of its economic history. Numerous southern states suffering from a drop in textile manufacturing turned to European and Asian recruiting, offering similar tax incentives as South Carolina an and a continued commitment to an open shop. Following the Upcountry's lead in recruiting Michelin North America, BMW Manufacturing Company and others in Upcountry South Carolina, the state of Alabama successfully courted Mercedes in the 1970s; Nissan and Volkswagen established plants in Tennessee in 1983 and 2011, and Kia in Georgia in 1984. Mercedes-Benz and Porsche established North American headquarters in Georgia in the early 2000s. By 2020, the South claimed nearly half the annual foreign direct investment in the United States, but "the acknowledged pioneer in international recruiting effort was South Carolina."[76]

The Upcountry was built on leadership. From the textile industrialists of the late nineteenth and early twentieth century to the Jewish entrepreneurs who established textile and clothing manufacturing well into the twentieth century, business leadership provided growth and vision. The civic leadership provided by Jewish mayors combined business savvy with political management and direction.

For the Jewish merchants, whose retail lives largely came to an end in the late twentieth century, their transition to a new economy was realized through their children and grandchildren who no longer relied on retail trade to make a living. Rather, these were college-educated Jews of a new era who became doctors, dentists, attorneys, educators, and upper-level managers. They too, would find a future in the modern economy of Upcountry South Carolina.

Epilogue

Jews have always made up a small minority of the population of the Upcountry (now referred to as "the Upstate"), but their impact on business and manufacturing far outweigh their numbers. Unlike their predecessors who arrived with a peddler's pack on their back, Jews now arrive carrying briefcases.

For nearly a century in upstate South Carolina, Jewish entrepreneurs and businesspeople dominated clothing manufacturing and retail trade. However, the changing nature of the textile industry represented one of the many changes transforming the region beginning in the mid-twentieth century affecting Jews equally with native-born manufacturers.

The dramatic decline in the textile and garment industries forced community leaders to seek industrial diversification. Aggressive recruiting conducted by upstate community leaders and local chambers of commerce laid the foundation for the establishment of international firms such as BMW and Michelin. By the early 1970s, economic historian Marko Maunula reports that "more than fifty percent of all international investment took place in the Greenville-Spartanburg area, making it the uncontested leader in foreign direct investment in the state, if not the entire nation."[1]

The Jewish business presence in the Upstate has largely vanished with the exception of several Jewish enterprises that launched in the late twentieth and early twenty-first century.[2] Most upstate Jews are no longer involved in growing the economy through retail; rather, they relocate to South Carolina for management positions in one of the many international companies in the Upstate. One interviewee estimated that nearly twenty-five percent of BMW's management in the late twentieth century was Jewish.[3]

Jewish newcomers establish practices as doctors, dentists, lawyers, and accountants, while others pursue careers in real estate and education. Responding to nationwide college recruiting, Jewish academics moved to the Upstate to teach at the region's many colleges and universities, offering classes in

English, business, communication, history, education and philosophy. Jewish professors accepting positions in the Upstate increased the Jewish population, but more importantly reflected a nationwide trend that occurred after the Civil Rights Act of 1964, which made employment discrimination illegal.

The Upstate attracts young professionals, transplants, and retirees with opportunities in economically robust communities. With its beautifully landscaped Main Street, Greenville boasts a multitude of sidewalk cafés, restaurants, and chic hotels, just as Max Heller envisioned. While Spartanburg has become a hub for higher education with five colleges and universities plus the Edward Via College of Osteopathy and the Sherman College of Chiropractic. An international airport located in Spartanburg County on the I-85 corridor connecting Spartanburg and Greenville provides easy access for the 545 foreign Upstate companies that make frequent business trips to Europe. For these reasons and more, the Upstate continues attracting Jews and others to its environs.

One of the more striking features of recent Jewish migrants to the Upstate are the number of intermarried couples. Unlike the early Jewish settlers in the Upcountry who considered marriage to another Jew one of the most important means of retaining Jewish identity, that belief has declined. That mid-twentieth century belief has changed, not only in the Upstate but nationwide. According to Rabbi Yossi Liebowitz, more than fifty percent of the congregants at Temple B'nai Israel in Spartanburg are intermarried couples. Similarly, Rabbi Sam Rose of Greenville's Temple Israel stated that only one of five weddings he performed recently were both Jews.[4]

In 1990, the Council of Jewish Federations published a population survey stating that "over one-half (fifty-two percent) of recent marriages that involved Jewish Americans were intermarriages and between 2005 and 2013, fifty eight percent of Jews were married to non-Jews."[5] Historian Edward Shapiro deftly defines intermarriage as an "insoluble dilemma since it stemmed from diminishing anti-Semitism and rapid social and economic mobility, which Jews welcomed."[6]

Liebowitz maintains that another sign of change among Jews who settle in the Upstate "is a shift to cultural Judaism as people are no longer interested in practicing their faith."[7] Thus, they may observe Passover and Chanukah, but they rarely attend services, in fact, many are unaffiliated with any congregation. Since the mid-1980s Greenville has swelled with newcomers, most from the Northeast. While more than 900 Jewish families live in the greater Greenville metropolitan area, most of them remain unaffiliated.

One Jewish institution currently attracts more Jews than any other in the Upstate: Chabad. The Chabad Center of Greenville & the Upstate claims 200 members, but hundreds more attend their events. Established in 2013 by Rabbi Leibel Kesselman, Chabad is Orthodox but does not insist that the people attending their events practice Orthodoxy. Their mission is to inspire unaffiliated Jews or Jews who have lost the fervor for their religion to reconnect. Chabad is not a membership-based institution, so Jews can participate without paying annual dues and pay a nominal fee for the events they do attend. Events take place in hotel ballrooms, for example, because there is no institutional structure. The large pool of people who participate in Chabad include established Jews as well as newcomers to the area, such as Brazilian, Argentinian, and Ukrainian Jews. Jason Hansen and Danielle Eisner and their two children attend nearly all the events that Chabad sponsors, even though they belong to two synagogues. Hansen refers to Chabad offerings as "Judaism a la carte," because participants can choose which events to attend and do not feel obligated to do more. Eisner remarks that there is no pressure on anyone to affiliate and people do not fear being shunned if they do not belong to Chabad. Furthermore, she noted that Chabad provides a "wow factor" to Jewish High Holy Days. Chabad makes Chanukah an amazing event with "Chanukah on Ice," a menorah ice sculpture featuring a firelit menorah on Main Street in Greenville.[8]

Chanukah on Main is an event Chabad has been sponsoring for years, drawing more than 600 people. According to Eisner and Hansen, Chabad attracts unaffiliated Jews to its events in an effort to inspire them to examine and renew their Judaism be it Orthodox, Conservatism, or Reform.[9] Amy Hammer, once a member of Beth Israel, left the congregation for Chabad and maintains that she enjoys their educational classes and the way they bring Jewish life into the community, providing outreach to unaffiliated Jews.[10]

Jews in the Upstate now take their place with a large immigrant population from all over the world who have come to work in a region once dominated by cotton mills and now the site of German, French, Swiss, Japanese, Italian, British, Austrian, and Belgian companies, making it a world-class center for manufacturing. International awareness and world-class skills are a priority in the Upstate as foreigners have made it their home. The sister cities of Greenville and Spartanburg are now the site of the largest per capita diversified foreign investment in the United States. Jews, in many ways, were forerunners to the diversification of the Upstate, both ethnically, religiously, and industrially and brought the skills and sometimes, even the companies, they started in Europe to the United States. Their legacy to the diversification of the Upstate is just now being realized.

GLOSSARY

BAT MITZVAH (Hebrew)—coming-of-age ritual for Jewish girls around the age of 12; parallel to bar mitzah for boys.

KASHRUT (Hebrew)—specific religious laws governing the selection and preparation of kosher food.

KOSHER (Hebrew)—ritually fit foods prepared to Torah and rabbinical traditions and supervision.

LANDSMAN (Yiddish): a fellow Jew who may share the same geographical origins.

MATZAH (Hebrew)—unleavened bread prepared for use at a seder.

MIKVAH (Hebrew)—a ritual bath used by men and women for conversion to Judaism, and women at the end of the menstrual cycle.

MINYAN (Hebrew)—a quorum of ten men and/or women over the age of thirteen required for a worship service.

MOHEL (Hebrew)—a Jewish person trained in the practice of circumcision.

SEDER (Hebrew)—the annual Passover meal celebrating the Exodus from Egypt.

SHOCHET (Hebrew)—a person officially certified to slaughter cattle and poultry according to Jewish law.

SHUL (Yiddish)—a reference to a house of worship and study; synagogue.

NOTES

INTRODUCTION

1. Nathan Shapiro interview with Caldwell Sims, South Carolina Writers Project, Union County Historical Society.

2. Charles, *The Narrative History of Union County, South Carolina*, 413.

3. Rosenberg Mercantile Co. records.

4. Weissbach, *Jewish Life*.

1: THE LURE OF SOUTH CAROLINA

1. Huhner, "The Jews of South Carolina: From the Earliest Settlement to the End of the American Revolution," 39–61.

2. Eli Evans, "Preface," to *Portion of the People*, xv.

3. Edgar, *South Carolina, A History* 62.

4. Bauman, *Dixie Diaspora*, 7.

5. Hagy, *This Happy Land*, 94.

6. Rosengarten and Rosengarten, *Portion of the People*, 81.

7. Encyclopedia of Southern Jewish Communities, Columbia, South Carolina, http:/www.isjl.org/.

8. Perlmutter, "Ebb and Flow," 15.

9. Hagy, *This Happy Land*, 195.

10. Joselit, "Land of Promise," 25. .

11. Before the Civil War, the South Carolina Piedmont was known as the backcountry. The same region was known as the Upcountry after the Civil War, and as the Upstate starting in the twentieth century.

12. South Carolina Jewish History-Jewish Virtual Library. https://www.jewishvirtual library.org/.

13. Koffman, "Occupational Turn." Review of Hasia R. Diner's *Roads Taken*.

14. Ibid., 82–83.

15. Diner, *Roads Taken*, ix.

16. Gerber, "Cutting Out Shylock," 615–637.

17. Walker, "Mineral Water," 1.

18. Zambone, *Daniel Morgan*, xv.

19. Vecchio, "From Slavery to Freedom," 108.

20. Huff, *Greenville*, 62.

21. Ford, *Origins of Southern Radicalism*, 7.

22. Ibid.

23. Ibid., 7–8.
24. Ibid., 9.
25. Huff, *Greenville*, 83.
26. Ford, *Origins of Southern Radicalism*, 12.
27. Vecchio, "From Slavery to Freedom," 108.
28. Huff, *Greenville*, 113.
29. O'Neill, "For the General Good," 13.
30. Ford, *Origins of South Radicalism*, 16.
31. Ibid., 38.
32. Ibid., 52.
33. Ibid., 243.
34. Ibid., 262.
35. Ibid., 221.
36. Edgar, *South Carolina*, 279.
37. Boyanski, *Reimagining Greenville,* 18.
38. Huff, *Greenville,* 63.
39. Leonard, *Our Heritage,* 10.
40. Hieke, *Jewish Identity,* 106.
41. Rosenberg and Rosenberg, *Portion of the People*, 124.
42. Rosenberg Mercantile Co. records. Reputedly, the Rosenbergs were "excessively conscientious toward their slaves, sanctioned their marriages, and went to great lengths to keep families together."
43. Judy Bainbridge, "Swandale and His Local Mansion House," *Greenville (SC) News,* March 2, 1917, 1D.
44. Ibid.
45. Hieke, *Jewish Identity,* 52.
46. Goldstein and Weiner, *On Middle Ground*, 59.
47. Ibid.
48. Walker, "Mineral Water," 7.
49. Ibid.
50. Ibid.
51. Ibid., 8.
52. Cooper, *Greenville, Woven,* 38.
53. Walker, "Mineral Water," 12.
54. Ibid., 15.
55. See http://www.Archives/library.cofc.edu.
56. Reprint of a letter written by Thomas Irvine in 1892, noting that his father, William Irvine, and Simon Swandale, "a northern man, had bought the Mansion House in Greenville and kept it together for four years. Father then sold out to Swandale and moved to Spartanburg again." Reprint in *Hampton Heights* by Vivian Fisher, 10.
57. Ibid., 40.
58. Bainbridge, "Swandale and His Local Mansion House." Swandale had a lucrative and successful business career in Greenville. Unfortunately, at the age of sixty-nine, he was "accused of dementia," in a verdict that "found him to be of unsound mind and memory

and incapable of conducting his own affairs." The action was initiated by his wife. Swandale's son, Dr. G. Tupper Swandale, became his father's guardian. Tupper remained in Greenville and became a leading Physician, "but his father died, forgotten and without an obituary in 1884."

59. Ford, *Origins of Southern Radicalism*, 216.

60. Ibid., 236.

61. Huff, *Greenville*, 120.

62. 1870 US Federal Census, *Ninth Census of the US* [database online] Provo, Utah, Ancestry.com.

63. Belton Oscar Mauldin, *Journal for 1860*, journal entry for December 19. Archives, Furman University, Greenville, SC, 104 of transcription.

64. Ibid.

65. Ibid., journal entry for January 26, 1860, 8 of transcription.

66. Ibid.

67. Rosen, *Jewish Confederates*, 267.

68. Ibid.

69. Letter from the Ku Klux Klan to Davidson which reads, "Owing to the fact that there is a good deal of dissatisfaction in Hahira to you as a citizen, and as you are not a desirable citizen in this community [*sic*] and we being notified of the fact, we command that you be absent from this town, with your belongings, not later than February the First. First warning. Second warning will not be in this form." Signed CITIZENS, Hahira, Georgia, January 1926. Original letter was in his daughter's (Jeanette Davidson Finkelstein) possession. A copy of the letter is in the author's possession.

70. Jeanette Davidson Finkelstein, interview with Diane Vecchio, June 29, 2009, Spartanburg, SC.

71. Jeanette Finkelstein, Obituary, *Spartanburg Herald*; Finkelstein interview with Diane Catherine Vecchio.

72. Mason, "Anti-Jewish Violence," 84.

73. Ibid.

74. See discussion of Jewish peddlers' whiteness in "Entering the Mainstream of Modern Jewish History" by Hasia Diner, 102.

75. Ibid.

76. Rosengarten and Rosengarten, *Portion of the People*, 6.

77. Mendelsohn, *Rag Race*, 60.

78. Shai Weissbach, *Jewish Life*, 36.

79. Atherton, "Itinerant Merchandising," 35–39.

80. Mendelsohn, *Rag Race*, 67.

81. Shevitz, *Jewish Communities*, 37.

82. Rabin, *Jews on the Frontier*, 26.

83. Diner, "Entering the," 86–108.

84. George Visanska Rosenberg, interview with Dale Rosengarten, September 2, 1996. Jewish Heritage Collection, Special Collections, Addlestone Library, College of Charleston, Charleston, SC (hereafter cited as JHC).

85. Rosenberg Mercantile Co. records.

86. Rosa From Poliakoff, interview with Dale Rosengarten, May 19, 1995, JHC.

87. Ibid.

88. Nathan Shapiro, interview with Caldwell Sims for the South Carolina Writers' Project (WPA), March 6, 1939, Union County Historical Society, 14.

89. Ibid.

90. Several historians discuss the impact of Jacob Epstein on peddlers and merchants in the South, including Deborah Weiner in her study *Coalfield Jews: An Appalachian History.*

91. Levy, *Jacob Epstein,* 4.

92. Ibid., 15.

93. Ibid., 17.

94. Ibid., 22.

95. Evans, *Provincials,* 81–82.

96. Weiner, *Coalfield Jews,* 25.

97. Diner, "Entering the Mainstream," 98.

98. Shapiro interview with Caldwell Sims, 14.

99. Ibid.

100. Coleman, *Five Petticoats,* 24.

101. Ibid.

102. Shapiro interview.

103. Mrs. Richard Glasson, interview with Caldwell Sims for the South Carolina Writers' Project (WPA), 1938, Kennedy Room, Spartanburg County Public Library, Spartanburg, SC.

104. Clark, *Pills, Petticoats, and Plows.* Citations refer to the reprint edition.

105. Ibid.

106. Jones, *Mama Learned Us,* 35–38.

107. Ibid., 28.

108. Ibid., 26, 29.

109. Ibid, 34.

110. Hertzberg, *Strangers Within,* 182–83.

111. Webb, "Jewish Merchants," 55–80.

112. Ibid., 59.

113. Jones, *Mama Learned Us,* 29.

114. Shapiro interview.

115. Ibid., 8.

116. Ibid., 12.

117. Ibid.

118. Coleman, *Five Petticoats,* 24.

119. 1896 *Johnson's City Directory,* Spartanburg, SC.

120. Rabin, *Jews on the Frontier,* 25.

121. Diner, "Entering the Mainstream," 97.

122. Louis Schmier, "Jews and Gentiles," 2.

123. Glanz, "Notes on Early Jewish," 119–36.

124. Diner, *Jews of the United States,* 101.

125. Poliakoff, "D. Poliakoff: 100 Years," 8–10.

126. Jeanette Davidson Finkelstein, interview with Diane Catherine Vecchio, June 29, 2009, Spartanburg, SC.

127. Huff, *Greenville,* 128.

128. Ibid., 129.

129. Ibid., 135.

130. Ibid., 135.

131. Rosen, *Jewish Confederates*, xiii.

132. Archiver, rootsweb.ancestry.com, accessed July 23, 2016.

133. "Death of an Old Citizen," *Greenville (SC) News*, May 1, 1889, 2.

134. Ibid.

135. 1860 Census, Greenville, SC, Roll M653, 407.

136. Barnett, *Jews of South Carolina*, 229.

137. US Federal Census for Charleston, SC, 1870, 1880, 1910.

138. Huff, *Greenville*, 138.

139. Ibid., 132–3.

140. Spartanburg District Court of Magistrates and Freeholders, Trial Papers ("Slaves and Free Blacks"), 1825–65.

141. Huff, *Greenville*, 151.

142. Rabinowitz, *First New South,* 37.

143. Ford, "Rednecks and Merchants," 301.

144. Huff, *Greenville*, 178.

145. Ford, "Rednecks and Merchants," 301.

146. O'Neill, "For the General Good," 13.

147. Carlton, *Mill and Town,* 18.

148. Ibid., 20.

149. Ibid.

150. Ibid.

151. Mendelsohn, *Rag Race*, 7.

152. Huff, *Greenville,* 180.

153. Foster and Montgomery, *Spartanburg: Facts, Reminiscences,* 265.

154. "Anderson: Historical Overview," *Encyclopedia of Southern Jewish Communities*, Goldring Waldenberg Institute of Southern Life.

155 Ibid.

156. Hieke, *Jewish Identity*, 66.

157. Ibid.

158. Crittenden, *Greenville Century Book,* 87–88.

159. Ibid.

160. Ibid. Hzrman is Hymen's original, non-anglicized name. Hereafter, original, non-anglicized names are listed behind the Americanized Jewish names in parentheses.

161. Hyman Endel Family Papers, South Carolina Room, Greenville Public Library, Greenville, SC.

162. Contributed by the South Carolina Room at the Greenville Public Library, "Clothes Made the Man," *Upstate Business Journal*, March 14, 2014, see https://upstatebusiness journal.com/profile/clothes.

163. "Mr. Endel Back," *Greenville (SC) News*, March 12, 1911, 5.

164. Ibid.

165. "Last Will and Testament of Hyman Endel and Francis Endel," Hyman Endel Family Papers.

166. South Carolina Room at the Greenville Public Library, "Clothes Made the Man."

167. "Esteemed Citizen Passes Away at His Home in City," *Greenville (SC) News*, August 19, 1925, 1.

168. In their study of the Jews of Baltimore, Goldstein and Weiner discuss the propensity for Jewish businesspeople to demand civic inclusion in their new American communities. They argue that for Jews "staking their claim to membership in the broader civil society" did not necessitate downplaying their ethnic and religious distinctiveness as Jews. See Goldstein and Weiner, *On Middle Ground*, 69.

169. Greenville city directories, 1877–99.

170. Edgar, *South Carolina Encyclopedia*, 911.

171. Carlton, *Mill and Town*, 24.

172. Hieke, *Jewish Identity*, 66.

173. Bauman, *Dixie Diaspora*, 191.

174. Goldstein and Weiner, *On Middle Ground*, 94.

175. "Last Will and Testament of Hyman Endel and Francis Endel," (Mr. and Mrs. Endel both specified that they wished to be buried in Baltimore.) Hyman Endel Family Papers, Greenville Public Library.

176. Jews are buried in a "Jewish Section" of Floyd Greenlawn Memorial Cemetery in Spartanburg.

2: FOUNDATIONS OF JEWISH ENTERPRISE IN THE UPCOUNTRY

1. Willis, "Textile Town," 21.

2. Edgar, *South Carolina*, 283.

3. Racine, "Boom Time," 39.

4. Edgar, *South Carolina*, 484.

5. Eelman, *Entrepreneurs*, 8.

6. Ibid., 41.

7. Ibid., 43. The "Piedmont" is another term used to identify Upcountry South Carolina.

8. Kohn, *Cotton Mills*, 65.

9. Racine, "Boom Time," 41.

10. Huff, *Greenville*, 189.

11. Belcher, *Greenville County*, 32.

12. Huff, *Greenville*, 235.

13. Ibid., 238–39.

14. Carlton, *Mill and Town*, 6.

15. Edgar, *South Carolina, A History*, 456.

16. Cann and Teter, "New England Textile Collapse," 147.

17. Ibid.

18. Carlton, *Mill and Town*, 65.

19. Huff, *Greenville*, 193.

20. Ibid., 198.

21. Ibid., 195.

22. Nicholas Theodore, interview with Diane Vecchio, October 15, 2007, Greenville, SC.

23. The first Greek immigrant to settle in Spartanburg was Nick Trakas.

24. Foster and Montgomery, *Spartanburg, Facts, Reminiscences,* 318–321.

25. Pruitt, *Things Hidden,* 42.

26. Cohen, *Cotton Capitalists;* Mendelsohn, *Rag Race;* and Diner, *Roads Taken.* All examine issues of ethnicity and social group affiliation of Jews.

27. Aldrich and Waldinger, "Ethnicity and Entrepreneurship," 111–35.

28. Cohen, *Cotton Capitalists,* 2.

29. Mendelsohn, *Rag Race,* 5.

30. Ibid., 2.

31. Jerry Muller, *Capitalism and the Jews,* 65.

32. Ibid., 69.

33. Ibid., 70.

34. Ibid., 12.

35. Ibid., 77.

36. Aldrich and Waldinger, "Ethnicity and Entrepreneurship," 114.

37. See Leonard Rogoff, *Down Home.*

38. Weiner, *Coalfield Jews,* 29.

39. 1900 US Federal Census.

40. 1910 and 1920 US Federal Census.

41. Ancestry.com; Greenville city directories, 1930–1940; Encyclopedia of Southern Jewish Communities, Greenville, SC; see https://www.isjl.org/.

42. "Jews in Spartanburg," chronology compiled by Joey Gainey from the *Spartanburg (SC) Herald,* Kennedy Room, Spartanburg County Public Library, and Spartanburg city directories, 1900–1930.

43. Ancesty.com; "Jews in Spartanburg" chronology; and Spartanburg city directories, 1910–1920.

44. Susan Jacobs, interview with Diane Vecchio, June 18, 2008, Spartanburg, SC.

45. Muller, *Capitalism and the Jews,* 91.

46. James Cobb (grandson of David Greenewald), interview with Diane Vecchio, November 8, 2007, Spartanburg, SC.

47. Harry Price, interview with Diane Catherine Vecchio, October 30, 2007, Spartanburg, SC.

48. Ibid.

49. Ibid.

50. Seymour Gray, interview with Diane Catherine Vecchio, December 10, 2007, Spartanburg, SC.

51. "Meyers Brothers Leave Newport News," *Newport News* (VA) *Time-Herald,* February 6, 1911.

52. 1930 US Federal Census, Ancestry.com.

53. Rosenberg Mercantile Co. records.

54. From, "Froms of Union," 14–16; See also death notice of Solomon Fram, *Union Times,* March 1, 1935, 83.

55. Ancestry.com.

56. Charles, *Narrative*, 297.

57. Meyer Drucker, interview with Diane Catherine Vecchio, November 9, 2019, Temple B'nai Israel, Spartanburg, SC.

58. Jews in Greenville, Folder, South Carolina Room, Greenville County Public Library.

59. Greenville, SC, City Council Minute Book 3, 1881–90. Meetings on 10.15.1886, 142 and 4.10.1887, 166.

60. Cohen, *Cotton Capitalists*, 7.

61. Gerber, "Cutting Out Shylock," 628–31.

62. Cohen, "Cotton, Capital," 112–36.

63. Cohen, "Cotton, Capital," 115, 116.

64. Shapiro interview.

65. Rogoff, *Down Home*, 100.

66. Cohen, *Coalfield Jews*, 27.

67. Ibid., 73.

68. Marsha Poliakoff, interview with Diane Catherine Vecchio, September 25, 2007, Spartanburg, SC.

69. Poliakoff, *Portraits of a People*, 31.

70. Ibid., 165.

71. Jacobs interview.

72. Ann Lurey, "From the Old Country," 10–11.

73. Jeff Zaglin (grandson of Charles Zaglin), interview with Diane Catherine Vecchio, June 26, 2009, Greenville, SC.

74. 1910 Spartanburg City Directory.

75. Information derived from Greenville city directories, US Census data, and interviews with Jeffrey Zaglin.

76. Nolan, *A Guide to Historic Greenville*, 91. On Greenville's Main Street between Coffee and Washington Streets, you can still see a sculpted rooster embedded into a building. According to Beverly Merritt, Sol Knigoff's granddaughter, sometime after leaving his hometown of Minsk, Sol met a stone carver and the two formed a friendship. After arriving at Ellis Island, Sol and his sculptor friend parted. The stone carver made a promise that after he established his business he would sculpt a rooster and send it to Sol as a token of the friendship they made on their way to America. The rooster is a Russian symbol for the fulfillment of wishes. The stone carver kept his promise and sent Sol the sculpted rooster, which he installed into the exterior wall at the top of his pawnshop; the building later burned, and the only thing Sol was able to salvage from the ruins was the sculpture. When he reopened his pawnshop in the present building, the rooster was proudly installed at the top of the façade.

77. Greenville City Directory, 1907.

78. Ibid.

79. Jacobs interview. See also Poliakoff, *Portraits of a People*, 128.

80. Marian Feinstein, interview with Diane Catherine Vecchio, December 14, 2009, Spartanburg, SC.

81. Alex Davis interview with Dale Rosengarten, February 28, 1997, College of Charleston Libraries.

82. Susan Zaglin, interview with Diane Catherine Vecchio, July 28, 2016, Greenville, SC.

83. Marion Feinstein, interview by Diane Catherine Vecchio, December 14, 2009, Spartanburg, SC.

84. The Industrial Removal Office (IRO) was created in 1901 by the Baron de Hirsch Fund to disperse Jews to cities and towns throughout the country. Fearing that a rise in anti-Semitism would occur because of the large concentration of Jews on the East Coast, the IRO resettled Jewish immigrants, especially the unemployed, in locations beyond the major cities of the Atlantic Seaboard.

85. Correspondence between Greenville merchants and the IRO, New York.

86. Woodward, *Origins of the New South,* 131.

3: CREATING COMMUNITY

1. The original congregation of Temple B'nai Israel in Spartanburg numbered approximately twenty-seven families. In Greenville, Congregation Beth Israel (Orthodox) started with twenty-five families, and the Temple of Israel (Reform) also organized with twenty-five families.

2. "Spartanburg, South Carolina," *Encyclopedia of Southern Jewish Communities,* accessed April 9, 2020, https://www.isjl.org/south-Carolina-spartanburg-encyclopedia .html.

3. Information collected from Spartanburg city directories, Ancestry.com, and Wachter, "In Search of Jewish Spartanburg," 4–7.

4. *The Southern Israelite,* March 24, 1927. Sisterhood files, Temple B'nai Israel.

5. Poliakoff, *Portraits of a People,* 7.

6. Rabbi Yossi Liebowitz, interview with Diane Catherine Vecchio, March 18, 2020, Spartanburg, SC.

7. Weissbach, *Jewish Life,* 175.

8. Wachter, "Dean Street Synagogue," Research on founders and synagogue unpublished document in author's possession, May 2006.

9. Goldstein, *Price of Whiteness,* 13.

10. For discussions on conflicts between German Jews and East European Jews, see for example, Goldstein and Weiner, *On Middle Ground;* Hertzberg, *Strangers Within;* Sorin, *Tradition Transformed;* Shevitz, *Jewish Communities;* and Weissbach, *Jewish Life.*

11. Bauman and Shankman, "Rabbi as Ethnic Broker," 202.

12. Sorin, *Tradition Transformed,* 101.

13. Goldstein and Weiner, *On Middle Ground,* 104–7.

14. Wachter, "Dean Street Synagogue," 3.

15. Goldstein and Weiner, *On Middle Ground,* 72.

16. Nadell and Sarna, *Women and American Judaism,* 4.

17. Poliakoff, *Portraits of a People,* 7.

18. Rogoff, *Down Home,* 180.

19. Steineke, "Dr. Rosa Gantt," 8–9.

20. *Southern Israelite.*

21. Poliakoff, *Portraits of a People,* 64.

22. *Southern Israelite.*

23. Poliakoff, *Portraits of a People*, 148–49.

24. Ibid., 151.

25. Ibid., 32.

26. Melinda Young, "Beth Israel's Synagogue Centennial Tells Greenville's History through World Wars, Main Street Commerce," *Greenville (SC) Journal*, June 24, 2016.

27. Alfieri, "Congregation Beth Israel," 4–5.

28. US Depart. of the Interior, National Park Service, National Registrar of Historic Place Registration Form. Application submitted to list the synagogue as an historic building. Temple B'nai Israel Folder, Kennedy Room, Spartanburg County Public Library.

29. Ibid.

30. Jack Bloom, interview with Diane Catherine Vecchio, June 17, 2008, Greenville, SC.

31. Letter from Jack Bloom to Marcie Cohen Ferris, 12 February 2002, in author's possession. See Ferris, *Matzoh Ball Gumbo,* 74–75.

32. Bloom, interview with Diane Catherine Vecchio.

33. Letter from Jack Bloom to Marcie Cohen Ferris.

34. Kaplan and Zaglin interview.

35. Zaglin, "Zaglins of Greenville," 6–7.

36. Bobbie Jean Rovner, Susan Zaglin, and Larry Zaglin, interview with Diane Catherine Vecchio, June 14, 2015, Greenville, SC.

37. Founding member Hyman Endel was born in Virginia to Russian Jewish parents; George Reisenfeld was of German descent; Philip Weinberger was born in Hungary; David Kohn was born in South Carolina to a Hungarian mother and a Bavarian father; Levy Rothschild was born in the German states; Isaac Jacobi was born in Baltimore to German parents. All information accessed on Ancestry.com, January 14, 2019.

38. In Greenville, Congregation Beth Israel (Orthodox) started with twenty-five families; although the Jewish community in Greenville was larger than the Spartanburg Jewish community, it was still relatively small.

39. "Temple of Israel Congregation to Soon Open Handsome Edifice in Greenville; Local Temple Was Organized in 1912," *Greenville (SC) Piedmont*, February 4, 1929, Folder: Religion: Judaism: Temple of Israel, South Carolina Room, Greenville County Library.

40. "Although Temple Is Not Old, Group Organized in 1911," *Greenville (SC) News*, January 12, 1947, 16.

41. Ibid.

42. "Brief History of the Temple of Israel," researched by Irving and Marjorie Abrams, South Carolina Room, Greenville Public Library.

43. The extraordinary accomplishments of southern Jewish female progressives are examined in the works of Leonard Rogoff, *Gertrude Weil;* Joan Marie Johnson, *Southern Ladies;* Amy Thompson McCandless, "Anita Politzer"; Belinda Friedman Gergel, "Irene Goldsmith Kohn."

44. MSS 1034–45, Hirschman Family Papers/Biographical Information 45A, South Carolina Historical Society, Addlestone Library, College of Charleston.

45. Love Rose Hirschmann Gantt, "Opening Doors: Women at the Medical University of South Carolina," Medical University of South Carolina, accessed December 17, 2019.

46. Ibid.

47. Services Today for Dr. Gantt," *Spartanburg (SC) Herald*, November 18, 1935, 8.

48. Huff, *Greenville*, 253.

49. Evans, *Provincials*, xiii.

50. Holt, *Magical Places*, 16.

51. Vincent Brook, "Jews in American Cinema and Media," https://www.oxford bibliographies.com/abstract/.

52. Ibid., 18.

53. Ibid.

54. US Federal Census records for 1910 and 1920, via ancestry.com; US city directories for Spartanburg, 1916.

55. Wachter, "Spartanburg's Jewish Stories," unpublished paper, in author's possession.

56. Improved Order of Red Men was modeled on aspects of American Indian Society and shaped its political identity around what it perceived to be American Indian values. National Museum of the American Indian, Washington, DC.

57. Cobb interview.

58. Hertzberg, *Strangers Within*, 168.

59. Shevitz, *Jewish Communities*, 89.

60. Weissbach, *Jews in Small-Town America*, 73.

61. Sterba, *Good Americans*, 6.

62. Ibid., 46.

63. 1920 and 1930 US Federal Census records and naturalization papers, via ancestry.com.

64. Wachter, "In Search of Jewish Spartanburg."

65. Poliakoff, *Portraits of a People*, 30.

66. Rosengarten and Rosengarten, *Portion of the People*, 78. See also US World War I draft registration cards, 1917–18.

67. Jewish New Year Observed Here," *Greenville (SC) News*, September 17, 1917, 8.

68. Poliakoff, *Portraits of a People*, 8.

69. "Tent and Trench."

70. Poliakoff, *Portraits of a People*, 182.

71. "Tent and Trench."

72. Foster and Montgomery, *Spartanburg*, 355.

73. Poliakoff, *Portraits of a People*, 235.

74. Alfieri, "Congregation Beth Israel," 4.

75. Jewish File, clippings from *Spartanburg (SC) Herald*, 1919, Kennedy Room, Spartanburg County Public Library.

76. "Cohen Commits Suicide While in Philadelphia," *Spartanburg (SC) Herald*, March 29, 1924, 3.

77. "David Greenewald is Laid to Rest," *Spartanburg (SC) Herald*, August 13, 1919, 8.

78. Ibid.

79. Obituary, Moses Greenewald, *Spartanburg Journal*, May 19, 1926, 4.

80. Obituary, Israel From, *Union Times*, March 1, 1935, 1.

81. Rebecca Winstock Rosenberg was the daughter of Moses Winstock, a Polish immigrant. Her husband, Abraham Rosenberg, was also born in Poland.

82. MSS 1122, Box 1, Folder 1 of the Winstock, Rosenberg, and Visanska Papers, South Carolina Historical Society, Addlestone Family Library, College of Charleston.

83. Shevitz, *Jewish Communities*, 105.

4: JEWISH BUSINESS AND INDUSTRY IN THE INTERWAR YEARS

1. Foster and Montgomery, *Spartanburg*, 408, and Huff, *Greenville*, 292.

2. Edgar, *South Carolina*, 485.

3. Foster and Montgomery, *Spartanburg*, 408.

4. Cann, "Improving Textile Town," 93.

5. Foster and Montgomery, *Spartanburg*, 409.

6. Ibid., 597.

7. Cann and Teter, "New England Textile Collapse, 146.

8. Foster and Montgomery, *Spartanburg*, 409.

9. Ibid., 412.

10. Ibid., 426.

11. Huff, *Greenville*, 295; Cann and Teeter, "New England Textile Collapse," 147.

12. Cann, "Improving Textile Town," 96.

13. Cann and Teter, "New England Textile Collapse," 147.

14. See for example: Carlton, *Mill and Town;* Eelman, *Entrepreneurs;* Ford, "Rednecks and Merchants"; 94–318, and Waldrep, *Southern Workers.*

15. Sarah Richardson, "Cone Family."

16. Weissbach, *Jewish Life.* 108.

17. Fahrer, *Home in Shalom'ville*, 66.

18. Theodore Kohn, US Civil War Soldier Records. Profiles, 1861–1865; US Federal Census 1880, 1990; US city directories, Orangeburg, SC, 1907, 1909.

19. See August Kohn Papers, University of South Carolina, University Libraries, Manuscripts (Kohn, August, 1868–1930), and Kohn, *Cotton Mills.*

20. Judith Bainbridge, "How Determined Businessman Built His Piedmont Shirt Co. into Industry Giant," *Greenville News*, July 16, 2020.

21. Judson Chapman, "Who's Who in Greenville," *Greenville (SC) Piedmont,* November 23, 1935, David Kohn Folder, South Carolina Room, Greenville Public Library.

22. "Returning from Wedding Trip" *The State* (Columbia, SC), April 16, 1912, 3.

23. Chapman, "Who's Who in Greenville."

24. Ibid.

25. Edgar, *South Carolina*, 456.

26. Belcher, *Greenville County,* 73. Belcher also notes that a modernized textile hall was built in 1964, and with the tremendous growth of the Upcountry's textile industry, international exhibitors from around the world attended the fair.

27. Chapman, "Who's Who in Greenville."

28. Ibid.

29. Ibid.

30. Mendelsohn, *Rag Race,* 207.

31. Dillon and Godley, "The Evolution of the Jewish Garment Industry, 1840–1940," *Chosen Capital*, edited by Kobrin, 2012; https://www.researchgate.net/publication/290542947.

32. Mendelsohn, *Rag Race*, 216.

33. Weissbach, *Jewish Life,* 108.

34. Fahrer, *Home in Shalom'ville*, 15, 69.

35. "Contracts Awarded," *Charlotte News*, August 18, 1941, 19.

36. Classifieds, *Chattanooga Daily Times*, October 23, 1932.

37. "Dixie Shirt Firm Is Soon to Close," *Greenville (SC) News,* May 29, 1948, 7.

38. "Dixie Shirt Company," advertisement for one hundred females, *Greenville (SC) News*, January 16, 1945, 19.

39. Help wanted ads for female and male help, *Greenville (SC) News*, June 26, 1932, 22; October 12, 1947, 4; December 4, 1947, 27, and *Chattanooga Daily Times*, October 23, 1932, 12.

40. Max Trout, interview with Diane Catherine Vecchio, March 30, 2021, Lake Bowen, Spartanburg County, SC.

41. "Textile Orders Reduced Here," *Greenville (SC) News*, August 18, 1945, 3.

42. "Dixie Shirt Firm Is Soon to Close," 7.

43. Harry Riemer, "Human Relations Saltzman's Greatest Pride," *Daily News-Record* (Harrisonburg, VA), May 18, 1953, 23–24.

44. "Silver Wings, An American Success Story." The Greenville businessmen who loaned money to Saltzman were Eugene Gillfillen, A. F. McKissick, J. F. Gallivan, H. J. Haynesworth, Curran Earle, J. W. Norwood, John Arrington Sr. and J. E. Sirrene.

45. Ibid.

46. Harry Abrams, 1920 Federal Census New York City; 1931 City Directory, Troy, New York;1940 Federal Census Greenville.

47. Fred Leffert, interview (son of Morris Leffert) with Diane Vecchio October 27, 2016, Greenville, SC; Obituary for Morris Leffert in *Greenville (SC) News,* January 20, 1990, 9.

48. 1920 US Federal Census, Brooklyn, New York.

49. Shepard Saltzman, Obituary, *Greenville (SC) News*, August 11, 1955, 18.

50. "Silver Wings: An American Success Story," *Daily News-Record* (Harrisonburg, VA), May 18, 1953.

51. "Piedmont Shirt Company Buys Out Kaynee Company," *Index-Journal* (Greenwood, SC), October 7, 1958, 3.

52. Solicitations for women workers at the Piedmont Shirt Company advertised in *Greenville (SC) News*, 1930s.

53. Riemer, "Human Relations," 23.

54. Ibid.

55. Victoria Morrow (granddaughter of Shepard Saltzman), phone interview with Diane Catherine Vecchio, March 10, 2018, New York, NY.

56. Ibid.

57. Mendelsohn, *Rag Race*, 209.

58. *The ISJL Encyclopedia of Southern Jewish Communities, Anderson, South Carolina.* ISJL - South Carolina Anderson Encyclopedia - Goldring/Woldenberg Institute of Southern Jewish Life.

59. Bodie McDowell, "Expansion Program Is Planned for Abbeville Shirt Plant," *Index-Journal* (Greenwood, SC), June 6, 1959, 1.

60. "SC Executive Faces Fraud Charges," *News and Observer*, (Raleigh, NC), Feb. 4, 1958, 3.

61. "Kaplan Faces Five-Year Jail Term Unless He Can Pay Banks," *Index-Journal* (Greenwood, SC), Feb. 21, 1959, 7.

62. Ibid.

63. "Former Abbeville Plant Official Begins Term," *Greenville (SC) News*, May 16, 1959, 3.

64. Irving Abrams, interview with Virginia Cain and Courtney Tollison Hartness, July 8, 2009, Upcountry History Museum, Greenville, SC.

65. Abrams interview with Courtney Tollison Hartness.

66. "Raycord Plans Spartan Plant," *Greenville (SC) News*, Nov. 20, 1986, 36.

67. Raycord Factory Outlet advertisement, *Greenville (SC) News*, May 6, 1948, 135.

68. Weissbach makes this clear in his study of *Jewish Life in Small-Town America*.

69. Ibid., 71.

70. Dubofsky and Dulles, *Labor in America,* 227–29.

71. Evans, *Provincials,* 28.

72. For the movement of Jews from urban America to suburbia see, for example: Roediger, *Working Toward Whiteness*; Cutler, *Jews of Chicago*.

73. Steve Richardson, "Woodruff," https://www.scencyclopedia.org/see/entries/woodruff.

74. "Jack Cohen and His Mule As They Went Down the Road," (no author) *Greenville News*, January 5, 1930, 21+.

75. Ibid.

76. Cobb interview.

77. Harry Price, "Prices' Store," 11–12.

78. Ibid.

79. US Federal Census, 1920 and 1930; Joe Wachter, "Spartanburg Jews," private compilation of Jews in Spartanburg.

80. Len Farmer, "Henry Blohm, Ernest Rosenberg Are Honored," *Index-Journal* (Greenwood, SC), December 5, 1984, 1.

81. US Federal Censuses 1930, 1940; Greenville city directories, 1917, 1924, 1931, 1935; Lurey, "From the Old Country," 11.

82. US Federal Censuses 1910, 1920, 1930; Spartanburg city directories, 1906, 1910, 1911.

83. 1930 and 1940 Federal Censuses, Greenville;.

84. South Carolina Naturalization Records, 1886–1921, Abe Smith (Abraham Schmidt), US Federal Census, 1940.

85. 1940 Federal Census, Abe Smith; Julius Smith.

86. 1930 Federal Census and 1940 Federal Census for Anderson; 1936 City Directory for Anderson, and the National Jewish Welfare Board.

87. Poliakoff, *Portraits of a People,* 32.

88. Louis H. Pollock, Obituary, *Palm Beach Post,* August 30, 1956, 10; Schochet and Fahrer, *Family Store,* 35.

89. All three families (Davis, Kaufman, and Zaglin) were related. Victor Davisan immigrant from the Isle of Rhodes, Greece married Molly Kaufman, a Rumanian immigrant and settled in Flint, MI. The couple moved to Greenville in 1922 to assist Molly's brother, Harry Kaufman, operating his auto parts business (Kaufman's). In 1926, Victor Davis opened his own auto parts business in Greenville. Henry R. Zaglin, owner of Zaglin's Auto Parts was also a member of the Davis family. Rovner, Zaglin, and Zaglin interview with Diane Catherine Vecchio. See also oral history interview with Alex Davis by Dale Rosengarten and Sandra Lee Kahn Rosenblum.

90. Rovner interview with Diane Catherine Vecchio.

91. Joe Wachter, "B'nai Israel Founders," in author's possession.

92. US Federal Censuses of 1900 and 1920. Greenville city directories for 1880, 1892, 1900, 1907, 1909, 1911, 1915, 1917; South Carolina death certificates, 1821–1968.

93. US Federal Census (1900, 1910, 1920); City directories for Spartanburg and Greenville (1880, 1900, 1913, 1914, 1915, 1917, and the 1920–29), and South Carolina Naturalization Petitions from 1884 to the 1929.

94. Harris, *Out to Work,* 123–24.

95. Prell, "Economic Turn," 2.]

96. Vecchio, *Merchants, Midwives, and Laboring Women,* 66–69.

97. Prell, "Economic Turn," 4.

98. Ibid., 67.

99. Ibid.

100. Federal Census data 1900, 1910, and 1920.

101. 1920 Federal Census.

102. 1910 Federal Census.

103. Ibid.

104. 1920 Federal Census.

105. Finkelstein interview.

106. 1910 Federal Census for Union, 1920 Federal Census for Spartanburg.

107. Weissbach, *Jewish Life,* 89.

108. Ibid., 90–91.

109. 1905 Spartanburg City Directory.

110. Blackwelder, *Now Hiring,* 3.

111. Ibid., 62.

112. Endelman, *Jewish Community,* 5.

113. 1920 and 1930 Federal Censuses, Greenville, SC.

114. 1930 US Federal Census, Greenville, SC.

115. Ibid.

116. 1920 US Federal Censuses, Spartanburg and Greenville, SC.

117. 1930 Federal Census, Anderson, SC.

118. Price, "Prices' Store for Men," 11–12.

119. Toll, *Making of an Ethnic Middle-Class,* 72.

120. Foster and Montgomery, *Spartanburg,* 432.

121. Waldrep, *Southern Workers*, 44.

122. George Chaplin, interview with Dale Rosengarten, September 27, 1995, Jewish Heritage Collection, College of Charleston; US Federal Census data, 1940, and 1954.

123. Goldstein and Weiner, *On Middle Ground*, 202.

124. Tanenbaum interview, with Diane Vecchio, April 29, 2021, Spartanburg, SC.

125. Goldstein and Weiner, *On Middle Ground*, 236–37.

126. Dan Epstein interview, with Diane Vecchio, October 23, 2020, Greenville, SC.

127. Rosa From Poliakoff, interview with Dale Rosengarten, May 1, 1995, Abbeville, SC. Jewish Heritage Collection, College of Charleston Library, MSS 1035-014, 7.

128. *Encyclopedia of Southern Jewish Communities*, Anderson, SC, https://www.isjl .org.

129. Jack Bloom interview, with Dale Rosengarten, February 26, 1997, Greenville, SC. Jewish Heritage Collection, College of Charleston.

130. Foster and Montgomery, *Spartanburg,* 438.

131. James Cobb, interview with Diane Catherine Vecchio, November 8, 2007, Spartanburg, SC.

5: THE PROMISE OF AMERICAN LIFE

1. Poliakoff interview.

2. Poliakoff interview, 12.

3. From, "Froms of Union," 14.

4. Baily, *Immigrants in the Land of Promise*, 146.

5. Weissbach, *Jewish Life*, 127.

6. Diane Vecchio, "Ties of Affection," 117–33.

7. Endelmann, *Jewish Community,* 116.

8. 1910, 1920, 1930 Federal Censuses, Spartanburg, SC.

9. 1910, 1920 Federal Censuses, Greenville, SC.

10. 1920 Federal Census, Greenville, SC.

11. Abbeville County Historical Society, *Images of America. Abbeville County*, (Charleston, SC: Arcadia, 2004), 54–55.

12. 1910, 1920 Federal Censuses, Spartanburg, SC.

13. 1910, 1920 Federal Censuses, Greenville, Anderson, Easley, Gaffney, Greenwood, and Union, SC.

14. Davis interview, 9.

15. Ibid., 10.

16. Ibid.

17. Bloom interview with Rosengarten.

18. Bodnar, Simon, and Weber, *Lives of Their Own,* 154.

19. Marinari, *Unwanted,* 5.

20. On Italian return migration see Caroli, "Italian Repatriation," Cerase, "Expectation and Reality," and Cinel, *National*.

21. Foner, *From Ellis Island,* 182.

22. Ibid., 182.

23. Heinze, "Critical Period," 138.

24. Heinze, "Critical Period," 131–66.

25. Sarah and Louis Fayonsky, Petitions for Naturalization, 1920.

26. Abraham Blumberg, Petition for Naturalization, papers submitted, 1920.

27. Abraham Shain, Petition for Naturalization, March 6, 1925, Greenville; Sam Lure naturalized in 1930.

28. 1910 Federal Census, Greenville, SC.

29. Information derived from Petitions for Naturalization, Spartanburg city directories, and Federal Censuses for Spartanburg, 1910, 1920, 1930.

30. Based on analysis of Jewish immigrant naturalization records and Federal Censuses.

31. Glenn, *Daughters of the Shtetl,* 66.

32. Kraut, *Huddled Masses,* 137.

33. Raphael, *Jews and Judaism,* 134.

34. Raphael, *Jews and Judaism,* 137. Historian Colin Greer argues that "rather than being an agent of Americanization schools preserved the status quo," in *The Great School Legend. A Revisionist Interpretation of American Public Education,* rev. ed. (NY: Penguin, 1976).

35. Kraut, *Huddled Masses,* 137.

36. Vecchio, *Merchants, Midwives, and Laboring Women,* 38.

37. Miriam Cohen found that "Italian parents tended to take children, particularly their daughters out of school as early as possible . . . time spent in the classroom diminished the daughter's ability to contribute to the family." See Cohen, *Workshop to Office,* 114–15.

38. Kathie Friedman-Kasaba's study of Italian and Jewish women in New York City in the late nineteenth and early twentieth centuries maintains that single Italian women supplemented their educations with classes in evening schools, business schools, or private dressmaking schools, viewing these institutions as far more relevant to their needs than the public high schools. See Friedman-Kasaba, *Memories of Migration,* 169.

39. Federal Censuses, Greenville, 1920, 1930; Greenville city directories, 1931, 1933, 1940, 1943.

40. *The Scribbler,* Spartanburg High School yearbooks, 1927–1939. Yearbooks provided by Dr. Russell Booker, former superintendent of schools, District 7, Spartanburg.

41. Federal Censuses Spartanburg; 1930, 1935, 1928, 1940.

42. Shapiro: USC school yearbooks, Wofford College, and World War II drafts cards.

43. Federal Census, Dillon, SC, 1930.

44. Federal Censuses, 1920, 1930, for the towns of Anderson, Abbeville, SC.

45. Carlton, *Mill and Town,* 260.

46. Diner, *New Promised Land,* 73.

47. Sorin, *Tradition Transformed,* 163.

48. Dinnerstein, *Anti-Semitism in America,* 158; see also Synott, *Student Diversity.*

49. Sorin, *Tradition Transformed,* 184.

50. Bloom interview with Rosengarten.

51. For example, Jack Bloom and his brother both attended Furman. Reuben Siegel attended Clemson College, Ernest Rosenberg attended the College of Charleston, Simon Hecklin attended Wofford, and Bill Shapiro attended Tulane.

52. Ida Lurey Bolonkin and Joan Bolonkin Meir, interview with Dale Rosengarten, March 9, 2014, St. Augustine, FL. Jewish Heritage Collection, MSS 1035–389, College of Charleston.

53. Klapper, *Jewish Girls Coming of Age,* 55.

54. "Rosenberg-Moise Engagement," *Greenville News*, September 20, 1942, 5.

55. "Miss Visanska Will Be Bride of Mr. Rothschild," *The Constitution* (Atlanta), August 21, 1932, 30.

56. 1900 Federal Census, Des Moines, IA; 1910, 1920 Federal Censuses, Spartanburg; 1913, 1916, and 1920 city directories, Spartanburg.

57. 1920 and 1930 Federal Censuses, Spartanburg; 1924 Spartanburg High Yearbook, and 1928 Spartanburg City Directory.

58. "Miss Poliakoff is married in Anderson Rites," *Greenville (SC) News*, June 18, 1939, 16.

59. "Rosa Poliakoff Obituary," *Index-Journal*, October 27, 1999, 4.

60. Sorin, *Tradition Transformed,* 162.

61. Ibid., 160.

62. Bloom, "History of the Jewish," 73–88.

63. Goldberg, "Being Jewish in Union," 16–17.

64. Poliakoff interview.

65. From, "All the Bases Covered," 19.

66. Bolonkin and Meir interview.

67. Davidson interview.

68. Ibid.

69. Bolonkin and Meir interview.

70. Diner, *Hungering for America,* 3.

71. Diner, *Hungering for America*, 155.

72. Ibid., 155–56.

73. Ferris, "Dining in the Dixie Diaspora," 227.

74. Ibid., 127.

75. Ibid., 228.

76. Diner, *New Promised Land,* 47.

77. Dianne Ashton, "Expanding Jewish Life," 47–69.

78. From, "The Froms of Union," 14–16.

79. Letter from Jack Bloom to Marcie Cohen Ferris, February 12, 2002, in author's possession. See also Ferris, *Matzoh Ball Gumbo,* 74–75.

80. Ferris, "Dining in the Dixie Diaspora," 232.

81. Jack Bloom interview with Diane Catherine Vecchio.

82. Edward Gray, interview with Diane Catherine Vecchio, December 10, 2009, Spartanburg, SC.

83. Feinstein interview.

84. Jacobs interview.

85. Linda Tannenbaum, interview with Diane Catherine Vecchio, January 19, 2010, Spartanburg, SC.

86. Ferris, "Dining in the Dixie Diaspora," 238.

87. Bauman, *New Vision,* 255.

6: THE UPCOUNTRY GOES TO WAR

1. Hartness, *World War II*, 13.

2. Ibid., 11.

3. Ibid., 15.

4. "Kaplan Faces Five-Year Jail Term Unless He Can Pay Banks," *Index-Journal* (Greenwood, SC), February 21, 1959, 7.

5. Jewish Americans in World War II: Statistics on Jewish American soldiers; New Orleans, LA: National WWII Museum, nationalww2museum.org.

6. Foster and Montgomery, *Spartanburg*, 487.

7. Hartness, *World War II*, 61.

8. Ibid., 61.

9. Ibid., 62.

10. Foster and Montgomery, *Spartanburg*, 496.

11. Maunula, *Guten Tag Y'All*, 13.

12. Turpin, et al., *When the Soldiers Came*, 153.

13. Ibid.

14. Hartness, *World War II*, 62.

15. Turpin, et al., *When the Soldiers Came*, 143.

16. See www.schistory.net/campcroft/people/plotkin.html.

17. Hartness, *World War II*, 19.

18. Ibid., 20.

19. Ibid.

20. Ibid., 18.

21. Feinstein interview.

22. Ibid.

23. Joe Wachter, telephone interview with Diane Catherine Vecchio, December 2, 2020.

24. Moore, *GI Jews*, 11.

25. Some members of Spartanburg's Temple who served during World War II include Ben Abelkop, Harold Cohen, Louis Cohen, Berry Cohen, Abram Feinstein, Seymour Feinstein, Jack Finkelstein, Robert Gilpin, Stanley Goldblatt, Lewis Katz, Irving Malinow, Stanley Malinow, Hyman Pollock, Manuel Pressman, Irving Price, Mitchell Price, William Price, Ralph Robkin, Eugene Shapiro, Sidney Shapiro, Seymour Silver, Joel Tanenbaum, Ralph Tanenbaum, and Junius White. Among the members of Congregation Beth Israel, Greenville, serving in the armed forces were Ralph Sarlin, Leon Shain, Ralph Lurey, Jack David, Sam Fay, Henry Gorman, Meyer Lurey, Louis Davis, Jack Bloom, Edward Morris, Carl Proser, Louis Zaglin, Harry Zaglin, Marion Zaglin, Jack Zaglin, Marvin Silverstein, Frank Gorman, Joel Lax, Alex Davis, Albert Levite, David Schmelzer, Herman Davidson, Harry Saltzman, and Alfred Kaufman. No compilation exists of men serving from Temple Israel in Greenville.

26. Moore, *GI Jews*, 47.

27. Jim Sudmeier, "Harold Cohen," https://Jimsudmeier.com/harold-cohen/#.

28. US World War II Army Enlistment Records, 1938–1946; 1940 Federal Census, Spartanburg, SC.

29. World War II Draft Card, Harvey Saltzman.

30. Samuel Lurey, Obituary, *Greenville (SC) News,* Aug. 14, 1961, 10.

31. "Sam Lurey," Lurey received his promotion to Lt. Col. in ceremonies at the US Army Civil Affairs School in Fort Gordon, GA. He was commissioned a 2nd Lt. in the Corps of Engineers in March 1943, *Greenville News,* August 14, 1961, 10; "Sam Lurey Obituary," *Greenville News,* Jan. 7, 2006, 21.

32. Dixie Hopper, "DAPCO Company Incorporated. A Solid Family Business," *Greenville Magazine,* April 1986, 35, personal collection of Bobbie Jean Rovner, Greenville, SC; Alex Davis, interview with Dale Rosengarten, Feb. 28, 1997, MSS 1035-131, Jewish Heritage Collection, Special Collections, Addlestone Library, College of Charleston, Charleston, SC.

33. Bloom interview.

34. Rabbi Zaglin's sons serving in the armed forces included Harry, Louis, Marion, and Jack. Zaglin, "Zaglins of Greenville," 6–7.

35. World War II Draft Cards, 1942–1947, Abram Rosenberg.

36. Neely, "Jews of Anderson," 8–10.

37. Irving Abrams, Obituary, *Greenville News,* July 22, 2020.

38. World War II Draft Cards, 1942–1947, Ralph Tanenbaum; 1940 US Census, Spartanburg.

39. Max Massey, Obituary, *Spartanburg Herald-Journal* (SC), April 13, 2018.

40. Massey, Obituary.

41. 1930 Federal Census, Orangeburg, SC; "Sol Abrams Dies, Funeral Today at 1," Sol Abrams Folder, South Carolina Room, Greenville Public Library; World War II Draft Cards, 1940–1947; University of South Carolina Yearbook, 1948.

42. Edward Poliakoff, "Aboard the Huddleston: WW II Diaries of Dr. A. Ellis Poliakoff, Cpt., US Army Medical Corps," *Jewish Historical Society of South Carolina,* jhssc .org/2015/05/27/.

43. Moore, *GI Jews,* 75.

44. Poliakoff, "Aboard the Huddleston," 4.

45. Moore, *GI Jews,* 142.

46. Poliakoff, Aboard the Huddleston," 7.

47. "Famed Tank Commander Promoted to Colonel," *Daily News Journal* (Murfreesboro TN), May 4, 1945, 1.

48. Blanche Gibbs, "Famous Fighter Comes Home. Col. Cohen Gave Nazis Unwanted Lessons," *Spartanburg (SC) Herald Journal*, October 28, 1945.

49. Sudmeier, "Harold Cohen," 2.

50. Angie Thompson, "Rue du Colonel Harold Cohen," *Tifton (GA) Gazette*, October 5, 2009, https://www.tiftongazette.com/archives/.

51. Ibid.

52. Sudmeier, "Harold Cohen," 2.

53. Harold Cohen, "Distinguished Service Cross Citation," https://jimsudmeier.com/.

54. Sudmeier, "Harold Cohen," 3.

55. Ibid., 3.

56. "Nazi's Stunned by Yank Speed," Front page headline of *Charlotte Observer,* March 17, 1945, 1.

57. Angie Thompson, "Farewell to a Hero," *Tifton (GA) Gazette*, August 15, 2006, https://www.tiftongazette.com/archives.

58. Sudmeier, "Harold Cohen," 5.

59. Sudmier, 4.

60. 1930 and 1940 Federal Censuses, Gaffney and Greenville SC.

61. *Greenville High School Yearbook*, 1938.

62. US World War II Army Enlistment Records, 1938–1946.

63. Greenville City Directory, 1942.

64. "Fliers Downed in Hong Kong Raid Reach American Lines," *Fort Worth Star-Telegram*, November 15, 1942, 29.

65. Ben Samuel, "Jews in Uniform," *Wisconsin Jewish Chronicle* (Milwaukee, WI), March 3, 1944, 9.

66. "Walker's Club," Library of Congress, Office of War Information, https://www.loc.gov/item/2017697698.

67. "Lt. Sher Killed in Action," *Greenville News,* September 9, 1943, 14.

68. "Morton Sher," https://www.honorstates.org/index.php?id=80027.

69. "Memory of Flier Will Be Honored," *Greenville News*, November 8, 1943, 8.

70. Nathan Belth, *Fighting for America.*

71. Ibid.

72. Shapiro, *Time for Healing,* 15.

7: JEWISH GARMENT MANUFACTURING

1. Maunula, *Guten Tag, Y'All,* 34.

2. Ibid., 14.

3. Ibid., 34.

4. Ibid.

5. David Carlton, "Textile Town Settles In, 1950 to 1974," *Textile Town, Spartanburg County, South Carolina*, ed. Betsy Wakefield Teter (Spartanburg, SC: Hub City Writers Project, 2002), 210.

6. Huff, *Greenville,* 389.

7. Carlton, "Textile Town Settles In," 212.

8. Ibid., 213.

9. Ibid., 210.

10. Huff, *Greenville,* 389.

11. The 1947 Taft-Hartley Act was a federal law that restricted the activities and powers of labor unions, thus, amending the Wagner Act. It passed over a veto by President Truman who called it a "Slave-labor bill." *First Amendment Encyclopedia,* mtsu.edu.

12. See https://nrtwc.org/facts/right-work-mean/.

13. James C. Cobb, *The South and America Since World War II* (New York: Oxford University Press, 2012), 57.

14. Cobb, *Industrialization,* 144.

15. Cobb, *Selling of the South,* 79.

16. Ibid., 90.

17. Woodward, *Origins of the New South,* 291.

18. Maunola, *Guten Tag Y'All,* 40.

19. "Frederick B. Dent, 97, Commerce Secretary and Nixon Ally, Dies," *New York Times,* www.nytimes.com/2019/12/16.

20. Carlton, "Textile Town Settles In," 213.

21. Kanter, *World Class,* 249.

22. Roger Milliken, Obituary, https://www.legacy.com/us/obituaries/nytimes/name/.

23. Maunula, *Guten Tag Y'All,* 33.

24. Philip Stone, "Making a Modern State: The Politics of Economic Development in South Carolina, 1938–1962," PhD diss., University of South Carolina, 2003, 202.

25. See Kanter, *World Class* and Maunula, *Guten Tag Y'All.*

26. Abernathy, et al., *A Stitch in Time,* 30.

27. Bodie McDowell, "New Abbeville County Plant to Begin Operating Dec. 1," *Index-Journal* (Greenwood, SC), November 13, 1959, 1; "Iva Manufacturing Company, *Greenville News,* February 13, 1963, 5; Robert Bohler, "Iva Manufacturing to Be Featured in Trade Magazine," *Greenville News,* April 7, 1988, 54; "Small Plant to be Established in McCormick," *Greenville News,* October 5, 1972, 4.

28. Mrs. A. H. Counts, "Prosperity Garment Plant Displays Growth at Open House," *Greenville News,* July 10, 1959, 3; "Old School Manufacturing Company in Prosperity, (1958) was a subsidiary of M. Setlow & Sons of Connecticut," *Greenville News,* December 28, 1958, 33; 1900 US Census, New Hartford, CT.

29. "Local Sportswear Company Expands," *Gaffney Ledger* (SC), January 3, 1973, 1.

30. Jewish-owned textile and garment factories in the Upcountry included M. Lowenstein & Sons, the Shore Company, Carolina Blouse Company, (later MacShore Classics), Iva Manufacturing, Clark Hill Mfg. Sportswear Unlimited, Raycord, Riegel Textiles, Maxon Shirts, Cutron Corporation, Emb-Tex, Kemco, Gaftan Sportswear, L&K, the Kreiger Corporation, Varat Enterprises, Williamston Pants Company, Carolina Converting Mills, Easley Textile Company, Swirl, Inc., Sportair Manufacturing, Salem Manufacturing, Westminster Manufacturing, Wendall Fabrics, Spectator, Inc., Spartan Undies, Butte Knit, and M. Setlow & Sons.

31. Chantelle Porter, "Famous Jewish Fashion Designers and Their Cultural Impact," https://bellatory.com/fashion-industry/Famours.

32. Robert Zieger, *Life and Labor,* 2.

33. Walker, *All We Knew Was to Farm,* 86.

34. Miller and Pozzetta, *Shades of the Sunbelt,* xiii.

35. South Carolina: Table 43. Economic Characteristics of the Population, by Sex, for Counties: Spartanburg, 1950, US Census, Population, 2, 40.

36. Belcher, *Greenville County,* 138.

37. Sandor Teszler, "Memoir," Ch. 1: Youth (unpublished memoir), Archives, Sandor Teszler Library, Wofford College Archives, Spartanburg, SC.

38. Ibid, Ch. 2: Productive Years, Europe.

39. Fenyo, *Hitler, Horthy, and Hungary,* 159.

40. Teszler, "Memoir," Ch. 2: Productive Years, Europe.

41. "Hungary After the Occupation," US Holocaust Memorial Museum, https://encyclopedia.ushmm.org/content/en/article/.

42. Carl Lutz was a Swiss diplomat in charge of representing the United States, Great Britain and other countries that had cut ties with Hungary. Lutz issued certificates for

Hungarian Jews to emigrate to Palestine, which amounted to the largest rescue operation of Jews during World War II. Lutz and his wife were designated "Righteous Among the Nations" by Yad Vashem. See Jewish Virtual Library, http://www.jewishvirtuallibrary.org.

43. Teszler, "Memoirs," Ch. 2, Productive Years, Europe.

44. Ibid.

45. Diner, *We Remember,* 156.

46. Immigration and Ship Manifest lists; Naturalization records for Akos Teszler, who changed his name to Tessler. Ancestry.com.

47. Teszler, "Memoirs," Ch. 3: Productive Years, America.

48. "Spartanburg Industries" supplement to *Spartanburg* (SC)*Herald* and *Spartanburg (SC) Journal,* March 15, 1968. Butte Knits Folder, Kennedy Room Archives, Spartanburg Public Library.

49. Teter, *Textile Town,* 251.

50. "Butte: A Native Giant Among Area's Industries," *Spartanburg Herald-Journal Business and Industrial Review,* March 13, 1971, C-10.

51. Teter, *Textile Town,* 251–53.

52. Poliakoff, *Portraits of a People,* 48. Spartan Undies was a New York-based United Merchants and Manufacturing company located in Spartanburg. It employed 250 workers and produced women's and girl's lingerie and sleepwear for discount department stores.

53. Ibid., 5.

54. Sylvia Rex, interview with Diane Catherine Vecchio, November 14, 2019, Spartanburg, SC.

55. Poliakoff, *Portraits of a People,* 48.

56. Teszler, "Memoirs," Ch. 3, Productive Years, America, 2.

57. Ibid.

58. "Butte Knitting Mills of Spartanburg: How It Grew," Spartanburg-Business, Butte Knits Folder, Kennedy Room, Spartanburg Public Library.

59. Teter, *Textile Town,* 252.

60. "Spartanburg Industries" Butte Knits Folder, Kennedy Room, Spartanburg Public Library.

61. "The Butte Knitting Mills Story," pamphlet collection, Kennedy Room, Spartanburg Public Library.

62. Poliakoff, *Portraits of a People,* 100.

63. Tanya Bordeaux Hamm, "Andrew Teszler. A Life Cut Short," in *Textile Town,* Spartanburg, SC, 252–53.

64. Poliakoff, *Portraits of a People,* 100.

65. Eleanor Garner Hannah, "Andrew Teszler: A Man Who Cared for People," *Spartanburg Herald-Journal,* May 9, 1971, B7.

66. Ibid.

67. Ibid.

68. Ibid.

69. Ibid.

70. Sandor Teszler Memoirs, Retirement, 1–2, Wofford College Archives.

71. "Atomic Radiation Lab for Test in Textile Field Opens at State," *News and Observer* (Raleigh, NC), November 4, 1958, I, 2.

72. "The Swirl Story," June 10, 2014. https://vintagefashionguild.org/fashion-history/.

73. Ibid.

74. Ibid.

75. "Jack Nachman, founder of Swirl Inc., dies at 76," private papers of Jack Cutchin of Easley, SC, in author's possession.

76. John Cutchin, interview with Diane Catherine Vecchio, January 2, 2021, Easley, SC.

77. "Breakfast to Bedtime Clothes," *Charlotte Observer,* October 29, 1967, Section E, 65.

78. "The Swirl Story," 4–5.

79. "Swirl," Fuzzylizzie Vintage, 4–5, https://vintage-fashionguild.org/label-resource /swirl/.

80. J. Michael Elliott, Obituary, "Bill Tice, 52, Creator of Stylish Clothing to Wear at Home," *New York Times,* March 29, 1995, Section A, 21.

81. "Suit Filed to Collect $770,753 from Former Owners of Clothing Manufacturer," *Greenville (SC) News,* March 20, 1991, 30.

82. "Pike Garments Stockholders Agree to Sell to Big Piedmont Company," *Troy* (AL) *Messenger,* June 17, 1953, 1.

83. Herbert Blueweiss, "Piedmont's Growth Called a Geometrical Progression," *Troy* (AL) *Messenger,* June 26, 1953, 3.

84. "Max Heller," *Greenville (SC) News,* March 4, 1962, 35.

85. Vecchio, "Max Moses Heller," 181–211.

86. Ibid.,186.

87. Ibid.

88. Harry Wiemer, "Deep Interest in Employees, Saltzman Trait," *Troy (AL) Messenger,* July 29, 1953, 7.

89. "Piedmont Shirt Company," File: "Textiles P-R." South Carolina Room, Greenville County Library.

90. J. A. C. Dunn, "Heller 1: "If You Remember At Me," *Charlotte (NC) Observer,* September 6, 1966. Max Heller Papers, Box 4, Folder 1, Furman University Special Collections (hereafter, FUSC).

91. Max Heller, interview with Dale Rosengarten and Sandra Lee Kan Rosenblum, Feb. 28, 1997, College of Charleston Library, Jewish Heritage Project. Lib-cat-cofc.edu /search.

92. One day, Heller was walking down the street when he felt a tap on the shoulder. He looked around to see a longtime friend from his sport club. "Hans," he said, "How good to see you." Hans pointed to the Jews scrubbing the street; "Over there, pig Jew, he yelled at Heller as he shoved him to the ground to scrub the streets. Dunn, Heller 2: "Luck and Good Weather," Max Heller Papers, Box 4, Folder 1, FUSC.

93. Heller interview with Rosengarten & Rosenblum.

94. Interview with Max Heller, 21. Max Heller Papers, Box 7, Folder 8. FUSC.

95. Ibid.

96. "Maxon Shirt: At 10-Year Mark It's a Thriving Company," *Boys' Outfitter Newsletter,* October 1957, 240. Max Heller Papers, Box 7, Folder 2, FUSC.

97. Ethel Steadman, "Heller, Man Behind Maxon," *Greenville (SC) News,* March 4, 1962, Max Heller Papers, Box 7, Folder 2, FUSC.

98. Ibid.

99. "Apparel Firm Buys Maxon Shirt Plant," *Greenville (SC) News,* April 2, 1971, Max Heller Papers, Mayoral Files, Box 4, Folder 2, FUSC.

100. Abe Hardesty, "David Krieger. Hard Work, Ingenuity Make American Dream Lifelong Reality for Textile Entrepreneur," *Greenville News,* January 25, 2006, 58.

101. "Miss Page Annette Miller, David Krieger Plan to Wed," *Circleville (OH) Herald,* August 16, 1972, 6.

102. Jim Du Plessis, "Emb-Tex Agrees to Receiver After Inventory Shortfall," *Greenville (SC) News,* April 10, 1991, 4D.

103. "Emb-Tex Doubles in Size," *Greenville News,* November 7, 1988, 23.

104. "Emb-Tex" File, Textiles E-1, South Carolina Room, Greenville County Library.

105. Hardesty, "David Krieger, Hard Work, Ingenuity" 58.

106. "Emb-Tex underfunded retirement, health insurance plans, officials say," Emb-Tex File, South Carolina Room, Greenville County Library.

107. "Carolina Blouse Demonstrates Outstanding Growth: Nearly 1700 Employees," *Greenville (SC) News,* January 8, 1960, 11.

108. "MacShore Classics," *Greenville (SC) News,* February 12, 1956, 122.

109. "Carolina Blouse Demonstrates Outstanding Growth," 11.

110. "Carolina Blouse Had 1500 Employees," *Greenville News,* February 12, 1956, 122.

111. "Polio No Handicap to this Veteran Salesman," *Greenville (SC) News,* August 27, 1958, 9.

112. "Once with 1,800 Employees," *Greenville (SC) News,* August 28, 2004, 17.

113. Ibid.

114. Marjorie W. Young, "The Lowenstein Story," in *Textile Leaders of the South,* (Anderson, SC: J. R. Young, 1963), 307–16. Kennedy Room, Spartanburg County Library.

115. Harry Riemer, "Trace Lowenstein Growth from 7 to 86 Employees," *Daily News-Record* (Harrisonburg, Virginia) December 6, 1946. Textile Workers Union of America Records, Wisconsin Historical Society, Madison, WI, hereafter WHS, Madison.

116. "The Lowenstein Story," 311.

117. Ibid.

118. Ibid.

119. Herbert James, "Lowenstein Dedicates Building Today, Marking Milestone," DNR, 3/1/55, TWUA papers, MSS 87, Box 106, WHS, Madison.

120. "M. Lowenstein Companies," Register of the M. Lowenstein Corporation Records, 1902–1982, Clemson University Archives.

121. Ibid.

122. David Carlton, "Textile Town Settles In, 1950 to 1974," in *Textile Town,* 219.

123. M. Lowenstein Corporation Records, MSS 134, Box 1, Mill Village Sale, 1949, July-September, Clemson University Archives; 1940 Federal Census, Anderson, SC; Anderson City Directory, 1946, "Obituary," *Greenville News,* February 15, 1991, 26.

124. Ibid.

125. Obituary, *Greenville (SC) News,* February 8, 1980, 5D.

126. "The Lowenstein Story," 312.

127. Minchin, *What Do We Need a Union For,* 31.

128. M. Lowenstein Companies, Register of the M. Lowenstein Corporation Records, Clemson University Archives.

129. "The Lowenstein Story," 312.

130. Ibid.

131. "Testimonial Dinner Will Honor Leon Lowenstein," *Gaffney (SC) Ledger,* June 4, 1953, 1.

132. "M. Lowenstein Report Wins Annual Award," September 15, 1957, TWUA Papers.

133. "The Lowenstein Story," 312.

134. M. Lowenstein Companies, Register of the M. Lowenstein Corporation Records, Clemson University Archives.

135. "The Lowenstein Story," 312–13.

136. Ibid.

137. Ibid., 325.

138. Ibid., 309.

139. John Value, "Leon Lowenstein: Dean of Textile Industry," *Boston Globe,* August 3, 1965, 14.

140. "Lowenstein Forms New Subsidiary," *American Textile Reporter,* November 15, 1956, TWUA reports, MSS 87, Box 109, "Lowenstein and Sons Financial Records, WHS, Madison.

141. Register of the M. Lowenstein Corporation, 1889–1986, MSS 134 M. Lowenstein Corporation Records, Clemson University Archives.

142. Cathy Silverman Lewson, interview with Diane Catherine Vecchio, May 18, 2021, Spartanburg, SC.

143. Ibid.

144. "Blacksburg Company Celebrates 50 years in the Fabric Industry," *Gaffney (SC) Ledger,* March 4, 1996, 1.

145. "Students Learn Vocation on the Job at Wendall," *Gaffney (SC) Ledger,* July 12, 1974, 1.

146. Maunula, *Guten Tag Y'All,* 16.

147. Ibid.

148. Ibid., 219.

149. "Greenville and Lincolnton Firms Ditch NRA Provisions: Piedmont Shirt Company and Spinning Mill Change Hours and Wages," *Greenville (SC) News,* May 30, 1935, 1.

150. "Statement Given by Shirt Company: Report All Strife over at Piedmont Shirt Company, Harmony Reigns," *Greenville (SC) News,* May 31, 1935, 13.

151. Ibid., 13.

152. "Judge Us Fairly," *Greenville (SC) News,* June 2, 1936, 18.

153. "Carolinas In Move to Keep NRA Features," *Charlotte (NC) News,* May 30, 1935, 4.

154. Mandell, *Corporation as Family,* 145.

155. "Piedmont Shirt Co. Ordered to Halt Employees' Union," *Index-Journal* (Greenwood, SC), June 3, 1939, 5.

156. "Reports Labor Act Violated: Trial Examiner Says Unions in Greenville Mill Company Dominated," *Charlotte (NC) Observer,* March 28, 1939, 8.

157. "Office Union Asks Vote at Textile Company," in *Roanoke Labor Journal,* July 22, 1937, TWUA Records, WHA, Madison.

158. "Spartanburg Firm is Fined in Court, *Greenville (SC) News,* August 18, 1942, 3.

159. Maunula, *Guten Tag Y'All,* 16.

160. Ibid., 19.

161. Ibid., 19–20.

162. Spartanburg: Petition opposing unionization is being circulated at Spartan Undies," *The Item* (Sumter, SC), June 4, 1964, 20.

163. MSS 129, Box 2, TWUA records, WHA, Madison.

164. Ibid., MSS 129, Box 2.

165. "3,000 Win Improved Conditions in Three Lowenstein Renewals," *Textile Labor,* September 3, 1949, Atlanta, MSS 87, Box 109, TWUA records, WHS, Madison. "Lowenstein and Sons," Financial, 1915–1957, TWUA records, Madison.

166. Ibid.

167. "Dixie Shirt Co. Ordered to Halt Anti-Union Acts," *Gaffney (SC) Ledger,* September 28, 1949, 6.

168. Carlton, "Textile Town Settles In," 228.

169. Teter, "Voices from the Village: Rosalie Tucker," in *Textile Town,* 236.

170. "Workers Back on Jobs at Spartanburg Plants," *Greenville (SC) News,* April 10, 1969, 3.

171. Teter, "Butte Knit. Decline of a Double-Knit Dynamo," 251.

172. Carlton, "Textile Town Settles In," 212–13.

173. "School Comes to Plant," *Colorado Springs Gazette-Telegraph,* May 8, 1969, 7.

174. "Butte 'Foots' the Bill," *Spartanburg Herald-Journal,* supplement, March 15, 1968, 10.

175. "Employees Socialize," *Spartanburg Herald-Journal,* supplement, March 15, 1968, 10.

176. Job and benefit advertisement for Piedmont Shirt Company, *Greenville (SC) News,* October 18, 1966, 79.

177. Maunula, *Guten Tag, Y'all,* 20.

178. Freidman, *Philadelphia Jewish Life,* xvi.

179. Goldstein and Weiner, *On Middle Ground,* 72.

180. In Spartanburg, for example, the textile leader Walter S. Montgomery (1866–1929) embarked on philanthropy in the early twentieth century when he provided funding for the Pellagra Hospital in 1913. Together with Mac Cates, they created a community foundation which continues to provide millions of dollars to charitable organizations in the county. Textile philanthropy soared in the 1940s with the creation of the Milliken Foundation, the Arcadia Foundation (Mayfair Mills), and the Arkwright Foundation. These and other textile companies funded community studies, scholarship programs, new school construction, etc. According to Betsy Wakefield Teter, their charity only accelerated in the latter part of the twentieth century. See Betsy Wakefield Teter, "Spreading the Wealth. A Century of Textile Philanthropy," in *Textile Town,* Spartanburg County, South Carolina, 296–298.

181. Hamm, "Andrew Teszler: A Life Cut Short," in *Textile Town*, Spartanburg, 253.
182. Ibid.
183. "New Library at Wofford Named for Sandor Teszler," *Spartanburg Herald Journal,* March 28, 1971. Sandor Teszler Folder, Wofford College Archives.
184. Sandor Teszler, Obituary, *Spartanburg (SC) Herald,* July 23, 2000, 1.
185. "B'nai B'rith Unit Meets in City, April 1–2," *Greenville (SC) News,* March 26, 1967, 11.
186. "Harry S. Abrams, Obituary," *Greenville (SC) News,* January 29, 1977, 22.
187. "Accepts Keys to Jewish Center," *Greenville (SC) News,* October 13, 1958, 6.
188. "Kaye on Committee Planning UJA Meet," *The Item* (Sumter, SC), March 7, 1956, 12.
189. "Leon Lowenstein, 93, Philanthropist Dies," *Miami News,* April 6, 1976, 6.
190. "Textile Executive Lowenstein, 92, Dies," *Greenville (SC) News,* April 7, 1976, 32.
191. Ibid.
192. Ibid.
193. Edgar, *South Carolina Encyclopedia,* 956.
194. Teter, "Textile Town in Transition," in *Textile Town,* 267.
195. Ibid., 276.
196. Ibid.

8: JEWISH–BLACK RELATIONS

1. "Colored Schools of County Show Material Improvement," *Spartanburg (SC) Herald,* January 14, 1919, 4.
2. Diner, *In the Almost Promised Land,* 125–127, 166. See also Diner, *Julius Rosenwald;* Ascoli, *Julius Rosenwald;* Feiler and Lewis, *A Better Life;* andStephanie Deutsch, *You Need a Schoolhouse: Booker T. Washington, Julius Rosenberg, and the Building of Schools for the Segregated South,* (Evanston, IL: Northwestern University Press, 2015).
3. Franklin and Moss, *From Slavery to Freedom,* 406.
4. Ascoli, *Julius Rosenwald,* 135.
5. Ibid., 141.
6. Diner, *Julius Rosenwald,* 162–64.
7. Ibid.,173–74.
8. Ibid.,174–75.
9. South Carolina Department of Archives and History, https://digital.library.sc.edu/exhibits/rosenwald/.
10. Lugene Gist, interview with Tom Cosby, January 6, 2007, Santuck, SC, https://digital.library.sc.edu/exhibits/rosenwald/.
11. Ibid.; and Mattie Sims Savage, interview with Tom Cosby, June 14, 2007, Union, SC, https://digital.library.sc.edu/exhibits/rosenwald/.
12. Diner, *Julius Rosenwald,* 174.
13. Ibid.
14. Diner, *Julius Rosenwald,* 145.
15. Webb, "Jewish Merchants and Black Customers in the Age of Jim Crow," 62.
16. Ibid
17. Hertzberg, *Strangers Within,* 183.

18. Webb, "A Tangled Web: Black-Jewish Relations in the Twentieth Century South," 192–209.

19. No retail shops existed in the Black Southside, but the neighborhood had a bustling business sector where Black entrepreneurs operated barber shops, eating establishments, funeral parlors, and grocery stores.

20. Hill and Lee, *South of Main*, 70.

21. Finkelstein interview with Diane Catherine Vecchio.

22. From, "The Froms of Union: Merchants on Main Street for 100 Years," 15.

23. Allan From, Panel discussion: "Hub City Reminisces," Annual Meeting of the Jewish Historical Society of South Carolina, November 10, 2019, Temple B'nai Israel.

24. Edward Gray, interview with Diane Catherine Vecchio, December 10, 2009, Spartanburg SC.

25. Dorothy Price Cohen, interview with Diane Catherine Vecchio, October 29, 2009, Spartanburg, SC.

26. Rovner, Zaglin, and Zaglin interview.

27. Goldfield, "A Sense of Place: Jews, Blacks, and White Gentiles in the American South," 58–79.

28. Gray interview.

29. Feinstein interview.

30. Maunula, *Guten Tag Y'All*, 27.

31. O'Neill, "Memory, History, and the Desegregation of Greenville, South Carolina," 286–99.

32. Felder, *Civil Rights,* 86.

33. Frady, *Jesse,* 83.

34. Huff, *Greenville,* 407.

35. Frady, *Jesse,* 137.

36. Ibid.

37. Patrick Obley, "How Jackie Robinson Ignited Greenville's Civil Rights Movement," *Sun-News,* (Myrtle Beach, SC), April 7, 2013, 1A and A14.

38. Ibid., see also "Business, Taxation, Racial Problems Loom," *The State,* (Columbia, SC), January 1, 1960, 17; and Robinson-Simpson, *Greenville County,* 51.

39. Jesse Jackson, interview with Diane Catherine Vecchio, October 30, 2013, Greenville, SC.

40. Ibid.

41. O'Neill, "Memory, History, and the Desegregation of Greenville," 290.

42. Brinson, *Stories of Struggle,* 189.

43. O'Neill, "Memory, History, and the Desegregation of Greenville," 290.

44. Ibid.

45. Ibid.

46. Ibid., 291.

47. Brinson, *Stories of Struggle,* 188.

48. Hill and Lee, *South of Main,* 73–74.

49. O'Neill, "Memory, History, and the Desegregation of Greenville," 290.

50. Damon Fordham, "Remembering the Lunch Counter Sit-in," in *South of Main,* 200–201.

51. Ibid.

52. Ibid., 200.

53. Maunula, *Guten Tag Y'All,* 29.

54. Bass and Nelson, *Orangeburg Massacre,* 10.

55. Ibid.

56. Ibid., 11.

57. Maunula, *Guten Tag Y'All,* 30.

58. Ballantyne, *New Politics,* 24.

59. Ibid., 43.

60. Ibid., 24.

61. Edgar, *South Carolina,* 537–38.

62. Ibid., 538.

63. Courtney Tollison, "Principles Over Prejudice: The Desegregation of Furman University, Wofford, Columbia, and Presbyterian Colleges," (master's thesis, University of South Carolina, 2001), 2.

64. O'Neill, "Memory, History, and the Desegregation of Greenville," 295.

65. Ibid., 296.

66. Bass and Nelson, *Orangeburg Massacre,* 11–12.

67. Robinson-Simpson, *Greenville County,* 40, 52.

68. Bass and Nelson, *Orangeburg Massacre*, 8–9.

69. "The Orangeburg Massacre," www.history.com/topics/1960s/.

70. Gutkowski, "The Evolution of Environmental (In)Justice in Spartanburg, South Carolina, 1900–2000," 938.

71. Ibid., 939.

72. Email exchange with Courtney Tollison Hartness, January 26, 2022.

73. Marc Dollinger, "From 'Hamans' to 'Torquemadas': Southern and Northern Jewish Responses to the Civil Rights Movement," in Bauman and Kalin, *Quiet Voices,* https://muse.jhu.edu/book/35916.

74. David Goldfield maintains that "during the civil rights era, many Jews remained on the sidelines." In smaller towns, especially, Jews rarely spoke out. Historian Stephen Hertzberg agrees, adding that "Jews were likely to adopt the attitudes and practices of their gentile neighbors," *(Strangers Within the Gate City).* Eric Goldstein echoes this sentiment in his study of Jews and race, noting that "most Jews in the South generally shied away from high profile political engagement with racial issues" *(The Price of Whiteness).*

75. Rabbi Burton Lee Padoll, interview with Dale Rosengarten, October 21, 1999, *Jewish Heritage Collection,* Oral Histories, College of Charleston, MSS. 1035–224, 11, https://lcdl.library.cofc.edu/lcdl/catalog/lcdl:36578.

76. From, panel discussion, "Hub City Reminisces."

77. Ibid.

78. Gary Poliakoff, interview with Diane Catherine Vecchio, September 30, 2021, Spartanburg, SC.

79. Leonard Dinnerstein, *Uneasy at Home,* 133.

80. Bauman and Kalin, *Quiet Voices.*

81. Ibid.

82. Ibid., 135.

83. Ibid., 138; see also Rabbi Allen Krause, who examined the opinions of southern Jewish rabbis in *To Stand Aside or Stand Alone: Southern Reform Rabbis and the Civil Rights Movement*, eds. Mark K. Bauman & Stephen Krause, (Tuscaloosa: University of Alabama Press, 2016). Krause believes that most Jews are "somewhat ambivalent about the whole issue but tending toward thoughts sympathetic to the Negro."

84. Bauman and Kalin, *Quiet Voices*; studies conducted by Leonard Dinnerstein, Marc Dollinger, and Allen Krause.

85. Leonard Dinnerstein, *Uneasy at Home,* 133.

86. Email exchange with Dale Rosengarten, January 21, 2022.

87. Rabbi Gerald Wolpe, interview with Dale Rosengarten, November 15, 1999, Charleston, SC., Jewish Heritage Collection, MSS. 1035–231, 13.

88. Ibid.,13.

89. Ibid.,13.

90. Ibid.,13.

91. Ibid.,15.

92. Ibid.,16.

93. Rabbi Burton Lee Padoll interview, 11.

94. Ibid.

95. Ibid.

96. Ibid., 11–12.

97. Rabbi Burton Lee Padoll, sermon, April 14, 1961, 3. https://lcdl.library.cofc.edu/.

98. Rabbi Burton Lee Padoll interview, 13.

99. Ibid., 14.

100. Ibid., 12.

101. Email exchange with Dale Rosengarten, January 21, 2022.

102. Dollinger, "From 'Hamans' to 'Torquemadas'."

103. See Northside rising, Spartanburg, SC.

104. Clay Turner, telephone interview with Diane Catherine Vecchio, November 12, 2021.

105. Yossi Liebowitz interview with Diane Vecchio, June 20, 2020, Spartanburg, SC.

106. See http://www.Templeofisrael.org/our-rabbi.

107. Frederickson, "Four Decades of Change: Black Workers in Southern Textiles, 1941–1981," 64.

108. Ibid., 65.

109. Judith Bainbridge, "How Black Workers Changed the Textile Industry in South Carolina," October 28, 2018, D1, https://www.greenvilleonline.com/story/news/2018/10/29/.

110. Teter, "Making History. The Battle to Desegregate," in *Textile Town*, 246.

111. Minchin, "Black Activism, the 1964 Civil Rights Act, and the Racial Integration of the Southern Textile Industry," 809–844.

112. Bainbridge, "How Black Workers Changed the Textile Industry in South Carolina"

113. Minchin, "Black Activism, the 1964 Civil Rights Act, and the Racial Integration of the Southern Textile Industry," 813.

114. Irving Abrams, interview with Dale Rosengarten and Sandra Lee Kahn Rosenblum, Greenville, SC., January 27, 1997, MSS 1035–28, Jewish Heritage Oral History Collection, College of Charleston Library, 45.

115. Ibid.

116. Victoria Morrow, phone interview with Diane Catherine Vecchio, March 10, 2018.

117. Max Heller, interview with Marvin Lare, "Champions of Civil and Human Rights in South Carolina," A Digital Exhibition by the Department of Oral History at the University of South Carolina, May 23, 2006, vol. 3, part 3, online.

118. Ibid., 188.

119. Heller, interview, US Holocaust Museum, September 24, 1998, 41.

120. Oakley Coburn, "Memories of Sandor Teszler," South Carolina Historical Society annual meeting, October 2020, Temple B'nai Israel, Spartanburg, SC.

121. Ibid.

122. Sandor Teszler, Memoirs, "America," Sandor Teszler Papers, Wofford College, Spartanburg, SC.

123. Ibid., 3.

124. Brenda Lee Pryce, interview with Diane Catherine Vecchio, April 27, 2021, Spartanburg, SC.

125. Ibid.

126. Ibid.

127. Ibid.

128. Ibid.

129. Minchin, "Black Activism, the 1964 Civil Rights Act," 816.

130. Pryce interview.

131. Belcher, *Greenville County*, 148.

132. "The State. Table 184, Detailed Industry of Employed Persons by Race and Sex, 1970," 680. US Department of Commerce. 1970 Census of the Population, vol. 1, part 42, South Carolina.

133. Max Heller, interview with Rosengarten and Rosenblum, 133.

134. Andrew Baker, "Max Moses Heller: Jewish Mayor in the Sunbelt South," 68.

135. Max Heller, interview with Bass and DeVries, A-0155-Southern Oral History Program Collection (#4007) at the Southern Historical Collection. The Louis Round Wilson Special Collection Library, UNC-Chapel Hill, December 3, 1974. https://dcr.lib.unc.edu/record/.

136. Vecchio, "Max Moses Heller: Patron Saint of Greenville's Renaissance," 181–211.

137. Ibid., 190.

138. See https://www.isjl.org/jewish-mayors-in-the-south.html.

139. Baker, "Max Moses Heller, "Jewish Mayor in the Sunbelt South," unpublished paper, 2.

140. Vecchio, "Max Moses Heller: Patron Saint of Greenville's Renaissance," 198.

141. Susan Heller Moses, "Max and Trude Heller: Giving Back to the Community," *Jewish Historical Society of South Carolina* 21, no. 2, (2016) 8–9.

142. "Politicians Can Look Back on 1972 As One of Most Eventful, Colorful Years," *Greenville (SC) News*, Max Heller Papers, Box 12, Scrapbooks 1969–1974, Clippings

and press from first term as mayor, Furman Special Collections, Duke Library, Furman University.

143. Baker, "Max Moses Heller: Jewish Mayor in the Sunbelt South" *Southern Jewish History*, 78. See also Dale Perry, "Housing, Sanitation Criticized at Meeting, *Greenville (SC) News*, October 12, 1973, Box 12, Heller Papers, Furman University.

144. Baker, "Max Moses Heller: Jewish Mayor in the Sunbelt South," 78; see also "City government did more Listening, Brick and Mortar," *Greenville (SC) Piedmont*, December 27, 1973, Heller Papers Box 16, Furman University.

145. Max Heller, interview with Jack Bass and Walter DeVries, for the Southern Historical Collection, Louis Round Wilson Special Collections Library, UNC-Chapel Hill, December 3, 1974. Interview #A-0155.

146. Willie Sullivan, "Leaders Feel Greenville Race Relations Improved," *Greenville (SC) News*, January 11, 1972, 3.

147. Ibid.

148. Vecchio, "Max Moses Heller, Patron Saint of Greenville's Renaissance," 199.

149. Ibid.

150. See https://scafricanamerican.com/honorees/lillian-brock-flemming.

151. Baker, "Max Moses Heller Jewish Mayor in the Sunbelt South," 21.

152. Vecchio, "Max Moses Heller, Patron Saint of Greenville's Renaissance199.

153. Lottie Gibson, interview with Marvin Lare, May 23, 2006, https://digital.library .sc.edu/.

154. Dunleavy and Mitchell interview with Diane Catherine Vecchio.

155. Su Su Johnson, interview with Diane Catherine Vecchio, January 12, 2022, Spartanburg, SC.

156. Mary Thomas, interview with Diane Catherine Vecchio, March 4, 2022, Spartanburg, SC.

157. Gutkowski, "The Evolution of Environmental (In)Justice in Spartanburg Carolina, 1900–2000," 924.

158. Ibid., 924–25.

159. Ibid., Gutkowski argues that "Arkwright illustrates how the South's legacy of racial discrimination often magnified the environmental impact of deindustrialization on African American communities. . . ." Spartanburg, a city experiencing a massive Sun Belt boom, suffered the decline of older industrial brownfield sites creating a toxic environment.

160. Ibid., 947.

161. William Barnet, interview with Diane Catherine Vecchio, January 25, 2022, Spartanburg SC.

162. Ed Memmott, telephone interview with Diane Catherine Vecchio, January 12, 2022, Spartanburg, SC.

163. Dunleavy interview.

164. Johnson interview.

165. Russell Booker, interview with Diane Catherine Vecchio, February 19, 2022, Spartanburg, SC.

166. Thomas interview.

167. The city secured funding from the Mary Black Foundation, the Spartanburg Housing Authority, BMW, Coca Cola, and other sources.

168. The C. C. Woodson Community Center provides Southside residents with a place to hold meetings, socialize, learn, and exercise. It features a swimming pool, an exercise room, a full-court basketball gym, a community room, a library and learning center, a teen center and health and wellness room; see https://cityofspartanburg.org/Facilities/Facility/Details/.

169. See http://www.knowitall.org/video/William-Barnet-legacy-leadership.

170. Barnet was also a major force behind the creation of the Citizen Scholars Program, a special initiative of the Spartanburg County Foundation to assist county students with academic potential for those who would not normally attend college. The seven-year program provides students with an adult mentor and academic support.

171. Kathryn Harvey, Facing Race Together "What I learned from Bill Barnet," Together SC. Allies for Good, April 13, 2021, https://www.togethersc.org/blog/.

172. Richardson is a businessman who established Hardees, Spartan Foods, and Flagstaff, all headquartered in Spartanburg, SC.

173. These include the City of Spartanburg, Spartanburg School District 7, Mary Black Foundation, Spartanburg County Foundation, Spartanburg Regional Healthcare System, Edward Via College of Osteopathic Medicine, the University of South Carolina Upstate, Spartanburg Methodist College, Wofford College, and the YMCA. Thomas also notes that every bank in Spartanburg has donated monies and believes fervently in the efforts of the NDG.

174. This $15 million community center includes a swimming pool, basketball courts, walking track, workout rooms, and meeting rooms. As a result of the redevelopment of the Northside, a reduction of crime by almost 80% occurred between 2011 and 2016. Thomas also clarified that while the Northside was historically a predominantly Black community, the NDG wants it to be diverse and inclusive, with Hispanic, Asians, and whites residing in the neighborhood. White community members are already living in the newly built homes and Hispanic and Asian grocery stores have opened on the Northside.

175. The center is designed to serve infants, toddlers, and preschoolers from different socio-economic and cultural backgrounds.

176. Booker interview.

177. Thomas interview.

178. Barnet interview.

179. Liebowitz interview.

180. Booker interview.

181. See https://cityofspartanburg.org/Facilities/Facility/Details/CC-Woodson-Community-Center-31.

182. "Mayor Junie White is our Mensch of the Months of September and October, See https://ourtemple.net/2018/10/01.

183. Johnson interview.

184. "Spartanburg Mayor Junie White Honored With Order of the Palmetto in His Last City Council Meeting," http://www.spartanburg.com/news/2022/12/.

185. See https://www.towleroad.com/2010/06/spartanburg-sc-mayor-junie-white-comes-out-for-lgbt-equality.

9: THE JEWISH ROLE IN A NEW ECONOMY

1. Jewish businesses still operating in Spartanburg in the 1950s and 1960s included Quality Bakery, Greenewalds Clothing Store and Prices' Mens Shop, Mangels Clothing, Gilbard's Dad and Lad, The Fashion, Silver's Five and Ten Cent Store, Saul's Ladies Ready to Wear, Marion's, The Men's Shop, Steins, Smith's Pawn and Music Store, the Standard Cloak Company, Orendolf Department Store, Jack's Shoe Store, The Style Shop, Elliot's Jewelry, Worthmore Clothing, Kosch & Grey Jewelers, Pearls Millinery, The Vogue, Holtan Appliance Store, Carolina Loan and Luggage, The Men's Shop, Sklar's Jewelry Store, and The Globe. David and Julian Spigel operated a real estate office and optometry practice. Max Massey, a World War II hero, owned the Kiddie Korner, a stylish children's clothing store. Eventually, his business grew to twenty-one stores throughout the South.

After serving in World War II, Harry Zaglin returned to Greenville and opened an army and navy store, a business still operating today by his son, Jeffrey in a new location. Bob Rovner established a fashionable men's store on Main Street in the mid-1950s. After receiving an MBA from Harvard in the early 1940s and serving in the US Army Air Corps, Rovner settled in Greenville and operated a men's clothing shop for twenty-seven years before retiring in 1980. Isidore Goldblatt, the proprietor of Rey's Jewelry Store, together with Morris Lurey, operated the New York Shoe Store. Gerald Rosenberg owned and operated the Industrial Scrap and Waste Company that employed several members of his family.

Following World War II, all three Davis sons returned from military duty to work in the family business, Davis Auto Parts, launched in 1926 by V. P. Davis. In 1958, Alex Davis was appointed president and treasurer of the company, and Louis became vice president. By then the firm had grown substantially and in 1974 the newly named DAPCO Company incorporated with eight auto parts stores throughout the Upcountry.

2. "Fedder's Fashion Will End a 58 Year Tradition in Easley," *Greenville (SC) News*, August 29, 1984, 23.

3. From, "The Froms of Union: Merchants on Main Street for 100 Years," 14–17.

4. Danny McNeill, "Abbeville Store Begins Second Hundred Years," *Index-Journal* (Greenwood, SC), October 12, 1972, 12.

5. Herby Rosenberg, Obituary, https://www.legacy.com/us/obituaries/indexjournal /name/.

6. See https://www.worldatlas.com/articles/first-shopping-malls-in-the-united-states .html.

7. "Upton Plans Changes for Meyers-Arnold," *Spartanburg Herald-Journal* (SC), June 12, 1987, Merchants Folder, Commerce, Box CO34, Kennedy Room, Spartanburg County Library.

8. Tanenbaum interview with Diane Catherine Vecchio.

9. Feinstein's family moved to Spartanburg after she had studied dance in New York.

10. "Miss Marion's School of Dance," booklet.

11. Obituary, "Beloved Miss Marion Dies," *Spartanburg Herald-Journal* (SC), May 7, 2017, B4.

12. Jose Franco, "Like Mother, Like Daughter, Sharing Talent and a Studio," *Spartanburg Herald-Journal* (SC), May 13, 2001, C1.

13. Einstein interview.

14. Federal censuses, Spartanburg, 1920, 1930, 1940.

15. Jacobs interview with Diane Catherine Vecchio.

16. See https://www.company-histories.com/One-Price-Clothing-Stores-Inc-Company -History.html.

17. Greg Myers, "Demand for Low-Price Clothing Spurts Growth," *Greenville (SC) News,* January 20, 1996, 34.

18. no author. "One Price Clothing Joins Stock Tables," *Greenville (SC) News*, July 8, 1987, 26.

19. Steve Matthews, "Clothing Chain Top Performer Among New Carolinas Offerings," *Charlotte Observer,* July 20, 1987, 28.

20. "5 Carolinas Firms on List of 200 Best" *Charlotte Observer*, October 31, 1989, 24.

21. Anne Perry, "USCS Honors 2 Duncan Residents for Community, Educational Strides," *Greenville (SC) News*, March 3, 1993, 53.

22. Rosengarten and Rosengarten, *Portion of the People,* 79.

23. These included Irene Krugman Rudnick of Aiken, Harriet Keyserling and William Keyserling of Beaufort, Hyman Rubin and Isadore Lourie of Columbia, Leonard Krawcheck and Arnold Goodstein of Charleston, Matthew Poliakoff of Spartanburg, and Sylvia Dreyfus of Greenville. Sol Blatt of Blacksville served as speaker of the house for more than three decades.

24. no author, "Hearings on Labor Bills Postponed," *Columbia Record,* March 8, 1949, 17.

25. "Stream Pollution Control Law Sought by Poliakoff, *Greenville (SC) News,* January 16, 1954, 16.

26. "House Passes Prayer Bill," *Greenville (SC) News,* June 2, 1977, 1.

27. L. D. Johnson, "Attack on Dreyfus Disturbing," Furman University Chaplain, *Greenville* (SC). *News and Piedmont,* correct. July 3, 1977, 2-F.

28. "A Sexist Bible?" *Greenville (SC) News*, February 28, 1981, 17.

29. "Iranians at Citadel Losing Aid," *Charlotte Observer, April 14, 1978, 21.*

30. Ibid. "Iranians at Citadel Losing Aid."

31. See https://www.isjl.org/jewish-mayors-in-the-south.html.

32. Morrow-Spitzer, "Free From Proscription and Prejudice," 5–41.

33. Neal R. Pierce, "He just wants to spend his time serving community," *Tampa Bay Times* (St. Petersburg), April 9, 1978, 71.

34. See https://www.opendurham.org/people/evans-eli-mutt.

35. Poland, *Greenville's Grand Design*, 19.

36. Max Heller, interview with Courtney Tollison, February 27, 2018, Greenville, SC.

37. Vecchio, "Max Moses Heller, Patron Saint of Greenville's Renaissance," 181–211.

38. Ibid., 193.

39. Ibid., 192.

40. Judith Bainbridge, "Max Heller Considered," *Greenville (SC) News,* March 13, 2017. Max Heller Papers, Box 10, Folder 17, FUSC.

41. Lacy Ford, "Economic Development and Globalization in South Carolina," 18–50.

42. Ibid., 21.

43. Ibid., 30.

44. Max Heller Papers. Box 7, Folder 3, FUSC.

45. See http://www.michelinman.com.

46. Kanter, *World Class*, 270.

47. Maunula, *Guten Tag Y'All*, 113.

48. At the same time, Spartanburg leaders were also attracting foreign investments to the county including Hoechst Celanese, Menzel, Zima, Hobourn Aero Components, Rieter Machine Works, Sulzer-Ruti, and Symtech, to name a few.

49. Kanter, *World Class,* 242.

50. Ibid.

51. William Barnet, interview with Diane Catherine Vecchio, July 14, 2021, Spartanburg; see also company pamphlet, "A History of William Barnet & Son, Inc."

52. William Barnet, II, "A History of William Barnet & Son, Inc., booklet.

53. Barnet, "A History of William Barnet."

54. Ibid.

55. Ibid.

56. Ibid.

57. Barnet interview with Vecchio.

58. Barnet, "A History of William Barnet."

59. Spartanburg-Biography-Barnett, 2001–2013 File Drawer 1, Pamphlet File Collection, Spartanburg County Library, Kennedy Archives.

60. Max Heller Papers, Box 1 (Congressional Campaign), Folder 1, FUSC.

61. "Heller Questions Campbell's Tactics," *Columbia Record*, October 1, 1986, 11. Max Heller Papers. Congressional/Gubernatorial Campaign Files, Box 65, Folder 1, FUSC.

62. Al Dozier, "Sprouse Attacks," *Greenville (SC) Piedmont*, November 2, 1978. Max Heller Papers, Congressional/Gubernatorial Campaign Files, Box 1, Folder 1, FUSC.

63. Dozier, "Sprouse Attacks."

64. One Greenvillian wrote to Sprouse and copied Heller saying, "I heard your comment concerning Mayor Heller's beliefs . . . and must say it is one of the lowest blows in the name of Christianity that I have heard recently. I too, am a Christian and would like to apologize to Mayor Heller on behalf of Christians, and Baptists in particular." Max Heller Papers, Box 1, Congressional Campaign, Folder 1, FUSC.

65. Ibid.

66. Andrew Baker, "Max Moses Heller: Jewish Mayor in the Sunbelt South," 65.

67. Kathy Dunleavy and Karen Mitchell, interview with Diane Catherine Vecchio, February 7, 2022, Spartanburg, SC.

68. Su Su Johnson, interview with Diane Vecchio, January 12, 2022, Spartanburg, SC.

69. Johnson interview.

70. Barnet Archives, William Barnet III, home office, Main St., Spartanburg, SC.

71. "Kiwanis Club salutes Barnet as its Citizen of Year, *Spartanburg (SC) Herald*, December 3, 2010, C3.

72. See www.knowitall.org/video/william-barnet-legacy-leadership.

73. Max and Trude Heller, interview with Dale Rosengarten.

74. Charles Sowell, "An inspiration, a teacher Max Heller papers. Box 7 Folder 3, FUSC.

75. Stipp, "Greenville, Heller Good for Each Other." Max Heller papers. Box 7, Folder 4.

76. Cobb, *South and America*, 205.

EPILOGUE

1. Maunula, *Guten Tag Y'All*, 86.

2. Businesses founded since the late 1990s and early 2000s include, for example, Cohen's Close Outs, an outlet and discount store operated by Jeff and Dee Dee Cohen, and Imagination Station, an upscale toy store founded by Mindy and Mark Slotin in Spartanburg. In 2006, Andy Lovenwirth moved to the region from Philadelphia and established Carolina Fresh Fish and Seafood in Boiling Springs. Robin Greenfield relocated to Greenville from Miami Beach in 2003 and opened Greenfield's Bagels and Kosher Deli, a favorite breakfast and lunch spot for hundreds of Greenvillians, who especially enjoy her corned beef pastrami on seeded rye. "Guide to Reubens," *Greenville (SC) News*, November 2, 2004, 72.

3. Dan Einstein, interview with Diane Catherine Vecchio, October 23, 2020, Greenville, SC.

4. Liebowitz interview. Rabbi Sam Rose interview, with Diane Vecchio, July 27, 2020, Greenville, SC.

5. "Pew survey of US Jews: soaring intermarriage, assimilation rates," *Jewish News*, http://www.jewishnewsva.org/.

6. Shapiro, *Time for Healing*, 232.

7. Liebowitz interview.

8. Danielle Eisner and Jason Hansen, telephone interview with Diane Vecchio, February 26, 2023.

9. Eisner and Hansen interview.

10. Amy Hammer interview, with Diane Vecchio, October 22, 2019, Greenville, SC.

BIBLIOGRAPHY

MANUSCRIPT COLLECTIONS

Adams, Irving and Marjorie. "A Brief History of the Temple of Israel," South Carolina Room, Greenville Public Library, Greenville, SC.

Abraham Wolfe Davidson Papers. Special Collections and Archives. Clemson University.

August Kohn Papers, Manuscript Collections, 1868–1930, South Caroliniana Library, University of South Carolina.Gantt Collection. Kennedy Room. Spartanburg County (SC) Library.

Hirschman Family Papers, 1910–1987. Special Collections, Addlestone Library. College of Charleston.Hyman Endel Family Papers. South Carolina Room, Greenville County Library, Greenville, SC.

Jewish Heritage Collection. Special Collections, Addlestone Library. College of Charleston.

Kennedy Room. Spartanburg County (SC) Public Library.

Max Heller Papers, Special Collections and Archives. Furman University. Rosenberg Mercantile Company Records (Abbeville, SC) 1861–1965. South Caroliniana Library. Manuscript Collection University of South Carolina.

Sisterhood Files. Temple B'nai Israel. Spartanburg, SC.

South Carolina Historical Society.

Sandor Teszler Papers, Sandor Teszler Library. Wofford College, Spartanburg, SC.

South Carolina Room. Greenville County (SC) Public Library System.

Temple B'nai Israel Folder. Kennedy Room. Spartanburg County (SC) Public Library.

Textile Workers Union of America (TUWA) Records. Wisconsin Historical Society.

Union County Historical Society. Union, SC.

William Barnet III Papers, office of William Barnet, Spartanburg, SC.

Winstock, Rosenberg, and Visanska Papers. South Carolina Historical Society. Addlestone Library. College of Charleston.

NEWSPAPERS AND PERIODICALS

Atlanta Constitution
Boston Globe
Charlotte News
Charlotte Observer
Chattanooga Daily Times
Colorado Springs Gazette-Telegraph
Circleville (OH) Herald
Columbia Record

Daily News Journal (Murfreesboro, TN)
Daily News-Record (Harrisonburg, VA)
Evening Star (Washington, DC)
Fort Worth Star Telegram
Gaffney (SC) Ledger
Greenville (SC) Journal
Greenville (SC) News
Greenville (SC) Piedmont
Index-Journal (Greenwood, SC)
Miami News
New York Times
Newport News (VA) Times-Herald
News and Observer (Raleigh, NC)
Palm Beach (FL) Post
Southern Israelite (Augusta, GA)
Spartanburg (SC) Herald Journal,
The State (Columbia, SC)
Sun-News (Myrtle Beach, SC)
Tampa Bay Times, (St. Petersburg, FL)
The Gazette, (Tifton, GA)
The Sumter (SC) Item
Troy (AL) Messenger
Union (SC) Times
Wisconsin Jewish Chronicle (Milwaukee, WI)

SECONDARY WORKS

Abbeville County Historical Society. *Images of America: Abbeville County.* Charleston, SC: Arcadia Publishing, 2004.

Abernathy, Frederick H., John T. Dunlop, Janice H. Hammond, and David Weil. *A Stitch in Time: Lean Retailing and the Transformation of Manufacturing: Lessons from the Apparel and Textile Industries.* New York: Oxford University Press, 1999.

Aldrich, Howard E., and Roger Waldinger. "Ethnicity and Entrepreneurship." *Annual Review of Sociology* 16 (1990): 111–35.

Alfieri, Victor. "Congregation Beth Israel: 100 Years and Counting." *Jewish Historical Society of South Carolina* 21, no. 2 (Fall 2016): 4–5.

Anbinder, Tyler. *City of Dreams: The 400-Year Epic History of Immigrant New York.* Boston, MA: Houghton Mifflin Harcourt, 2016.

Ascoli, Peter M. *Julius Rosenwald: The Man Who Built Sears, Roebuck and Advanced the Case of Black Education in the American South.* Indianapolis, IN: Indiana University Press, 2006.

Ashkenazi, Elliott. *The Business of Jews in Louisiana, 1840–1875.* Tuscaloosa: University of Alabama Press, 1988.

———. "Jewish Commercial Interests Between North and South: The Case of the Lehmans and the Seligmans." In *Dixie Diaspora: An Anthology of Southern Jewish History,* edited by Mark K. Bauman, 194–208. Tuscaloosa: University of Alabama Press, 2006.

Ashton, Dianne. "Expanding Jewish Life in America, 1826–1901." In *The Columbia History of Jews and Judaism in America,* edited by Marc Lee Raphael, 47–69. New York: Columbia University Press, 2008.

Atherton, Lewis. "Itinerant Merchandising in the Antebellum South." *Bulletin of the Business Historical Society* 19 (April 1945): 35–39.

Baily, Samuel L. *Immigrants in the Land of Promise: Italians in Buenos Aires and New York City, 1870–1914.* Ithaca, NY: Cornell University Press, 1999.

Baker, Andrew. "Max Moses Heller: Jewish Mayor in the Sunbelt South." *Southern Jewish History* 25 (2022): 59–98.

Ballantyne, David. *New Politics in the Old South: Ernest F. Hollings in the Civil Rights Era.* Columbia: University of South Carolina Press, 2016.

Barkan, Elliott, ed., *Immigration, Incorporation, Integration, and Transnationalism: Interdisciplinary and International Perspectives.* New Brunswick, NJ: Transaction, 2007.

Barnett, Elzas. *Jews of South Carolina.* Philadelphia, PA: J. B. Lippincott, 1905.

Bass, Jack, and Jack Nelson. *The Orangeburg Massacre.* First published 1996. Macon, GA: Mercer University Press, 2002.

Bauman, Mark K., ed. *Dixie Diaspora: An Anthology of Southern Jewish History.* Tuscaloosa: University of Alabama Press, 2006.

———, ed. *A New Vision of Southern Jewish History: Studies in Institution Building, Leadership, Interaction, and Mobility.* Tuscaloosa: University of Alabama Press, 2019.

———. ed. "Southern Jewish Women and Their Social Service Organizations." *Journal of American Ethnic History* 22, no. 3 (Spring 2003): 34–78.

Bauman, Mark K., and Arnold Shankman. "The Rabbi as Ethnic Broker: The Case of David Marx." In *A New Vision of Southern Jewish History: Studies in Institution Building, Leadership, Interaction, and Mobility,* edited by Mark K. Bauman, 201–12. Tuscaloosa: University of Alabama Press, 2019.

Bauman, Mark K., and Berkeley Kalin, eds. *The Quiet Voices: Southern Rabbis and Black Civil Rights, 1880s to 1990s.* Tuscaloosa: University of Alabama Press, 1997.

Bauman, Mark K., and Stephen Krause, eds. *To Stand Aside or Stand Alone: Southern Reform Rabbis and the Civil Rights Movement.* Tuscaloosa: University of Alabama Press, 2016.

Bayor, Ronald, ed. *Race and Ethnicity in America: A Concise History.* New York: Columbia University Press, 2003.

Belcher, Ray. *Greenville County, South Carolina: From Cotton Fields to the Textile Center of the World.* Charleston, SC: History Press, 2006.

Belth, Nathan. *Fighting for America: An Account of Jewish Men in the Armed Forces, from Pearl Harbor to the Italian Campaign.* New York: National Jewish Welfare Board, 1944.

Blackwelder, Julia Kirk. *Now Hiring: The Feminization of Work in the United States, 1900–1995.* College Station: Texas A & M University Press, 1997.

Bloom, Jack L. "A History of the Jewish Community of Greenville, South Carolina." *The Proceedings and Papers of the Greenville County Historical Society, 1998–2005* 12 (2005): 73–88.

Bodnar, John. *The Transplanted: A History of Immigrants in Urban America.* Bloomington: Indiana University Press, 1977.

Bodnar, John, Roger Simon, and Michael Weber. *Lives of Their Own: Blacks, Italians, and Poles in Pittsburgh, 1900–1960.* Urbana: University of Illinois Press, 1976.

Boyanski, John, with Knox White. *Reimagining Greenville: Building the Best Downtown in America.* Charleston, SC: History Press, 2013.

Breibart, Solomon. *Explorations in Charleston's Jewish History.* Charleston, SC: History Press, 2005.

Brinson, Claudia Smith. *Stories of Struggle: The Clash over Civil Rights in South Carolina.* Columbia: University of South Carolina Press, 2020.

Cann, Katherine. "Improving Textile Town 1910 to 1929." In *Textile Town: Spartanburg County, South Carolina,* edited by Betsy Wakefield Teter, 89–119. Spartanburg, SC: Hub City Writers Project, 2002.

Cann, Katherine, and Betsy Wakefield Teter. "The New England Textile Collapse: A Southern Migration Begins." In *Textile Town: Spartanburg County, South Carolina,* edited by Betsy Wakefield Teter, 146–48. Spartanburg, SC: Hub City Writers Project, 2002.

Carlton, David L. *Mill and Town in South Carolina, 1880–1920.* Baton Rouge: Louisiana State University Press, 1982.

Caroli, Betty Boyd. *Italian Repatriation from the United States, 1900–1914.* New York: Center for Migration Studies, 1973.

Cerase, Francesco. "Expectation and Reality: A Case Study of Return Migration from the United States to Southern Italy." *International Migration Review* 8, no. 2 (1974): 245–62.

Charles, Allan D. *The Narrative History of Union County, South Carolina.* Spartanburg, SC: Reprint, 1987.

Cinel, Dino. *The National Integration of Italian Return Migration 1870–1929.* Cambridge: Cambridge University Press, 1991.

Clark, Thomas. *Pills, Petticoats, and Plows: The Southern Country Store.* Indianapolis, IN: Bobbs-Merrill, 1944, reprint 1989.

Cobb, James C. *Industrialization and Southern Society, 1877–1984.* Lexington: University Press of Kentucky, 1984.

————. *The Selling of the South: The Southern Crusade for Industrial Development, 1936–1990.* Urbana: University of Illinois Press, 1993.

————. *The South and America since World War II.* New York: Oxford University Press, 2012.

Cohen, Michael R. "Cotton, Capital, and Ethnic Networks: Jewish Economic Growth in the Postbellum Gulf South." *American Jewish Archives* 64, no. 1–2 (2012): 113–36.

————. *Cotton Capitalists: American Jewish Entrepreneurship in the Reconstruction Era.* New York: New York University Press, 2017.

Cohen, Miriam. *Workshop to Office: Two Generations of Italian Women in New York City, 1900–1950.* Ithaca, NY: Cornell University Press, 1992.

Coleman, Caroline Sprouse. *Five Petticoats on Sunday.* Greenville, SC: Hiott Press, 1962.

Cooper, Nancy Vance Ashmore. *Greenville: Woven from the Past.* Sun Valley, CA: American Historical Press, 2000.

Crittenden, S. S. *The Greenville Century Book: Comprising an Account of the Settlement of the County, and the Founding of the City of Greenville, S.C.* Greenville, SC: Press of Greenville News, 1903.

Cutler, Irving. *The Jews of Chicago: From Shtetl to Suburb.* Urbana: University of Illinois Press, 1996.

Deutsch, Stephanie. *You Need a Schoolhouse: Booker T. Washington, Julius Rosenwald, and the Building of Schools for the Segregated South.* Evanston, IL: Northwestern University Press, 2015.

Diner, Hasia R. "Entering the Mainstream of Modern Jewish History: Peddlers and the American Jewish South." In *Jewish Roots in Southern Soil: A New History,* edited by Marcie Cohen Ferris and Mark I. Greenberg, 86–108. Waltham, MA: Brandeis University Press, 2006.

———. *Hungering for America: Italian, Irish, and Jewish Foodways in the Age of Migration.* Cambridge, MA: Harvard University Press, 2001.

———. *In the Almost Promised Land: American Jews and Blacks, 1915–1935.* Baltimore, MD: Johns Hopkins University Press, 1997.

———. *The Jews of the United States, 1654–2000.* Berkeley: University of California Press, 2004.

———. *Julius Rosenwald: Repairing the World.* New Haven, CT: Yale University Press, 2017.

———. *A New Promised Land: A History of Jews in America.* New York: Oxford University Press, 2003.

———. *Roads Taken: The Great Jewish Migration to the New World and the Peddlers Who Forged the Way.* New Haven, CT: Yale University Press, 2015.

———. *We Remember with Reverence and Love: American Jews and the Myth of Silence after the Holocaust, 1945–1962.* New York: New York University Press, 2009.

Dinnerstein, Leonard. *Anti-Semitism in America.* New York: Oxford University Press, 1994.

———. *The Leo Frank Case.* New York: Columbia University Press, 1987.

———. *Uneasy at Home: Antisemitism and the American Jewish Experience.* New York: Columbia University Press, 1987.

Dubofsky, Melvyn, and Foster Rhea Dulles. *Labor in America: A History.* 6th ed. Wheeling, IL: Harlan Davidson, 1984.

Edgar, Walter. *South Carolina: A History.* Columbia University of South Carolina Press, 1998.

———. *The South Carolina Encyclopedia.* Columbia: University of South Carolina Press, 2006.

Eelman, Bruce W. *Entrepreneurs in the Southern Upcountry: Commercial Culture in Spartanburg, S.C., 1845–1880.* Athens: University of Georgia Press 2008.

Egelman, William, William Gratzer, and Michael D'Angelo. "Italian-Jewish Intermarriages: The Italian American Spouse." *Italian Americana* 23 (Winter 2005): 94–105.

Endelmann, Judith E. *The Jewish Community of Indianapolis, 1849 to the Present.* Bloomington: Indiana University Press, 1984.

Evans, Eli. *The Provincials: A Personal History of Jews in the South.* Chapel Hill: University of North Carolina Press, 2005.

Fahrer, Sharon C. *A Home in Shalom'ville: The History of Asheville's Jewish Community*. Asheville, NC: History @ Hand Publishing, 2016.

Feiler, Andrew, and John Lewis. *A Better Life for Their Children: Julius Rosenwald, Booker T. Washington, and the 4,978 Schools that Changed America*. Athens: University of Georgia Press, 2021.

Felder, James L. *Civil Rights in South Carolina: From Peaceful Protests to Groundbreaking Rulings*. Charleston, SC: History Press, 2012.

Fenyo, Mario. *Hitler, Horthy, and Hungary: German-Hungarian Relations, 1941–44*. New Haven, CT: Yale University Press, 1972.

Ferris, Marcie Cohen. "Dining in the Dixie Diaspora: A Meeting of Region and Religion." In *Jewish Roots in Southern Soil: A New History*, edited by Marcie Cohen Ferris and Mark I. Greenberg, 226–54. Waltham, MA: Brandeis University Press, 2006.

———. *Matzoh Ball Gumbo: Culinary Tales of the Jewish South*. Chapel Hill: University of North Carolina Press, 2010.

Ferris, Marcie Cohen, and Mark I. Greenberg, eds. *Jewish Roots in Southern Soil: A New History*. Waltham, MA: Brandeis University Press, 2006.

Fisher, Vivian B. *Hampton Heights of Spartanburg: Its History, Houses, and People*. Spartanburg, SC: Everbest, 2011.

Foner, Nancy. *From Ellis Island to JFK: New York's Two Great Waves of Immigration*. New Haven, CT: Yale University Press, 2000.

Ford, Lacy. "Economic Development and Globalization in South Carolina." *Southern Cultures* 13 (Spring 2009): 18–50.

———. *Origins of Southern Radicalism: The South Carolina Upcountry, 1800–1860*. New York: Oxford University Press, 1991.

———. "Rednecks and Merchants: Economic Development and Social Tension in the South Carolina Upcountry, 1865–1900." *Journal of American History* 71, no. 2 (September 1984): 294–318.

Forsberg, Aaron. "Eisenhower and Japanese Economic Recovery: The Politics of Integration with the Western Trading Bloc, 1952–1955." *Journal of American-East Asian Relations* 5, no. 1 (Spring 1996): 57–75.

Foster, Vernon, and Walter Montgomery. *Spartanburg: Facts, Reminiscences, Folklore*. Spartanburg, SC: Reprint, 1998.

Frady, Marshall. *Jesse: The Life and Pilgrimage of Jesse Jackson*. New York: Random House, 1996.

Franklin, John Hope, and Alfred A. Moss Jr. *From Slavery to Freedom: A History of African Americans*. 7th ed. New York: McGraw Hill, 1994.

Frederickson, Mary. "Four Decades of Change: Black Workers in Southern Textiles, 1941–1981." In *Workers' Struggles, Past and Present: A Radical American Reader*, edited by James Green, 62–82. Philadelphia, PA: Temple University Press, 1983.

Freidman, Murray. *Philadelphia Jewish Life, 1940–2000*. Philadelphia, PA: Temple University Press, 2003.

Freidman-Kasaba, Kathi. *Memories of Migration: Gender, Ethnicity, and Work in the Lives of Jewish and Italian Women in New York, 1870–1924*. Albany, NY: SUNY Albany Press, 1996.

Friddle, Linda, ed. *Famous Greenville Firsts.* Greenville, SC: Metropolitan Arts Council, 1986.

From, I. Allan. "All the Bases Covered: Memories of My Childhood in Union." *Jewish Historical Society of South Carolina* 24, no. 2 (Fall 2019): 17–19.

———. "The Froms of Union: Merchants on Main Street for 100 Years." *Jewish Historical Society of South Carolina,* 24, no. 2 (Fall 2019): 14–16.

Gabaccia, Donna. *From the Other Side: Women, Gender, and Immigrant Life in the U. S. 1820–1990.* Bloomington: Indiana University Press, 1994.

Gerber, David. "Cutting Out Shylock: Elite Anti-Semitism and the Quest for Moral Order in the Mid-Nineteenth Century American Marketplace." *Journal of American History* 69, no. 3 (December 1982): 615–37.

Gergel, Belinda Friedman. "Irene Goldsmith Kohn: An Assimilated 'New South' Daughter and Jewish Women's Activism in Early Twentieth-Century South Carolina." In *South Carolina Women: Their Lives and Times, Volume 2,* edited by Marjorie Julian Spruill, Valinda W. Littlefield, and Joan Marie Johnson, 190–214. Athens: University of Georgia Press, 2010.

Gergel, Belinda Friedman, and Richard Gergel. *In Pursuit of the Tree of Life: A History of the Early Jews of Columbia, South Carolina, and the Tree of Life Congregation.* Columbia, SC: Tree of Life Congregation, 1996.

Glanz, Rudolf. "Notes on Early Jewish Peddling in America." *Jewish Social Studies* 7, no. 2 (April 1945): 119–36.

Glazier, Jack. *Dispersing the Ghetto: The Relocation of Jewish Immigrants across America.* Ithaca, NY: Cornell University Press, 1998.

Glenn, Susan M. *Daughters of the Shtetl: Life and Labor in the Immigrant Generation.* Ithaca, NY: Cornell University Press, 1990.

Goldberg, Gloria From. "Being Jewish in Union." *Jewish Historical Society of South Carolina* 24, no. 2 (Fall 2019): 16–17.

Goldfield, David. "A Sense of Place: Jews, Blacks, and White Gentiles in the American South." *Southern Cultures* 3, no. 1 (Spring 1977): 58–79.

Goldstein, Eric L. *The Price of Whiteness: Jews, Race, and American Identity.* Princeton, N.J: Princeton University Press, 2006.

Goldstein, Eric L., and Deborah Weiner. *On Middle Ground: A History of the Jews in Baltimore.* Baltimore, MD: Johns Hopkins University Press, 2018.

Grady, Timothy P., and Melissa Walker. *Recovering the Piedmont Past: Unexplored Moments in Nineteenth-Century Upcountry South Carolina History.* Columbia: University of South Carolina Press, 2013.

Greer, Colin. *The Great School Legend: A Revisionist Interpretation of American Public Education.* Revised ed. New York: Penguin Books, 1976.

Gurock, Jeffrey S. "American Judaism between the Two World Wars." *The Columbia History of Jews and Judaism in America,* edited by Marc Lee Raphael, 93–113. New York: Columbia University Press, 2008.

Gutkowski, Andrew. "The Evolution of Environmental (In)Justice in Spartanburg, South Carolina, 1900–2000." in *Journal of American History* 106, no. 4 (March 2020): 923–48.

Hagy, James W. *This Happy Land: The Jews of Colonial and Antebellum Charleston.* Tuscaloosa: University of Alabama Press, 1993.

Hammack, David, Diane Grabowski, and John Grabowski, eds. *Identity, Conflict, and Cooperation: Central Europeans in Cleveland, 1850–1930.* Cleveland, OH: Western Reserve Historical Society, 2002.

Harris, Alice Kessler. *Out to Work: A History of Wage-Earning Women in the United States.* New York: Oxford University Press, 1982.

Hartness, Courtney Tollison. *World War II in Upcountry South Carolina: "We Did Everything We Could."* Charleston, SC: History Press, 2019.

Heinze, Andrew R. "The Critical Period: Ethnic Emergence and Reaction, 1901–1929." In *Race and Ethnicity in America: A Concise History,* edited by Ronald H. Bayor, 131–66. New York: Columbia University Press, 2003.

Hertzberg, Steven. *Strangers Within the Gate City: The Jews of Atlanta, 1845–1915.* Philadelphia, PA: Jewish Publication Society of America, 1978.

Hieke, Anton. *Jewish Identity in the Reconstruction South: Ambivalence and Adaptation.* Berlin: De Gruyter, 2013.

Hill, Beatrice, and Brenda Lee. *South of Main.* Spartanburg, SC: Hub City Press, 2005.

Holt, Marion Peter. *Magical Places: The Story of Spartanburg's Theaters and Their Entertainment, 1900–1950.* Spartanburg, SC: Hub City Press, 2004.

Huff, Archie Vernon, *Greenville: The History of the City and County in the South Carolina Piedmont.* Columbia: University of South Carolina Press, 1995.

Huhner, Leon. "Francis Salvador: A Prominent Patriot of the Revolutionary War." *American Jewish Historical Society* 9 (1901): 107–22.

———. "The Jews of South Carolina: From the Earliest Settlement to the End of the American Revolution." *American Jewish Historical Society* 12 (1904): 39–61.

Johnson, Joan Marie. *Southern Ladies, New Women: Race, Region, and Clubwomen in South Carolina, 1890–1930.* Gainesville: University Press of Florida, 2004.

Jones, Lu Ann. *Mama Learned Us to Work: Farm Women in the New South.* Chapel Hill: University of North Carolina Press, 2002.

Joselit, Jenna Weissman. "Land of Promise: The Eastern Jewish Experience in South Carolina." In *A Portion of the People: Three Hundred Years of Southern Jewish Life,* edited by Theodore Rosengarten and Dale Rosengarten, 22–30. Columbia: University of South Carolina Press, 2001.

Kanter, Rosabeth Moss. *World Class: Thriving Locally in the Global Economy.* New York: Simon & Schuster, 1995.

Klapper, Melissa. *Jewish Girls Coming of Age in America, 1860–1920.* New York: New York University Press, 2005.

Koffman, David. "The Occupational Turn in American Jewish History." *Journal of American Ethnic History* 36, no. 1 (Fall 2016): 82–86.

Kohn, August. *The Cotton Mills of South Carolina, 1907: Letters Written to the* News and Courier. Charleston, SC: Nabu, 2010.

Korn, Bertram W. *American Jewry and the Civil War.* Philadelphia, PA: Atheneum Press, 1970.

———. "Jews and Slavery in the Old South, 1789–1875." In *Jews in the South,* edited by Leonard Dinnerstein and Mary Palsson, 41–52. Baton Rouge: Louisiana State University Press, 1973.

Kraut, Alan M. *Goldberger's War: The Life and Work of a Public Health Crusader.* New York: Hill and Wang, 2003.

———. *The Huddled Masses: The Immigrant in American Society, 1880–1921.* Wheeling, IL: Harlan Davidson, 1982.

Kugelmass, Jack. *Jews, Sports, and the Rites of Citizenship.* Urbana: University of Illinois Press: 2007.

Kurlansky, Mark. *Hank Greenberg: The Hero Who Didn't Want to Be One.* New Haven, CT: Yale University Press, 2013.

Le May, Michael, and Elliott R. Barkan, eds. *U. S. Immigration and Naturalization Laws and Issues: A Documentary History.* Westport, CT: Greenwood Press, 1999.

Leonard, Michael. *Our Heritage: A Community History of Spartanburg County, S. C.* Spartanburg, SC: Spartanburg Herald and Journal, 1983.

Levy, Lester. *Jacob Epstein.* Baltimore, MD: Maran Press, 1978.

Lurey, Ann. "From the Old Country to the Upcountry: The Lurey Family Story." *Jewish Historical Society of South Carolina* 21, no. 2 (Fall 2016): 11.

———. "From the Old Country to the Upcountry: Tracking the Switzers from Ariogola to America." *Jewish Historical Society of South Carolina* 21 no. 2 (Fall 2016): 10.

Mandell, Nikki. *The Corporation as Family: The Gendering of Corporate Welfare, 1890–1930.* Chapel Hill: University of North Carolina Press, 2002.

Marinari, Maddalena. *Unwanted: Italian and Jewish Mobilization against Restrictive Immigration Laws, 1882–1965.* Chapel Hill: University of North Carolina Press, 2020.

Mason, Patrick Q. "Anti-Jewish Violence in the New South." *Southern Jewish History* 8 (2005): 77–119.

Maunula, Marko. *Guten Tag Y'all: Globalization and the South Carolina Piedmont, 1950–2000.* Athens: University of Georgia Press, 2009.

McCandless, Amy Thompson. "Anita Pollitzer: A South Carolina Advocate for Equal Rights." In *South Carolina Women: Their Lives and Times, Volume 2,* edited by Marjorie Julian Spruill, Valinda Littlefield, and Joan Marie Johnson, 166–89. Athens: University of Georgia Press, 2010.

McMillan, Samuel Lucas. "The Globalization of Spartanburg: A Story of Local Leaders and State Supporters." *Journal of Political Science* 43 (2015): 73–98.

Mendelsohn, Adam D. *The Rag Race: How Jews Sewed Their Way to Success in America and the British Empire.* New York: New York University Press, 2016.

Miller, Randall M., and George E. Pozzetta, eds. *Shades of the Sunbelt: Essays on Ethnicity, Race, and the Urban South.* New York: Greenwood Press, 1988.

Minchin, Timothy J. "Black Activism, the 1964 Civil Rights Act, and the Racial Integration of the Southern Textile Industry." *Journal of Southern History* 65, no. 4, (November 1999): 809–44.

———. *What Do We Need a Union For: The TWUA in the South, 1945–1955.* Chapel Hill, NC: University of North Carolina Press, 1997.

Moore, Deborah Dash. "Freedom's Fruit." In *A Portion of the People: Three Hundred Years of Southern Jewish Life,* edited by Theodore Rosengarten and Dale Rosengarten, 10–21. Columbia: University of South Carolina Press, 2001.

———. *GI Jews: How World War II Changed a Generation.* Cambridge, MA: Belknap Press of Harvard University Press, 2004.

————. "Jewish Migration to the Sunbelt." In *Shades of the Sunbelt: Essays on Ethnicity, Race, and the Urban South,* edited by Randall M. Miller and George E. Pozzetta, 41–52. New York: Greenwood, 1988.

Morawska, Ewa. *Insecure Prosperity: Jews in Small-Town Industrial America, 1880–1940.* Princeton, NJ: Princeton University Press, 1996.

Morrow-Spitzer, Jacob. "Free From Proscription and Prejudice: Politics and Race in the Election of One Jewish Mayor in Late Reconstruction Louisiana." *Southern Jewish History* 22 (2019): 5–41.

Muller, Jerry. *Capitalism and the Jews.* Princeton, NJ: Princeton University Press, 2010.

Nadell, Pamela, and Jonathan Sarna. *Women and American Judaism: A Historical Perspective.* New York: Brandeis University Press, 2001.

Neely, Alyssa. "The Jews of Anderson, South Carolina: Merchants and Manufacturers." *Jewish Historical Society of South Carolina* 15, no. 1 (Spring 2010): 7–10.

Nolan, John M. *A Guide to Historic Greenville, South Carolina.* Mount Pleasant, SC: History Press, 2008.

O'Neill, Stephen. "For the General Good of the Churches: Furman University and Slavery: Task Force Report on Furman and Slavery." Greenville, SC: Furman University, 2018.

————. "Memory, History, and the Desegregation of Greenville, South Carolina." In *Toward the Meeting of the Waters: Currents in the Civil Rights Movement of South Carolina during the Twentieth Century,* edited by Winfred B. Moore and Orville Vernon Burton, 286–99. Columbia: University of South Carolina Press, 2008.

Perlmutter, Martin. "Ebb and Flow: Georgetown's Jewish History." *Jewish Historical Society of South Carolina* 22, no. 2 (Fall, 2017): 15.

Poland, Tom. *Greenville's Grand Design* Publishing Resources Group Inc., 2015.

Poliakoff, Ed. "D. Poliakoff: 100 Years on the Square." *Jewish Historical Society of South Carolina* 24, no. 1 (Spring 2019): 8–10.

Poliakoff, Marsha. *Portraits of a People. A History of Jewish Life in Spartanburg, SC.* Self-published, Marsha Poliakoff, 2010.

Prell, Riv-Ellen. "The Economic Turn in American Jewish History: When Women (Mostly) Disappeared." *American Jewish History* 103, no. 4 (October 2019): 485–512.

Price, Harry. "Prices' Store for Men: 'Ends Your Quest for the Best.'" *Jewish Historical Society of South Carolina* 24, no. 2 (Fall 2019): 11–12.

Pruitt, Dwain C. *Things Hidden: An Introduction to the History of Blacks in Spartanburg.* City of Spartanburg Community Relations Office, 1995.

Rabin, Shari. *Jews on the Frontier: Religion and Mobility in Nineteenth-Century America.* New York: New York University Press: 2017.

Rabinowitz, Howard. *The First New South, 1865–1920.* Arlington Heights, IL: Harlan Davidson, 1992.

Racine, Philip. "Boom Time in Textile Town: 1880 to 1909." In *Textile Town: Spartanburg County, South Carolina,* edited by Betsy Wakefield Teter, 37–59. Spartanburg, SC: Hub City Writers Project, 2002.

Raphael, Marc Lee. *Jews and Judaism in a Midwestern Community: Columbus, Ohio, 1840–1975.* Columbus, OH: Columbus Historical Society, 1979.

Richardson, Sarah. "The Cone Family Exemplified Jewish Immigration in the South by Encouraging Industrial and Cultural Progress." https://www.historynet.com/afamily -fortune-made-of-whole-cloth.

Roberts, Giselle, and Melissa A. Walker. *Southern Women in the Progressive Era: A Reader.* Columbia: University of South Carolina Press, 2019.

Robinson-Simpson, Leola Clement. *Greenville County, South Carolina,* Black America Series. Charleston, SC: Arcadia, 2007.

Roediger, David R. *Working Toward Whiteness: How America's Immigrants Became White: The Strange Journey from Ellis Island to the Suburbs.* New York: Basic Books, 2005.

Rogoff, Leonard. *Down Home: Jewish Life in North Carolina.* Chapel Hill: University of North Carolina Press, 2010.

———. *Gertrude Weil: Jewish Progressive in the New South.* Chapel Hill: University of North Carolina Press, 2017.

Rosen, Robert N. *The Jewish Confederates.* Columbia: University of South Carolina Press, 2000.

Rosengarten, Theodore, and Dale Rosengarten, eds. *A Portion of the People: Three Hundred Years of Southern Jewish Life.* Columbia: University of South Carolina Press, 2001.

Schmier, Louis. "Jews and Gentiles in a South Georgia Town." In *Jews of the South, Selected Essays from the Southern Jewish Historical Society,* edited by Samuel Proctor and Louis Schmier with Malcolm Stern, 1–16. Macon, GA: Mercer University Press, 1984.

Schneider, Dorothy, and Carl Schneider. *American Women in the Progressive Era, 1900–1920.* New York: Facts on File, 1993.

Schochet, Jan, and Sharon Fahrer, eds. *The Family Store: A History of Jewish Businesses in Downtown Asheville, 1880–1990.* Asheville, NC: History @ Hand Publications, 2006.

Shapiro, Edward S. *A Time for Healing: American Jewry Since World War II.* Baltimore, MD: Johns Hopkins University Press, 1992.

Shevitz, Amy Hill. *Jewish Communities on the Ohio River: A History.* Lexington: University Press of Kentucky, 2007.

Sorin, Gerald. *Tradition Transformed: The Jewish Experience in America.* Baltimore, MD: Johns Hopkins University Press, 1997.

Stein, Regina. "The Road to Bat Mitzvah in America." In *Women and American Judaism: Historical Perspectives,* edited by Pamela S. Nadell and Jonathan Sarna, 223–34. Waltham, MA: Brandeis University Press, 2001.

Steineke, Brad. "Dr. Rosa Gantt: A Medical Pioneer." Spartanburg County Public Libraries Publication (Winter 2019), 8–9.

Sterba, Christopher. *Good Americans: Italian and Jewish Immigrants during the First World War.* New York: Oxford University Press, 2003.

Synott, Marsha Graham. *Student Diversity at the Big Three: Changes at Harvard, Yale, and Princeton since the 1920s.* New York: Routledge, Taylor & Francis Group, 2013.

Teter, Betsy Wakefield, ed. *Textile Town: Spartanburg County, South Carolina.* Spartanburg, SC: Hub City Writers Project, 2002.

Toll, William. *The Making of an Ethnic Middle-Class: Portland Jewry over Four Generations*. Albany, NY: SUNY Press, 1983.

Turpin, Susan, Carolyn Creal, Ron Crawley, and James Crocker, eds. *When the Soldiers Came to Town: Spartanburg's Camp Wadsworth (1917–19) and Camp Croft (1941–45)*. Spartanburg, SC: Hub City Writers Project, 2004.

Vecchio, Diane C. "From Slavery to Freedom: African American Life in Post-Civil War Spartanburg." In *Recovering the Piedmont Past: Unexplored Moments in Nineteenth-Century Upcountry South Carolina History,* edited by Timothy P. Grady and Melissa Walker, 107–34. Columbia: University of South Carolina Press, 2013.

———. "Max Moses Heller: Patron Saint of Greenville's Renaissance." In *Doing Business in America: A Jewish History,* edited by Steven Ross, Hasia R. Diner, and Lisa Ansell, 181–211. West Lafayette, IN: Purdue University Press, 2018.

———. *Merchants, Midwives, and Laboring Women: Italian Migrants in Urban America*. Urbana: University of Illinois Press, 2006.

———. "New Jewish Women: Shaping the Future of a 'New South' in the Palmetto State." *Journal of Southern Jewish History* 23 (2020): 43–75.

———. "Ties of Affection: Family Narratives in the History of Italian Migration." *Journal of American Ethnic History* 25, nos. 2–3 (2006): 117–33.

Vecoli, Rudolph J. "Cult and Occult in Italian American Culture: The Persistence of a Religious Heritage." In *Immigrants and Religion in Urban America,* edited by Randall M. Miller and Thomas Marzik, 25–47. Philadelphia, PA: Temple University Press, 1977.

———. "Peasants and Prelates: Italian Immigrants and the Catholic Church." *Journal of Social History* 2 (Spring 1969): 217–86.

Wachter, Joe. "Dean Street Synagogue, 1917–1961." *Jewish Historical Society of South Carolina* 11, no. 2 (Fall 2006): 4.

———. "In Search of Jewish Spartanburg." *Jewish Historical Society of South Carolina* 24, no. 2 (Fall 2019): 4–7.

Waldrep, G. C. *Southern Workers and the Search for Community: Spartanburg County, South Carolina*. Urbana: University of Illinois Press, 2000.

Walker, Melissa. *All We Knew Was to Farm: Rural Women in the Upcountry South, 1919–1941*. Baltimore, MD: Johns Hopkins University Press, 2000.

———. "Mineral Water, Dancing and Amusements: The Development of Tourism in the Nineteenth-Century Upcountry." In *Recovering the Piedmont Past: Unexplored Moments in Nineteenth-Century Upcountry South Carolina History,* edited by Timothy P. Grady and Melissa Walker, 6–24. Columbia: University of South Carolina Press, 2013.

Webb, Clive. "Jewish Merchants and Black Customers in the Age of Jim Crow." *Southern Jewish History* 2 (1999): 55–80.

———. "A Tangled Web: Black-Jewish Relations in the Twentieth Century South." In *Jewish Roots in Southern Soil: A New History,* edited by Marcie Cohen Ferris and Mark I. Greenberg, 192–209. Waltham, MA: Brandeis University Press, 2006.

Weiner, Deborah. *Coalfield Jews: An Appalachian History*. Urbana: University of Illinois Press, 2016.

Weissbach, Lee Shai. *Jewish Life in Small-Town America: A History*. New Haven, CT: Yale University Press, 2005.

Wenger, Beth. *New York Jews and the Great Depression: Uncertain Promise.* New Haven, CT: Yale University Press, 1996.

Wilhelm, Cornelia. *The Independent Orders of B'nai B'rith and True Sisters: Pioneers of a New Jewish Identity, 1843–1914.* Detroit, MI: Wayne State University Press, 2011.

Willis, Jeffrey. "Textile Town Pioneers, 1816 to 1879." In *Textile Town: Spartanburg County, South Carolina,* edited by Betsy Wakefield Teter, 15–27. Spartanburg, SC: Hub City Writers Project, 2002.

Woodward, C. Vann. *Origins of The New South, 1877–1913.* Baton Rouge: Louisiana State University Press, 1971.

Zaglin, Jeff. "The Zaglins of Greenville: A Jewish-American Saga." *Jewish Historical Society of South Carolina* 21, no. 2 (Fall 2016): 6–7.

Zambone, Albert Louis. *Daniel Morgan: A Revolutionary Life.* Yardley, PA: Westholme, 2018.

Zieger, Robert. *Life and Labor in the New New South.* Gainesville, FL: University Press of Florida, 2012.

DISSERTATIONS AND THESES

Burnham, Leah Cannon. "The Power of Pearls: Memoir of a Russian Jewish Immigrant to the American South." Master's thesis, Clemson University, 2016.

Stone, Philip. "Making a Modern State: The Politics of Economic Development in South Carolina, 1938–1962." PhD diss., University of South Carolina, 2003.

Tollison, Courtney. "Principles Over Prejudice: The Desegregation of Furman University, Wofford, Columbia, and Presbyterian Colleges." Master's thesis, University of South Carolina, 2001.

INDEX

Page numbers in *italics* refer to illustrations.

Abe Goldberg's Clothing, 84
Abelkop, Larry, 184
Abelkop, Susan, 184
Abelkop family, 92
Abe Smith's Pawnshop and Music Store, 84
abolitionism, 20
Abrams, Anita, 77, 90, 100
Abrams, Anna, 113
Abrams, Creighton, 114–16
Abrams, Harry, 77, 80, 133, 149–50
Abrams, Helen, 90
Abrams, Irving, 80, 112, 150, 169
Abrams, Lewis, 113
Abrams, Salomon, 113
Acanfora, Richard, 127
Adelman, David, 127
AFL-CIO, 145
Aleo Manufacturing, 140
Aleph Zadik Aleph (AZA), 103
Allen, Mel, 109
Allen Brothers & Arcus, 87
Amalgamated Clothing Workers of America, 144
American Cigar Company, 91
American Revolution, 10–11
American Trim Products, 136, 137
anti-Semitism, 6, 8, 17–18, 118, 134, 151, 176, 193–94
Arcadia Mills, 35, 71
Arkwright Mill, 35
Arrow Steel Products, 184–85
Ashkenazim, 8
Atlanta, 34
Attaway, Ruth Cleveland, 139
Atwater, Lee, 193

August, Hyman, 40, 42, 53, 84, 85, 95, 98
August, Sadie, 84, 95, 100
automotive industry, 9
Axelrod, Lori Feinstein, 185

Bailey, C. William, 90
Bailey, Rosie, 90
Baily, Samuel, 95
Bainbridge, Judith, 72, 168
Baker, Andrew, 173
Ballantyne, David, 161
Baltimore, 15, 32–34
Baltimore Bargain House, 21
Baltimore Clothing Store, 17
Barnet, Meyer, 191
Barnet, Tom, 192
Barnet, Valerie Manatis, 197
Barnet, William, 175–81, 188, 191–97
Bass, Jack, 160
Bates, William, 34
Batesville Mill, 35
Battery Clothing Store, 68, 84
Battle of Gettysburg (1863), 26
Battle of Seven Pines (1862), 26
Bauman, Mark, 7, 32, 55
Beene, Geoffrey, 132
Belarus, 20
Belk Department Store, 90
Berlin, Bernard, 42, 54
Berlin, Hyman, 45
Berlin, Philip, 45
Berwick's Iron Works, 13
Beth Israel (Greenville), 57–58, 150, 167
Beth Israel Cemetery Association, 60
Bicoff, Sam, 84

Black–Jewish relations, 6, 18, 19, 23, 96, 105–6, 153–81
Blackwelder, Julia Kirk, 89, 124
Bloom, Amelia, 59, 95
Bloom, Anna, 90
Bloom, Clara, 90
Bloom, Ella, 88
Bloom, Harris, 41, 90, 95
Bloom, Henry, 48
Bloom, Jack, 59, 96, 101, 105, 111
Bloom, Julius, 48, 66, 90, 95
Bloom, Louisa, 48, 49, 90
Bloom, Melvin, 101
Bloom, Minnie, 48, 49, 90
Bloom, Sam, 24, 25, 48
Bloom's Department Store, 41, 43, 48, 66, 67, 93, 95
Blotcky, Annae Kramer, 63–64, 102
Blotcky, Abraham G., 53, 63–64
Blum, Julius, 127
Blumberg, Abraham, 65, 98
Blumberg, Mrs. Abraham, 60
Blumberg, Joe, 100
Blumberg, Julius, 100
Blumberg, Rosina, 100
BMW, 191, 198, 199
boarding, 88–89, 90–91, 94–95
Bobrow, Abraham, 87
Bobrow, Morris, 42
Bolonkin, Ida Lurey, 104
Booker, Russell, 177, 179, 180
Brafman, Samuel, 17, 46
Brill, Harry, 53, 68, 89
Brill Electric Company, 53, 54, 84
Broadway Shoe Store, 48, 84, 85
Brooks, Preston, 16
Brown v. Broad of Education (1954), 161
Bruck, Lajos, 128
Burlington Industries, 120
Butler, Mrs., 59
Butler Guards, 26, 66
Butte Knitting Mills, 2, 126–30, *127, 128,* 143, 147, 171
Byrnes, James F., 108

Calhoun, John C., 11, 16
Calhoun, Mrs. John C., 16

Campbell, Carroll, 193
Camp Croft, 108–10
Campel, Rebecca, 100
Campel, Rose, 100
Camperdown Mills, 35
Camp Sevier (Greenville), 66
Camp Wadsworth (Spartanburg), 66, 67
Cann, Kathy, 70
Carlton, David, 28, 35, 36, 120, 143
Carolina Blouse Company, 137–38
Carolina Clinchfield and Ohio Line, 34
Carolina Country Club, 151
Carolina Hide and Junk, 90
Carolina Mercantile Company, 40, 53, 54
Carr, Lewis, 26
carriage making, 13, 16
Catawbas, 10
cattle, 11
Caul, Margaret, 110
Chabad, 201
Chaplin, Morris, 91–92
Charlotte, 34
Chennault, Claire, 118
Cherokees, 10
Chesnee Mill, 120
Chicago Bargain House, 84
Chick Springs (hotel), 15
child labor, 36, 70, 101
Chiquola Manufacturing Company, 140
Cinderella Shoe Shop, 84, 85
citizenship, 97–98
Civil Rights Act (1964), 160, 169, 200
civil rights movement, 6, 157–72
Civil War, 25–27
Clark, Thomas, 22
Clark-Schwebel Fiberglass, 141
Classic Mills, 140
Clyburn, James, 172
Cobb, James, 120, 121, 191
Coburn, Oakley, 170
Cohen, Deborah, 47
Cohen, Dorothy, 156
Cohen, Eli (Elija), 82
Cohen, Fannie, 82, 95
Cohen, Harold, 107, 111, 114–16
Cohen, Jacob (Jack), 68, 74, 82, 145
Cohen, Jay, 22

Cohen, Judith, 100

Cohen, Mark, 39

Cohen, Max, 42, 50, 53, 74, 82, 95, 111, 122

Cohen, Michael R., 38, 46

Cohen, Mordecai, 7

Cohen, Philip M., 45

Cohen, Samuel, 56, 166–67

Cohen, Susan, 186

Cohen, Vivian, 90

Cohen's Chain Stores, 82, 83

Cohen's Department Store, 84

Coleman, Caroline, 22

Concept 1970s (fashion label), 132

Cone, Caesar, 72

Cone, Moses, 72

Congregation Beth Israel (Greenville), 57–58, 150, 167

Congress of Industrial Organizations (CIO), 145

Converse College, 32

Converse Mill, 35

Cook, Annie, 105

Copel, Louis, 39

corn, 11

cotton, 4, 11, 16, 27–28, 70, 107

The Cotton Mills of South Carolina (Kohn), 72

Covington Mills, 140

Daniel, Charles E., 121, 159, 161, 195

Darby, Jerry, 130

Darby, Viola, 130

Davidson, Abraham, 98

Davidson, Pauline, 86

Davidson, Samuel, 18, 21, 25, 88

Davidson's, 43, 85

Davis, Alex, 64, 96, 111

Davis, Jack, 111

Davis, Louis, 111

Davis, Victor, 49, 111

Davis Auto Supply (Davis Battery & Electric Company), 43, 47, 86, 111, 112

Davis family, 47, 96

Day, Zora Louise, 139

DeForest, John William, 27

de la Renta, Oscar, 132

DeLeon, Mordecai, 187

Dent, Frederick "Rick," 121, 151

desegregation, 158–73

Diner, Hasia, 8, 19, 20, 24, 126, 153, 154, 155

Dinnerstein, Leonard, 101, 164–65

Dixie Shirt Company, 42, 53, 74–75, 80, 107, 145, 146–47

D'Lugin, Abe, 47

D'Lugin, Jacob, 47

Draper Textile Machinery Company, 71

Drayton Mill, 35

Dreifus, Samuel, 39, 46

Dreyfus, Susan, 187

Drucker, Morris, 45

Du Bois, W. E. B., 155

Duncan Mill, 120

Dunleavy, Kathy, 176–77

Earle, Willie, 157

Easley Textile Company, 131

Edgar, Walter, 34, 70, 161

educational attainment, 99–100

Ehrenstein, Andrew, 128

Ehrenstein, Gabriel, 128

Ehrenstein, Magda, 128

Eichhorn, David, 108–9

Einstein, Simon, 17

Eisenmann, Isak, 14

Eisner, Danielle, 201

Elks Club, 5

Emb-Tex, 136–37

Emory, Olin, 159–60

Endel, Fannie, 30, 33

Endel, Hyman, 29–31, 32, 33, 50, 60, 64

Endel, Moses, 29

Endelmann, Judith, 95

England, English, 7, 10

entrepreneurship, 37–40

Entwistle Manufacturing Company, 140

Epstein, Jacob, 1, 21, 46–47

Epstein, William, 123

Equal Employment Opportunity Commission (EEOC), 169

erosion, 12

Evans, Eli, 63, 81

Evans, Mutt, 188

Fairforest Finishing Company, 71
Fair Labor Standards Act (1938), 145
Family Shoe Store, 83, 85
Faulkner, Thomas, 174
Fayonski, Louis, 39, 98
Fayonski, Minnie, 48
Fayonski, Mrs. Louis, 60
Fayonsky, Harry, 95
Fayonsky, Sarah, 98
Fedders Fashions, 183
Feinstein, Marian (Fink), 49, 105, 110, 157,
    185
Feinstein, Seymour, 110
Felder, James, 157
Fenyo, Mario, 125
Ferris, Marcie Cohen, 104, 105
Finkelstein, Jacob, 104
Finkelstein, Jeanette Davidson, 18, 48, 49,
    104, 156, 183
firearms manufacturing, 11, 13, 16
Flamm, Michael, 84–85
Fleishman, Alvin, 111
Fleishman and Klyne, 47
Fleishman, Nathan, 47, 92
Fleishman, Rosa, 88, 98
Fleishman, Samuel, 98
Fleming, Lillian Brock, 175
flour mills, 16
Floyd, John, 82
Foner, Nancy, 97
foodways, 104–6
Ford, Lacy, 11, 12, 16, 190
Fork Shoals Mill, 35
Foster, B. B., 12
Foster, George, 159
Fox's, 184
Franklin, John Hope, 153
Franklin School, 179, 195
fraternal organizations, 64–65, 69
Freedman, Lou, 48
Freedmen's Bureau, 27
Fram, Solomon, 45
Friedberger, Myer B., 45
Friedlander, Helen, 100
Friedman, Shirley, 76
From, Allen, 103, 105, 156, 163–64
From, Bertha, 45

From, Harry, 183
From, Israel, 20, 25, 45, 68, 98
From, Lena, 94
From, Mary, 94
From (Poliakoff), Rosa, 21, 92, 94, 102
From, Sarah, 94
Froms Department Store, 43, 183
Funkenstein, Louis, 111
Furman, Alester, 195
Furman University, 12, 26

Gaffney Maid, 145
Gaftan Sportswear, 123
Galicia, 20
Gantt, Harvey, 161
Gantt, Rosa Hirschmann, 56–57, 61, 66, 69
Gantt, Robert, 62
Gantt, Solomon, 61
garment industry, 119–52; civic involvement
    and, 148–51; consolidation in, 132–42;
    decline of, 151, 182, 199; innovation in,
    124–32; labor relations in, 142–48
Gaston, Dorothy, 147
Geffen, Lottie, 65
Geisberg, Florie, 90
Geisberg, Sadie, 90
Geisberg family, 96
Gelburd, Selmen, 100
Geller, Lou, 127
Gerber, David, 9
Germans, 10, 14, 39
Gibson, Lottie, 175
Gibson, W. F., 174
GI Jews (Moore), 118
Gilliam family, 24
Gist, Lugene, 154
Gittleson, Israel, 31, 45–46
Glenn Springs Hotel (resort), 16
Glickman, Morris, 48
Glickman's Broadway Shoes, 84
Globe Clothing House, 30
Globe Sample Company, 53
Globe Textile Store, 84
Goldberg, Abraham, 31, 40, 50, 54, 68, 88,
    98
Goldberg, Esther, 88, 98
Goldberg, Gloria From, 103

Goldberg, Kate, 89
Goldberg's Clothing Store, 53, 88
Goldbloom, Harold, 74
Goldfield, David, 156
Goldman, Barry, 127
Gold Rush, 24
Goldstein, Eric, 15, 55, 92, 148
Goldstein, Harry, 48
Goldstein, Joseph, 42, 53
Goldstein, Louis, 48
Goldstein's Shoe Store, 84, 85
Gow, Seymour, 67
Granby and Olympia Mills, 140–41
Gray, Edward, 105, 156
Gray, Seymour, 44
Great Depression, 70, 91, 92, 150
Great London Clothing House, 29
Greek Revival, 56
Greeks, 36–37, 51, 98
Green, Lee, 19
Greene, Herman, 174
Greene, Nathanael, 11
Greenewald, David, 31, 43, 53, 68, 82
Greenewald, Hannah, 43
Greenewald, Isaac, 31, 43, 53, 63, 65
Greenewald, Jacob, 43
Greenewald, Max, 31, 43, 53, 63, 64
Greenewald, Moses, 31, 43, 53, 68, 82
Greenewald family, 47, 96
Greenewald's, 31, 40, 43, 51, 82, 93, 156
Greenville Pawn Shop, 48
Greenwald, Seymour, 127
Greenwoods, 43
Gregg Community Center, 178
grist milling, 13
Gruber, Frances, 30
Gutkowski, Andrew, 163, 176

Hale's Jewelers, 86
Hammer, Amy, 201
Hampshire Underwear and Hosiery, 71
Hansen, Jason, 201
Harris Bloom and Sons, 84
Hayek, Friedrich A., 38
Hecklin, Alice, 90, 100
Hecklin, Barney, 53, 83, 85
Hecklin, Gussie, 95

Hecklin, Ida, 90
Hecklin, Rose, 57
Hecklin, Samuel, 53, 83, 85, 88, 95
Hecklin, Sarah, 90
Hecklin, Simon, 83, 101
Hecklin Shoes, 54
Heike, Anton, 13
Heller, Max, 78, 133, 134–35, 170, 196, 197, 200; political career of, 172–75, 188–91, 193, 195–96
Heller, Paula, 134
Heller, Trude, 133, 196
Hertz, Erwin, 89
Hertzberg, Steven, 23, 155
Hieke, Anton, 29, 32
Highland Manufacturing, 74
Hill, Beatrice, 160
Hipps family, 195
Hirsch, Isaac W., 26
Hirschmann, Lena Nachman, 61–62
hogs, 11
Hollings, Ernest "Fritz," 161, 162
homeownership, 94–97, 139
Hudson, R. C., 73
Hudson and Kohn, 73
Huff, A. V., 12, 63
Huguenot Mill, 35
Hutchings, Thomas, 34
Hyman, August, 88
Hyman, Sadie, 88

Improved Order of Red Men, 64
indigo, 7
industrialization, 9, 33, 70
Industrial Removal Society, 50
inflation, 26
Inman Mill, 35
intermarriage, 104, 200
International Ladies' Garment Workers' Union (ILGWU), 143, 145, 147
Invisibles (gang), 17
Irish, 9, 37
ironmaking, 13
Irvine, William H., 16
Irwin, Art, 146
Isaacs, Abraham, 17, 26, 32, 36
Iseman, Simon, 31

Italians, 9, 37, 87
Iva Manufacturing Company, 123

Jack's Economy Store, 156, 182
Jackson, Andrew, 11
Jackson, Jesse, 6, 157–58, 174–75
Jacobi, Isaac, 39, 48, 50, 60
Jacobi, Mrs. Isaac, 60
Jacobi Electric, 84
Jacobs, Camille, 73
Jacobs, Henry, 48–49, 185–87
Jacobs, Joseph, 53
Jacobs, Susan, 105–6, 186
Jacobs, Sylvia, 186
JaLog Industries, 145
jewelry stores, 85–86
Jewish–Black relations, 6, 18, 19, 23, 96,
    105–6, 153–81
Jewish education, 103–4
Jewish Legion, 65
Jewish Life in Small-Town America (Weiss-
    bach), 5
Jewish Welfare Board, 65–66
Johnson, George Dean, 151
Jonathan Logan, Inc., 1, 126, 145, 147
Jones, Lu Ann, 23
Judson Mills, 71, 73

Kanorovitz, Harris, 48
Kanter, Rosabeth Moss, 121, 191
Kantor, Harris, 47
Kantor, Mendel, 47
Kantor Company, 47, 50
Kaplan, Gustave, 79
Kaplan, Joseph, 79–80
Kaplan, Julius, 79
Karditz family, 96
kashrut, 53, 57, 104–5
Kassler, Irene, 94
Kaufman, Harry, 49
Kaufman, Molly, 49
Kaufman Brothers, 86
Kaynee Company, 78
Kemco Company, 137
Kennedy, John F., 120, 168
Kennedy, Mitch, 178
King, Bob, 158

Kissinger, Henry, 109
Klein, Anne, 124
Kline, Charles, 48
Kline, Rosa, 48
Kline, Sarah, 48
Klyne, Phillip, 47, 92
Knigoff, Adolph, 48
Knigoff, Solomon, 48
Koch, Ed, 109
Kohn, Abraham, 24
Kohn, August, 72
Kohn, David, 60, 72–73
Kohn, Theodore, 72
Korn, Bertram, 18
Kosch and Gray Jewelers, 43, 51, 182
kosher food, 53, 57, 104–5
Kozlow, Anne, 197
Kraut, Alan, 99
Krieger, David, 136–37
Krieger, Herman, 136
Krieger, Morris, 136
Krieger, Page, 137
Krieger Corporation, 133
Ku Klux Klan, 18, 97, 161, 170

L & K Dyeing and Finishing Plant, 123
L. Schonwetter's Clothing Store, 87
labor relations, 2, 91, 120, 130, 142–48
Ladies Fur Shop, 87
Lauren, Ralph, 124
Lawson's Fork Creek Mill, 35
Lee (Pryce), Brenda, 160, 171–72
Lee, Harry, 59
Lee, Stella Coln, 171
Leffert, Morris, 77
Lehman Brothers, 46
Lenworth Corporation, 140
Lesser, Carrie, 29
Lesser, Dora, 29
Lesser, Harry, 29
Lesser, Leo, 29
Lesser, Martha, 29
Lesser, Michael, 28–29
Lesser, Morris A., 29
Lesser, Sadie, 29
Levin, Abraham, 52, 53, 98
Levinson, Samuel, 46

Levite, Meyer, 53
Levy, Abigail, 17
Levy, L. L., 17
Levy, Morris, 60
Lewkowicz brothers, 123
Lewson, Cathy, 142
Liebowitz, Yossi, 167, 179–80, 200
Limestone Springs (hotel), 15
Lincoln, Abraham, 25
Lindo, Moses, 7
Lions Club, 5
Lithuania, 20
Loef, Samuel, 42, 53
Loef's Pressing and Hat Blocking Parlors, 53
Lowenberg, Joe, 17
Lowenburg, David, 46
Lowenstein, Abram, 138–39, 140
Lowenstein, Leon, 138–41, 146, 150
Lowenstein, Louis, 133, 138
Lowenstein, M., & Sons, 138–41, 144–45
Lowenstein, Morris, 138
Lowenstein Cotton and Storage Company, 141
Lucille (cook), 105
Lucky Seven (investment club), 47
lunch counter sit-ins, 159–60
Lurey, Anne, 58
Lurey, Milton, 74
Lurey, Morris, 42, 83
Lurey, Samuel, 42, 98, 101, 111
Lurey family, 96
Lureys, 43
Lutz, Carl, 125
lynching, 157

Macshore Classics, Inc., 137–38
Macy's, 37
Malinow, Stanley D., 111
Mallinow, Meyer, 64
malls, 182
Mandell, Nicki, 144
Manhattan Pawn Shop, 48
Mann (Price), Dora, 43, 66, 90, 95
Mansion House, 15, 16
Manus brothers, 47
Marie (housekeeper), 106
Marinari, Maddalena, 97

Mark, Harris, 29, 30
Marsh, Harry, 39
Mason, Patrick Q., 19
Massell, Sam, 188
Massey, Max, 112
Maunola, Marko, 119, 122, 143, 157, 160, 199
Mauldin, Belton, 17–18
Maxon Shirt Corporation, 135–36, *135*, 170
Mayer, Abraham, 24
Mayfair Mills, 121
Mazure, Maurice, 60
McBee, Vardry, 12, 25
McCary, Moses, 14
McDowell, Andie, 195
McNair, Robert, 194
McPherson, E. L., 163
Medical University of South Carolina, 61
Meir, Joan Bolonkin, 103, 104
Memmott, Ed, 176
Mendelsohn, Adam, 8, 20, 28, 38, 74
Menzer, Melinda, 168
Merrimack Manufacturing Mills, 139
Meyers, Alex, 44, 60
Meyers, Ben, 44
Meyers, Lewis, 44
Meyers, Manus, 44, 60
Meyers, Noland, 44
Meyers-Arnold Co., 44, *44*, 67, 184
Meyerson, Abraham, 40
Meyerson, Louis, 53
Michelin, 190, 198, 199
mikvahs, 59
Miller, Joseph, 42
Milliken, Roger, 121–22
Milliken, Seth, 122
Milliken and Company, 121–22
Mills, Mary, 134
Mills Manufacturing, 36
Minchin, Timothy, 169, 172
Minnie (cook), 105
Miss Marian's Dance Studio, 49, 110, 185
Mitchell, Harold, 176
Monaghan Mill, 36
Monsanto Company, 130
Moore, Deborah Dash, 110, 113, 114, 118
Morgan, Daniel, 32

Morris, Abraham, 42, 48, 186
Morris, Sylvia, 48
Morrow, Martin, 79, 133–34, 148
Morrow, Victoria, 79
Morrow-Spitzer, Jacob, 188
Moses, Isaiah, 7
Mostel, Zero, 109
Muller, Jerry, 38, 42–43
Myerson, Abe, 54

NAACP, 157–58
Nachman, Jack, 125, 131
Nachman, Jeffrey, 132
Nachman, Lawrence, 132
Nachman, Louis, 131
Nadell, Pamela, 56
National Labor Relations Board (NLRB),
    144–45, 146–47
Native Americans, 24
Netherlands, 7
New York Bazaar, 40, 43, 50, 82
New York City, 5, 9, 15, 34, 74, 77–78
New York Loan Office, 40, 42
New York Pawn Shop, 50
New York Shoe Store, 83–84
Nicholl, A., 17
Nicholls-Crook Plantation House, 12
Nichols, Frank, Jr., 156
Nixon, Richard M., 121
Northside Initiative, 178–81, 195

Olympia Mills, 129–30
O'Neill, Sean, 12, 27
O'Neill, Steve, 159, 161–62
One-Price Clothing, 49, 186
opportunity structures, 37
Orangeburg massacre (1968), 162–63
Orr Mills, 133, 146
Orthodox Judaism, 52–53, 55, 57, 59

Pacific Mills, 71, 140
Pacolet Mill, 35
Pacolet Springs, 15
Padoll, Burton, 163, 165–66
Palmetto House, 15
paper mills, 16
Parker, Lewis W., 36

Parker Cotton Mills Company, 36, 73
Patton, George S., 114, 136
pawn shops, 48, 92
Peace, Roger, 195
Peace Center for the Performing Arts, 189
peaches, 70
Pelham Mill, 35
People's Dry Goods Company, 100
Pero, Jerome, 54
Piedmont Club, 151, 194
Piedmont Manufacturing Company, 35,
    74–80, 75, 76, 107, 133–35, 143–44, 148
Plisse Corporation of America, 140
Plotkin, Philip, 109
pogroms, 8
Poinsett Club, 151, 194
Poland, Poles, 9, 20
Poliakoff, Abraham Ellis, 113–14
Poliakoff, Arthur, 113
Poliakoff, Benjamin, 50
Poliakoff, David, 21, 25, 113
Poliakoff, Ella, 113
Poliakoff, Eunice, 102
Poliakoff, Eva, 94
Poliakoff, Gary, 164
Poliakoff, Marion, 113
Poliakoff, Marsha, 47, 57
Poliakoff, Matthew, a87
Poliakoff, Myer, 102, 113
Poliakoff, Rosa (From), 21, 92, 94, 102
Poliakoff, Samuel, 113
Poliakoffs, 43
Pollacks Shoes, 53
Pollock, Lois, 100
Pollock, Lou, 85
Pollock's Shoe Store, 85
Porter family, 24
Portugal, 7
Prell, Riv-Ellen, 87–88
Price, Anne, 44, 100
Price, Bill, 66, 100
Price, Dora (Mann), 43, 66, 90, 95
Price, Harry, 40, 43–44, 50, 53, 64, 66, 82, 95
Price, Harry, Jr., 44
Prices Store for Men, 43, 50, 51, 90, 100, 156,
    182, 183
Print Mills, 120

Pridgeon, J. Leon, 160
Pritzker, Jay, 189
Pryce, Brenda Lee, 160, 171–72
Prospect Hill (resort), 15
public schools, 99, 179
Purpose-Built Communities, 178, 195

Rabinowitz, Howard, 27
railroads, 12–13, 27, 34
Raisin, Jacob, 52
Raphael, Marc Lee, 99
Raycord Company, 80
Reconstruction, 27
Reedy River Mill, 35
Reeves Brothers, 120
Reform Judaism, 30, 52–53, 55, 60
Re-Genesis (environmental group), 176
Reisenfeld, George, 60
resorts, 15–17
Rex, Sylvia, 128
Reynolds, Evie, 139–40
Reyzilovich, Tsale, 48
Rice, Ernest, 166
Richard, Carole Moore, 160
Richardson, Jerry, 178
right-to-work law, 120, 190
Riley, Richard, 190, 195
roadbuilding, 12
Robinson, Jackie, 158
Rock Hill Printing & Finishing Company,
    139, 140
Rogoff, Leonard, 39, 47, 67
Romania, 20
Rose, Sam, 167–68, 200
Rosen, Robert, 26
Rosenberg, Abraham, 14, 68, 83
Rosenberg, Cele, 102
Rosenberg, Ernest, 83
Rosenberg, Herby, 183
Rosenberg, Rebecca Winstock, 68
Rosenberg, Solomon, 96
Rosenberg, Wolf, 1, 2, 45
Rosenberg & Company, 1, 45
Rosenberg family, 13
Rosenberg Mercantile Company, 43, 183
Rosenblum, Abram, 111–12
Rosenblum family, 96

Rosenfeld, Cyvia, 92
Rosenfeld, William, 92, 185
Rosenfeld-Einstein and Associates Insurance
    Agency, 92, 185
Rosengarten, Dale, 19, 166
Rosengarten, Theodore, 19
Rosenthal, Abraham, 31
Rosenwald, Julius, 153–55
Rotary Club, 5
Rothschild, Levy, 39, 46, 48, 50, 60, 87
Rothschilds, Fannie, 88
Rovner, Bobbie Jean, 156
Ruffin, Edmund C., 16
Russia, 8, 39

Sachs, Aaron, 102
Saltzman, Anna, 78
Saltzman, Dorothy, 78
Saltzman, Harvey, 111
Saltzman, Jennie, 76
Saltzman, Nathan, 76, 77
Saltzman, Shepard, 80, 111, 122, 144; Black
    workers hired by, 169–70; death of, 79;
    early life of, 76; national expansion by, 78,
    133; New York City network of, 77–78;
    refugees aided by, 133, 134
Saltzman, Shirley, 79
Salvador, Francis, 187
Sample Shoe Store, 53, 83, 85
Sampson, Donald, 158
Samuel, Morris, 46
Sarlin family, 96
Sarlins Department Store, 183
Sarna, Jonathan, 56
Savage, Mattie Sims, 154
Saxon Mill, 35, 120
Schahub, Harry, 88–89
Schonwetter, Arnold, 48, 50
Schraibman, Aaron, 31, 39
Schwartz, David, 1–2, 126, 128, 145
Schwartz, Julius, 53
Schwartz, Siegfried, 48
Scots-Irish, 4, 8, 10
scrap metal, 48, 66, 111, 183
Sears, Booker, 160
Segal, Irene, 179
Sellers, Cleveland, Jr., 162–63

Sephardim, 8
Setlow, Herbert, 123
Setlow, Joseph, 123
Seward, J. L., 18
Shain, Abraham, 98
Shain, Mrs. Leon, 59
Shannon Knit, 129, 171
Shapiro, Edward, 118, 200
Shapiro, Eugene, 100
Shapiro, Herbert, 100
Shapiro, Nathan, 1, 2, 21–24, 25, 45, 47,
    88–89
Shapiro family, 96
Sheftall family, 96
Sher, Celia, 116
Sher, David, 116
Sher, Morton, 116–18
Sherman, Jacob, 50
Sherman, William T., 26
Shevitz, Amy Hill, 64
Shirtmaster, 79, 107
shoe manufacturing, 9
shoe stores, 85
shopping malls, 182
Shore, Max, 133, 137–38, 150
Siegel, Abe, 84
Siegel, Bessie, 84
Siegel, Marvin, 127
Siegel, Max, 84
Siegel, Reuben, 84
Siegel, Sam, 84
Siegel, Sol, 84
Siegel Brothers Jewelry Store, 84
Silverman, Abraham, 87
Silverman, Alan, 141–42
Silverman, Frank, 142
Simon, Abraham, 64
Skalowski family, 96
Skalowsky's Jewelry Store, 92
Slater Mill, 120
Slaters, Samuel, 71
slavery, 11, 12, 20, 27
Slovaks, 9
Smiley, Harry, 57
Smith, Abe, 84, 100
Smith, Julius, 84
Smith family, 96

soil exhaustion, 12
Sokoloff, Vladimir, 109
Sonenberg, Joseph, 17, 29
Sorin, Gerald, 55, 101, 102
South Carolina Manufacturing Company, 13
Southern Bleachers, 120
Southern Railroad, 34
Southern Textile Exposition (1915), 73
Spain, 7
Spartan Mills, 178
Spartan Undies, 145
Spiegel, D. M., 86
Spiegel Brothers, 86
Spigel, Daisey, 102
Spigel, Dana, 102
Spigel, David, 102
Spigel, Joseph, 53
Spigel family, 96
Spofford Mills, 140
Springfield Baptist Church, 162
Springs Industries, 141
Sprouse, Don, 193
Standard Cloak Company, 42, 48, 50, 186
steelmaking, 9
Steinberg, Hank, 185
Steinberg, Jack, 185
Sterba, Christopher, 65
Sterling High School, 162
Stevens, J. P., and Company, 120
Stone, Eugene, 136
Stone, Philip, 122
Stotsky, Mrs. Nathan, 59
strikes, 91, 140, 144, 146
Sudmeier, Jim, 115–16
Surasky, Abraham, 19
Swandale, Simon, 14, 16, 26, 32
Swedes, 10
Swirl, Inc., 131–32
Switzer, Bessie, 88
Switzer, Ida, 48
Switzer, Israel, 48
Switzer, Louis, 24, 31, 39
Switzer, Maurice, 88
Switzer family, 96

Tacapau Mills, 71
Taft-Hartley Act (1947), 120

tailoring, 49–50
Talley, James, 163, 175
Tanenbaum, Harry, 92
Tanenbaum, Linda, 106
Tanenbaum, Ralph, 112
Tanenbaum, Rick, 184–85
Tanenbaum, Saul, 185
Tanenbaum family, 184
tax incentives, 2, 120
Temple B'nai Israel (Spartanburg), 31,
    52–57, 127
Temple of Israel (Greenville), 30, 57, 60–61,
    73, 150
Teszler, Akos, 126
Teszler, Andrew, 1–2, 119, 125, 126–30,
    147–49, 171
Teszler, Joseph, 125
Teszler, Lidia, 125, 126, 129, 170
Teszler, Otto, 1, 119, 125, 126, 130, 131
Teszler, Sandor, 119, 125–26, 129–30, 149,
    170–71
Teter, Betsy Wakefield, 151, 168
Textile Hall, 73
textile industry, 28, 33, 50; decline of, 91,
    130, 151, 152, 182, 199; during Great
    Depression, 91; industrialization and, 9,
    11, 37–38; Jewish migration linked to, 34,
    72–73; segregation in, 168; southward
    migration of, 35, 36, 70, 71–72, 74–80;
    during World War II, 107
Textile Workers Union of America (TWUA),
    145, 146
Thomas, Mary, 176, 177, 179
Thomas, Tony, 178
Tice, Bill, 132
Timmons family, 195
tinworks, 16
tobacco, 11
Tobin, Jack, 127
Toll, William, 91
Tollison Hartness, Courtney, 107, 161
Toney, William, 15
tourism, 15
Trout, Max, 76
Truman, Harry, 126
Tucapau Mill, 35
Tucker, Rosalie, 147

Tukey, Richard, 190–91
tzedakah, 47

Ukraine, 20
University of South Carolina Upstate, 179,
    186–87, 194
Uprising of 1934, 140, 143
urbanization, 9

Valley Falls, 71
Vanderbilt Shirt Company, 74
Victor-Monaghan Mills, 120
Visanska, Florette, 102
Visanska, George, 20–21, 45, 95–96
Visanska family, 13
Vogue (clothing store), 48, 50
Volpin, Mrs. Alexander, 60

Wachter, Joseph H., 86, 110
Waddell, Edmund, 15
Waddell, Mrs., 59
Wagner Act (1935), 144
Wald, Rosa, 72
Walker, Joe, 154
Walker, Melissa, 15
Walker House Hotel, 15
Wamsutta Mills, 140
Ware, T. Edwin, 12
Washington, Booker T., 153
Wearever Fabrics Corporation, 140
Webb, Clive, 23, 155
Weil, Isaac, 29, 31, 46, 64
Weiner, Deborah, 15, 21, 39, 55, 92,
    148
Weintraub, Philip, 42, 53–54
Weinberger, Phil, 60
Weinman, Jack, 138
Weissbach, Lee Shai, 5, 53, 74, 81, 89
Wellman Industries, 131
Wendall Fabrics Corporation, 141–42
Wendlowsky, Isadore, 142
West, John C., 149
Weston, Celia, 185
wheat, 11
White, Junie, 177–78, 179–80, 188
White, Knox, 195
Whitney Mill, 35

Whot, Joe, 37
Williams, Peggy, 147–48
Williamson, Thomas, 12
Williamston Shirt Company, 135
Wings Boyswear, 78, 79
Wings Shirt Company, 78, 79
Winstock, Moses, 14
Winstock, Rebecca, 14
Winstock family, 13–14
Wise, Isaac Meyer, 105
WItz, Sam, 127
Wofford College, 32, 43, 83
Wolpe, Gerald, 165
Women and American Judaism (Nadell and
    Sarna), 56
women's suffrage, 62
Woodruff Cotton Mill, 82
Woodside, John, 36
Woodson Community Center, 177
Woodward, C. Vann, 50, 121
Woodward, Mrs. A. Y., 130
Works Progress Administration (WPA), 21
World War I, 65–67, 69, 73
World War II, 5, 107–18

Wyche, C. C., 80
Wyche, Tommy, 195

Yiddish language, 55
Yoffe family, 184
Yoffe, Michael, 185
Yoffe, Thelma, 185
Young Men's Hebrew Association (YMHA),
    59

Zaglin, Charles, 57–58, 58, 59, 66, 111
Zaglin, Freida, 48, 49
Zaglin, Harry, 48, 111
Zaglin, Jack, 111
Zaglin, Jeff, 51, 59
Zaglin, Larry, 156
Zaglin, Louis, 111
Zaglin, Marion, 111
Zaglin, Morris, 59–60
Zaglin, Susan, 156
Zaglin family, 96
Zaglin-Kaplan, Frieda, 59
Zaglins, 43
Zalensky's, 87